Touching Feeling

Edited by Michèle Aina Barale,

Jonathan Goldberg, Michael Moon,

and Eve Kosofsky Sedgwick

Touching Feeling

Affect, Pedagogy, Performativity

EVE KOSOFSKY SEDGWICK

DUKE UNIVERSITY PRESS

Durham & London

2003

© 2003 Duke University Press

All rights reserved.

Designed by Amy Ruth Buchanan. Typeset in Dante by Tseng
Information Systems, Inc. Library of Congress Cataloging-in-
Publication Data appear
on the last printed page of this book.

Frontispiece: photograph of Judith Scott.
Copyright © 1999 by Leon Borensztein. Reprinted by
permission. The epigraph at the beginning of "Interlude,
Pedagogic" is titled "Hope" from *The Complete Poems* by Randall
Jarrell. Copyright © 1969, renewed 1997 by Mary
von S. Jarrell. Reprinted by permission of Farrar,
Straus and Giroux, LLC.

THE DISTRIBUTION OF THIS BOOK
IS SUPPORTED BY A GENEROUS GRANT
FROM THE GILL FOUNDATION.

for T. W. M.

with my ridiculous love

CONTENTS

ACKNOWLEDGMENTS

Gratitude is not, in Silvan Tomkins's terms, an affect but a complex emotion. Complex as it is, to me it also seems one of the happiest and most simply self-rewarding. Michael Moon has been the spur to this project in a million ways he will and won't recognize, each of them a new form of beauty — at least new to me. My adorable partner, Hal Sedgwick, and parents, Leon and Rita Kosofsky, are thankable beyond thanks. The interlocutors whose ideas have provided an endless resource for this work include Stephen Barber, Lauren Berlant, Judith Butler, Mary Campbell, Jonathan Flatley, Adam Frank, Jonathan Goldberg, Tim Gould, David Kosofsky, Joe Litvak, Melissa Solomon, Andy Parker, Cindy Patton, Shannon Van Wey, and Josh Wilner. Then there are Alan Astrow, Mark Bauer, Laverne Berry, Mandy Berry, Rafael Campo, Tyler Curtain, Cathy Davidson, Eric Dishman, Jennifer Doyle, Denise Fulbrook, Claudia Gonson, Joe Gordon, Janet Halley, Neil Hertz, Marsha Hill, Jim Kincaid, Wayne Koestenbaum, Nina Kopesky, Songmin and Noam Ray Kosofsky, Adam, Daniel, and Rosemary Lebow, Meredith McGill, Gregory Mercurio, José Muñoz, Joan Richardson, Mary Russo, Barbara Herrnstein Smith, Greg Tomso, Dan and Karen Warner, Carolyn Williams, Carrie and Joe Hill Wilner, Eric Winer, and Ken Wissoker, all among the friends whose care has nourished me through these good years. The impermanent floating nonsectarian sangha that sustains my Buddhist imagination, besides Hal and Michael and Mary C., includes Sharon Cameron, Don Lopez, Tina Meyerhoff, Nancy Waring, and, beaming her kindness, Mary Moon.

Touching Feeling is a palimpsest of previously published and unpublished material. Although I have felt free to revise, the essays appear in the order in which they were originally written. The main borrowings from published materials are as follows.

The interlude appeared as part of "Socratic Raptures, Socratic Ruptures: Notes toward Queer Performativity," in *English Inside and Out,* ed. Jonathan Kamholtz and Susan Gubar (New York: Routledge, 1992).

A version of Chapter 1 was published as "Queer Performativity in the New York Edition Prefaces," in *Henry James's New York Edition: The Construction of Authorship,* ed. David McWhirter (Stanford: Stanford University Press, 1996), after appearing first in two parts: "Inside Henry James: Toward a Lexicon for *The Art of the Novel,*" in *Negotiating Lesbian and Gay Subjects,* ed. Monica Dorenkamp and Richard Henke (New York: Routledge, 1995), and "Queer Performativity: Henry James's *The Art of the Novel,*" GLQ 1.1(1993).

Adam Frank and I first published a version of Chapter 3 in *Critical Inquiry* (winter 1995); it later appeared as the introduction to Frank and Sedgwick, eds., *Shame and Its Sisters: A Silvan Tomkins Reader* (Durham, NC: Duke University Press, 1995).

A version of Chapter 4 appeared as part of the introduction to Sedgwick, ed., *Novel Gazing: Queer Readings in Fiction* (Durham, NC: Duke University Press, 1997).

Chapter 5 was commissioned for Donald S. Lopez Jr., ed., *Critical Terms for the Study of Buddhism* (Chicago: University of Chicago Press, forthcoming).

Some paragraphs on performativity from the introduction and Chapters 1 and 2 are borrowed from Andrew Parker's and my introduction to our coedited *Performativity and Performance* (New York: Routledge, 1995). The discussion of Henry James's anal eroticism in Chapter 1 both continues and borrows from the discussion of *The Wings of the Dove* in *Tendencies* (Durham, NC: Duke University Press, 1993).

INTRODUCTION

Much of the writing in *Touching Feeling* originally appeared in other contexts. But this collection of essays also represents a distinct project, one that has occupied a decade's work, which has nonetheless, and with increasing stubbornness, refused to become linear in structure. I think it is best described as a project to explore promising tools and techniques for nondualistic thought and pedagogy.

No doubt the ambition of thinking other than dualistically itself shaped the project's resistance to taking the form of a book-length, linear argument on a single topic. A lot of voices tell us to think nondualistically, and even what to think in that fashion. Fewer are able to transmit how to go about it, the cognitive and even affective habits and practices involved, which are less than amenable to being couched in prescriptive forms. At best, I'd hope for this book to prompt recognition in some of the many people who successfully work in such ways; and where some approaches may be new or unarticulated, a sense of possibility. The ideal I'm envisioning here is a mind receptive to thoughts, able to nurture and connect them, and susceptible to happiness in their entertainment.

Especially since the 1960s any number of Western academic, popular, and professional discourses have been cumulatively invoking nondualistic approaches in physics, gender and sexuality, art, psychology and psychoanalysis, deconstruction, postcolonial relations, pedagogy, religion and spirituality, race, mind-body problematics, the recovery movement, and science studies, among many other areas. But of course it's far easier to deprecate the confounding, tendentious effects of binary modes of thinking—and to expose their often stultifying perseveration—than it is to articulate or model other structures of thought. Even to invoke *non*dualism, as plenty of Buddhist sutras point out, is to tumble right into a dualistic trap. I've always assumed that the most useful work of this sort is likeliest to occur near the boundary of what a writer can't figure out how to say readily, never mind prescribe to others: in the Jacoblike wrestling—or t'ai chi, as it may be— that confounds agency with passivity, the self with the book and the world, the ends of the work with its means, and, maybe most alarmingly, intelligence with stupidity. If so, maybe there's been something encouraging in the structural recalcitrance of *Touching Feeling*.

Among the forms of stubbornness this book embodies (yes, I'm a Taurus), one of the most obvious is its fixation on a small number of theoretical texts, all of them in print by 1990. I'm fond of observing how obsession is the most durable form of intellectual capital. More or less explicitly, all these essays explore a sense of exciting and so far unexhausted possibility—as well as frustration—stirred up by four difficult texts: J. L. Austin's *How to Do Things with Words,* the introductory volume of Michel Foucault's *History of Sexuality,* Judith Butler's *Gender Trouble,* and the first three volumes of Silvan Tomkins's *Affect Imagery Consciousness* (excerpted in Tomkins, *Shame*). Additionally, except for the less-known work of Tomkins, the essays respond to the critical and pedagogical receptions and uses of those influential texts— respond to them often with what has been, for me at least, a vitalizing if sometimes coarse or unlovely exasperation. What I wish were equally evident (maybe it is in some places) is plain gratitude at the privilege of being an interlocutor in conversations I've experienced as so politically, intellectually, and imaginatively crucial.

At the same time, one of the cumulative stories told by *Touching Feeling* may be of a writer's decreasing sense of having a strong center of gravity in a particular intellectual field. Such encounters as those with mortality and with Buddhism, which shape the two last chapters, have had some slip-slidy effects, for better or worse, on the strong consciousness of vocation that made a book like *Epistemology of the Closet* sound confident of its intervention on contemporaneous scenes of sexuality and critical theory. By contrast, the work I've done in parallel with *Touching Feeling* over the past decade has included several editorial experiments in collaboration; a poetry book; the extended, double-voiced *haibun* of *A Dialogue on Love;* a lot of cancer journalism; and, increasingly, the nonlinguistic work of textile art. At the same time, interestingly, my classroom life has grown consistently more textured and relaxed. While I've struggled to make room in *Touching Feeling* for a sense of reality that would exclude none of these elements, I've also had to ungrasp my hold on some truths that used to be self-evident — including the absolute privilege of the writing act itself.

In her celebrated poem "One Art," Elizabeth Bishop's repeated refrain is "The art of losing isn't hard to master." In its insistence on a purgative aesthetic, it's the one poem of hers I've never liked; I picture it on a refrigerator magnet, say, urging dieters not to open the door. A more congenial version to me would invoke the art of *loosing:* and not as one art but a cluster of related ones. Ideally life, loves, and ideas might then sit freely, for a while, on the palm of the open hand. I would have liked *Touching Feeling* to be as open as that, and even as concentrated. In this introduction I can only unfold a few of the main topoi that have failed to become either dispensable or quite placeable during its writing.

PERFORMATIVITY AND PERFORMANCE

Touching Feeling is rooted in an intransigent fascination with some effects and implications surrounding J. L. Austin's foundational work on performative utterances. While the concept of performativity has propelled notably divergent trains of thought in several disciplines, I have been most responsive to one line that extends through Derrida to the early work of Judith Butler, a line that proved particularly influential in the development of gender studies and queer studies throughout the 1990s.

The "queer" potential of performativity is evidently related to the tenuousness of its ontological ground, signaled by the fact that it begins its intellectual career all but repudiated in advance by the coiner of the term. Austin introduces performativity in the first of his 1955 Harvard lectures (later published as *How to Do Things with Words*), only to disown it somewhere around the eighth. He disowns or dismantles "performativity," that is, as the name of a distinct and bounded category of utterances that might be opposed to the merely "constative" or descriptive, noting that "every genuine speech act is both" (147). Thus the use that deconstruction has had for "performativity" begins with the recognition of it as a property or aspect common to all utterances. Linguistics and analytic philosophy, by contrast, in spite of Austin's demurral, long remained interested in the process of classifying utterances as performatives versus constatives.

Yet, as Shoshana Felman points out in *The Literary Speech Act,* Austin's own performance in these lectures is anything but a simple one. One of their sly characteristics is a repeated tropism toward, an evident fascination with, a particular class of examples of performative utterance. Presented first as pure, originary, and defining for the concept; dismissed at the last as no more than "a marginal limiting case" of it, if indeed either the examples or the concept can be said to "survive" the analytic operation of the lectures at all (Austin 150); nonetheless reverted to over and over as if no argument or analysis, no deconstruction or dismantlement could really vitiate or even challenge the self-evidence of their exemplary force—these sentences are what Austin's work installs in the mind as performativity tout court, even while rendering nominally unusable the concept of performativity tout court. Famously, these are a cluster of sentences about which "it seems clear that to utter the sentence (in, of course, the appropriate circumstances) is not to *describe* my doing [a thing] . . . or to state that I am doing it: it is to do it" (3). Examples include "I promise," "I bequeath . . . ," "I christen . . . ," "I apologize," "I dare you," "I sentence you . . . ."

In the present book, departing from Austin's usage, I refer to these exemplary instances as *explicit performative utterances.* They have several syntactic and semantic features in common: they are in the (1) first-person singular (2) present (3) indicative (4) active; (5) the verb in each one names precisely the act (in Austin's term, the illocution) that the utterance itself performs; and (6) the adverb "hereby" could be inserted in each of them without distorting their form or meaning. Thus, "I [hereby] apologize" apologizes, "I [hereby] sentence" sentences, and so on.

If the category *explicit performative utterance* proves clarifying at all, it will not do so by sweeping the table clear of dubious cases. There are plenty of sentences whose force seems unproblematically performative in a classically Austinian sense but that violate each of the above rules. "The meeting is adjourned" violates 1 and 4, for example; "The court will come to order" violates 1 and 2; "You're out" violates 1 and 5; "Present!" violates 1, 2, and 3, if not also 6.

But the point of the narrowed category is not to introduce yet another level at which to play the game of seeking exceptions and of teasing out qualifying from nonqualifying utterances. Instead, I think the category is more useful in a spatialized mode of thought. If, as Austin himself says, there is finally no yes/no distinction between performative and nonperformative utterances, then it could be more helpful to imagine a maplike set of relations: a map that might feature *explicit performative utterances,* conforming strictly to rules 1 through 6, at its middle, and a multitude of other utterances scattered or clustered near and far, depending on the various ways they might resemble or differ from those examples. In Chapter 2 of *Touching Feeling,* "Around the Performative," I go further with this spatializing impulse, positing a new class of *periperformative* utterances whose complex efficacy depends on their tangency to, as well as their difference from, the explicit performatives.

Even this broad level of interest in the forms of performative language represents a departure from the deconstructive/queer lineage to which I referred earlier. For from Jacques Derrida to Judith Butler, the trajectory of literary and gender theory has angled increasingly away from (what might be called) the grammatical moment, or the grammatical impulse, in discussions of performativity. Let me oversimplify here in positing that both deconstruction and gender theory have invoked Austinian performativity in the service of an epistemological project that can roughly be identified as antiessentialism. Austinian performativity is about how language constructs or affects reality rather than merely describing it. This directly *productive* aspect of language is most telling, for antiessentialist projects, when the utterances in question are closest to claiming a simply descriptive relation to some freestanding, ostensibly extradiscursive reality. Analogously in the area of history, the same antiessentialist projects have foregrounded Foucault's repeated demonstrations of the *productive* force both of taxonomies and disciplines that have claimed to be simply descriptive and of prohibitions whose apparent effect is simply to negate. That language itself can be productive of reality is a primary ground of antiessentialist inquiry.

To that degree, both deconstruction and gender theory seem to have an interest in unmooring Austin's performative from its localized dwelling in a few exemplary utterances or kinds of utterance and showing it instead to be a property of language or discourse much more broadly. You could caricature Derrida as responding to Austin's demonstration of explicit performatives by saying, "But the only really interesting part of it is how all language is performative"; and Judith Butler as adding, "Not only that, but it's most performative when its performativity is least explicit—indeed, arguably, most of all when it isn't even embodied in actual words."

I have no quarrel to make with these powerful demonstrations, nor indeed with the antiessentialism that impels them. I would remark, though, on how both Derrida's and Butler's performativities, because they are in the service of an antiessentialist epistemological motive, can seem to be cast in the reverse image of the hypostatized grammatical taxonomies that have characterized, for example, John Searle's or Emil Benveniste's positivistic uses of Austin. That is to say, Derrida and Butler seem to emerge from a juncture at which Austin's syntactic taxonomies, which were originally both provisional and playful, can persist only as reductively essentializing; the move from *some* language to *all language* seems required by their antiessentialist project. Perhaps attending to the textures and effects of particular bits of language, as I try to do in many of these essays, requires a step to the side of antiessentialism, a relative lightening of the epistemological demand on essential truth.

I have also taken a distinct step to the side of the deconstructive project of analyzing apparently nonlinguistic phenomena in rigorously linguistic terms, as when Butler analyzes a particular gestural style as a variety of performative utterance ("Performative" 272–73). Like much deconstructive work, *Touching Feeling* wants to address aspects of experience and reality that do not present themselves in propositional or even in verbal form alongside others that do, rather than submit to the apparent common sense that requires a strict separation between the two and usually implies an ontological privileging of the former. What may be different in the present work, however, is a disinclination to reverse those priorities by subsuming nonverbal aspects of reality firmly under the aegis of the linguistic. I assume that the line between words and things or between linguistic and nonlinguistic phenomena is endlessly changing, permeable, and entirely unsusceptible to any definitive articulation. With Wittgenstein, however, I have an inclination to deprecate the assignment of a very special value, mystique, or thingness to meaning and language. Many kinds of objects and events *mean,* in many heterogeneous ways and contexts, and I see some value in not reifying or mystifying the linguistic kinds of meaning unnecessarily.

Up to this point I have been treating performativity as if its theoretical salience all came directly from work on speech acts following Austin. Yet in many contemporary usages, especially in gender and cultural studies, it seems to be tied primarily to, motivated primarily by the notion of a performance in the defining instance theatrical. Butler's early work articulates an invitation to, in her words, "consider gender . . . as . . . an 'act,' as it were, which is both intentional and performative, where 'performative' itself carries the double-meaning of 'dramatic' and 'non-referential' " ("Performative" 272–73). "Performative" at the present moment carries the authority of two quite different discourses, that of theater on the one hand, and of speech act theory and deconstruction on the other. Partaking in the prestige of both discourses, it nonetheless, as Butler suggests, means very differently in each. The stretch between theatrical and deconstructive meanings of "performative" can seem to span the polarities of nonverbal and verbal action. It also spans those of, at either extreme, the *extroversion* of the actor (aimed entirely outward toward the audience) and the *introversion* of the signifier (if "I apologize" only apologizes, "I sentence" only sentences, and so on). Michael Fried's opposition between theatricality and absorption seems custom-made for this paradox about "performativity": in its deconstructive sense performativity signals absorption; in the vicinity of the stage, however, the performative is the theatrical. But in another range of usages, a text such as Lyotard's *The Postmodern Condition* uses "performativity" to mean an extreme of something like *efficiency*—postmodern representation as a form of capitalist efficiency—while, again, the deconstructive "performativity" of Paul de Man or J. Hillis Miller seems to be characterized by the *dis*linkage precisely of cause and effect between the signifier and the world. At the same time, it's worth keeping in mind that even in deconstruction, more can be said of performative speech acts than that they are ontologically dislinked or introversively nonreferential. Following on de Man's demonstration of "a radical estrangement between the meaning and the performance of any text" (298), one might want to dwell not so much on the nonreference of the performative but rather on (what de Man calls) its necessarily "aberrant" (301) relation to its own reference: the torsion, the mutual perversion, as one might say, of reference and performativity. The first two chapters of *Touching Feeling* are especially involved with this unsettling aberrance between performativity and theatricality: the first in the lifelong, profound, and unrequited longing with which Henry James fantasized about the British theater; the second in an analysis of bourgeois marriage and chattel slavery as two versions of mobile theater — of the traveling proscenium — in nineteenth-century narrative.

BEYOND, BENEATH, AND BESIDE

I have already indicated that, for all its interest in performativity, the thrust of *Touching Feeling* is not to expose residual forms of essentialism lurking behind apparently nonessentialist forms of analysis. Nor is it to unearth unconscious drives or compulsions underlying the apparent play of literary forms. Nor again is it to uncover violent or oppressive historical forces masquerading under liberal aesthetic guise.

Without attempting to devalue such critical practices, I have tried in this project to explore some ways around the topos of depth or hiddenness, typically followed by a drama of exposure, that has been such a staple of critical work of the past four decades. *Beneath* and *behind* are hard enough to let go of; what has been even more difficult is to get a little distance from *beyond,* in particular the bossy gesture of "calling for" an imminently perfected critical or revolutionary practice that one can oneself only adumbrate.

Instead, as its title suggests, the most salient preposition in *Touching Feeling* is probably *beside.* Invoking a Deleuzian interest in planar relations, the irreducibly spatial positionality of *beside* also seems to offer some useful resistance to the ease with which *beneath* and *beyond* turn from spatial descriptors into implicit narratives of, respectively, origin and telos.

Beside is an interesting preposition also because there's nothing very dualistic about it; a number of elements may lie alongside one another, though not an infinity of them. *Beside* permits a spacious agnosticism about several of the linear logics that enforce dualistic thinking: noncontradiction or the law of the excluded middle, cause versus effect, subject versus object. Its interest does not, however, depend on a fantasy of metonymically egalitarian or even pacific relations, as any child knows who's shared a bed with siblings. *Beside* comprises a wide range of desiring, identifying, representing, repelling, paralleling, differentiating, rivaling, leaning, twisting, mimicking, withdrawing, attracting, aggressing, warping, and other relations.

Spatializing disciplines such as geography and anthropology do, though, have the advantage of permitting ecological or systems approaches to such issues as identity and performance. For instance, the anthropologist Esther

Newton includes in *Mother Camp,* her 1972 study of female impersonators in the United States, the floor plans of two drag clubs (71, 89). The plans are part of her field data on shows at each venue, and one of the strengths of her spatially precise analysis is an extra alertness to the multisided inter-actions among people "beside" each other in a room. Thus, while a per-former in one kind of room remains alone onstage and afterwards does no mixing with the audience, the performer in the other room remains in near-constant interaction with the band leader, club manager, members of the audience, and other performers both older and younger, in and out of vari-ous kinds of drag, amateur and professional. The effect underlines Newton's continuous assumption that drag is less a single kind of act than a hetero-geneous system, an ecological field whose intensive and defining relation-ality is internal as much as it is directed toward the norms it may challenge. When Butler draws on Newton's work at the end of *Gender Trouble,* on the other hand, the ecological attention to space collapses in favor of a temporal emphasis on gender as "stylized repetition" and "social temporality" (J. But-ler 140–41). With the loss of its spatiality, however, the internally complex field of drag performance suffers a seemingly unavoidable simplification and reification. In fact, I think this loss of dimension may explain why many early readers, wrongly, interpreted Butler's discussion as prescribing a sim-plistic voluntarity. Although temporal and spatial thinking are never really alternative to each other, I've consistently tried in *Touching Feeling* to push back against an occupational tendency to underattend to the rich dimension of space.

RUSES OF THE REPRESSIVE HYPOTHESIS

The jokes that stick in people's minds are the ones they don't quite get. *Touching Feeling* displays, I think, something like that relation to Foucault's *History of Sexuality, Volume 1.* Foucault's volume reminds me of a joke be-cause its argument is so promising and economical; my sense of not getting it comes from the way its very elegance seems also to make its promise unfulfillable.

To me, the almost delirious promise of the book is most attached to Fou-cault's identification of the "repressive hypothesis" and his suggestion that there might be ways of thinking around it. According to the repressive hy-pothesis that Foucault deprecates, the history of sexuality could only be that of the "negative relation" between power and sex, of "the insistence of the rule," of "the cycle of prohibition," of "the logic of censorship," and of "the uniformity of the apparatus" of scarcity and prohibition: "Whether one attributes it to the form of the prince who formulates rights, of the father who forbids, of the censor who enforces silence, or of the master who states the law, in any case one schematizes power in a juridical form, and one defines its effects as obedience" (82–85). Foucault, on the other hand, though he is far from claiming "that sex has not been prohibited or barred or masked or misapprehended since the classical age" (12), is more struck by the proliferation of modern discourses of sexuality than by their suppression. Or, more interestingly, he perceives that there may really be no "rupture" between "repression and the critical analysis of repression" (10); responding to the paradox of a society "which speaks verbosely of its own silence, [and] takes great pains to relate in detail the things it does not say" (8), he sees the modern period as defined, to the contrary, by "the multiplication of discourses concerning sex in the field of exercise of power itself: an institutional incitement to speak about it, and to do so more and more; a determination on the part of agencies of power to hear it spoken about, and to cause it to speak through explicit articulation and endlessly accumulated detail" (18). Thus, the would-be liberatory repressive hypothesis itself comes to be seen as a kind of ruse for mandating ever more of the oppressive verbal proliferation that had also gone on before and around it.

For a project of getting away from dualistic modes of thinking—especially about sex—what better point of departure than this discussion of the repressive hypothesis? Yet in reading Foucault's book more carefully, and especially in seeing the working out of its problematics in the writing of other scholars, it seemed increasingly clear that Foucault's book was divided against itself in what it wanted from its broad, almost infinitely ramified and subtle critique of the repressive hypothesis. I knew what I wanted from it: some ways of understanding human desire that might be quite to the side of prohibition and repression, that might hence be structured quite differently from the heroic, "liberatory," inescapably dualistic righteousness of hunting down and attacking prohibition/repression in all its chameleonic guises. If the critical analysis of repression is itself inseparable from repression, then surely to think with any efficacy has to be to think in some distinctly different way.

Foucault's searchingly critical analysis of the persistence of the repressive hypothesis through so many, supposedly radical and discontinuous discourses—Marxist, psychoanalytic, and libertarian, as well as liberal—certainly indicates that the project of thinking otherwise remained a prime motivation of his study. And to a considerable extent, his writings after this volume attempt to carry that project further. But the triumphally charismatic rhetorical force of *Volume 1* also suggests that Foucault convinced himself—certainly he has convinced many readers—that that analysis itself represented an exemplary instance of working outside of the repressive hypothesis. Rather than working outside of it, however, *Volume 1*, like much of Foucault's earlier work, might better be described as propagating the repressive hypothesis ever more broadly by means of displacement, multiplication, and hypostatization.

If my evaluation is accurate, here is a possible taxonomy of the most common ways of (mis?)understanding Foucault's discussion of the repressive hypothesis. Recent theorists seem to feel sure they understand his volume as arguing one of the following:

1. Even beyond the repressive hypothesis, some version of prohibition is still the most important thing to understand. But it operates through *producing* rather than through eliminating things/kinds of persons/behaviors/subjectivities.

2. Even beyond the repressive hypothesis, some version of prohibition is still the most important thing to understand. But it operates through *internalized* and apparently voluntary mechanisms, rather than through external, spectacular negative sanctions.

3. Even beyond the repressive hypothesis, some version of prohibition is still the most important thing to understand. But it bubbles up through *multiple*, often minute channels and discourses rather than through a singular law imposed from above.

4. Even beyond the repressive hypothesis, some version of prohibition is still the most important thing to understand. But it operates through a single, *transcendental* prohibition (language itself, say, or the Name of the Father) rather than through local, explicit ones.

5. Even beyond the repressive hypothesis, some version of prohibition is still the most important thing to understand. But it operates by disguising itself as *nature* (i.e., as essence). Nature and essentialism are, and have always been, the defining ruses of repression/prohibition.

It seems clear that, however heuristically powerful these trains of thought may be, none of them can fulfill Foucault's implicit promise: that there might be ways of stepping outside the repressive hypothesis, to forms of thought that would not be structured by the question of prohibition in the first place. But then, why would anyone hope to do so? Given the plain reality of prohibition, which Foucault admits, as a feature of every human discourse, let alone those of sexuality, it seems as though interest in side-stepping the repressive hypothesis could spring only from naïveté, whether willful or sincere: from a terminal reluctance to face reality.

But in responding so strongly to Foucault's implicit promise, I was actually not moved by the fantasy of a world without repression or prohibition. My discontent with the interpretations listed above is not, either, that they are too pessimistic or insufficiently utopian. Instead, impressed by Foucault's demonstration of the relentlessly self-propagating, adaptive structure of the repressive hypothesis, I came to see a cognitive danger in these interpretations: a moralistic tautology that became increasingly incapable of recognizing itself as such.

Or better than "tautology," drawn from the static language of logic, might be a systems description. Say that attempts to step aside from the repressive hypothesis, based on continuing rigorous study of its protean inclusivity, form an insoluble loop of positive feedback. It's as if A and B are in bed together under a dual-control electric blanket, but with the controls accidentally reversed: if A gets cold and turns up the temperature, B's side of the blanket will get warmer, whereupon B will turn down the temperature, making A's side even colder, so A turns up the temperature further — on B's side, and so on ad infinitum.

Chapter 4 of *Touching Feeling* analyzes such conceptual feedback loops — self-reinforcing, in Silvan Tomkins's terms, as opposed to self-fulfilling — in greater detail. Briefly, in the case of Foucault's volume and its effects, I would say that his analysis of the pseudodichotomy between repression and liberation has led, in many cases, to its conceptual reimposition in the even more abstractly reified form of the hegemonic and the subversive. The seeming ethical urgency of such terms masks their gradual evacuation of substance, as a kind of Gramscian-Foucauldian contagion turns "hegemonic" into another name for the status quo (i.e., everything that *is*) and defines "subversive" in, increasingly, a purely negative relation to that (an extreme of the same "negative relation" that had, in Foucault's argument, defined the repressive hypothesis in the first place). It's the same unhelpful structure that used to undergird historical arguments about whether a given period was one of "continuity" or "change." Another problem with reifying the status quo is what it does to the middle ranges of agency. One's relation to *what is* risks becoming reactive and bifurcated, that of a consumer: one's choices narrow to accepting or refusing (buying, not buying) this or that manifestation of it, dramatizing only the extremes of compulsion and voluntarity. Yet it is only the middle ranges of agency that offer space for effectual creativity and change.

A goodish Foucauldian subject, I'm rather abashed that *Touching Feeling* includes so little sex. A lot of the reason is the quotidian chance of my own life, as cancer therapy that aims to blot up every trace of circulating estrogen makes sexuality a less and less stimulating motive of reflection. It's also seemed, with the strategic banalization of gay and lesbian politics as well as their resolute disavowal of relation to the historical and continuing AIDS epidemic, as though in many areas the moment may be past when theory was in a very productive relation to sexual activism.

The closest this book comes to a sustained, directly sexual thematic is in Chapter 1, in a discussion of Henry James's fascination with the image of a hand that penetrates a rectum and disimpacts or "fishes out" the treasure imagined as collecting there. In an essay that has influenced me a lot, Renu Bora uses James's intense fecal interest as his point of departure for a remarkably productive discussion of the whole issue of texture. He develops the observation that to perceive texture is always, immediately, and de facto to be immersed in a field of active narrative hypothesizing, testing, and re-understanding of how physical properties act and are acted upon over time. To perceive texture is never only to ask or know What is it like? nor even just How does *it* impinge on *me?* Textural perception always explores two other questions as well: How did it get that way? and What could I do with it? These are the kind of intrinsically interactive properties that James J. Gibson called "affordances" in his 1966 book, *The Senses Considered as Perceptual Systems,* and, like Tomkins's work on affect, this approach to perception owes a great deal to the postwar moment of cybernetics and systems theory.

As Bora's essay shows, I haven't perceived a texture until I've instantaneously hypothesized whether the object I'm perceiving was sedimented, extruded, laminated, granulated, polished, distressed, felted, or fluffed up. Similarly, to perceive texture is to know or hypothesize whether a thing will be easy or hard, safe or dangerous to grasp, to stack, to fold, to shred, to climb on, to stretch, to slide, to soak. Even more immediately than other perceptual systems, it seems, the sense of touch makes nonsense out of any dualistic understanding of agency and passivity; to touch is always already to reach out, to fondle, to heft, to tap, or to enfold, and always also to understand other people or natural forces as having effectually done so before oneself, if only in the making of the textured object.

Walter Benjamin characterized one way of exploiting the reversible properties of textural objects and subjects when he wrote, "Even if a bourgeois is unable to give his earthly being permanence, it seems to be a matter of honour with him to preserve the traces of his articles and requisites of daily use in perpetuity. The bourgeoisie cheerfully takes the impression of a host of objects. For slippers and pocket watches, thermometers and egg cups, cutlery and umbrellas it tries to get covers and cases. It prefers velvet and plush covers which preserve the impression of every touch. For the . . . style of the end of the second empire, a dwelling becomes a kind of casing" (46). "This style views [the dwelling] as a kind of case for a person and embeds him in it together with all his appurtenances, tending his traces as nature tends dead fauna embedded in granite. One should not fail to recognize that there are two sides to this process. The real or sentimental value of the objects thus preserved is emphasized. They are removed from the profane eyes of nonowners, and in particular their outlines are blurred in a characteristic way. It is not strange that resistance to controls, something that becomes second nature to asocial persons, returns in the propertied bourgeoisie" (46–47).

Going from Victorian plush to postmodern shine, Bora notes that "smoothness is both a type of texture and texture's other" (99). His essay makes a very useful distinction between two kinds, or senses, of texture, which he labels "texture" with one x and "texxture" with two x's. Texxture is the kind of texture that is dense with offered information about how, substantively, historically, materially, it came into being. A brick or a metalwork pot that still bears the scars and uneven sheen of its making would exemplify texxture in this sense. But there is also the texture—one x this time—that defiantly or even invisibly blocks or refuses such information; there is texture, usually glossy if not positively tacky, that insists instead on the polarity between substance and surface, texture that signifies the willed erasure of its history. One consequence of Bora's treatment of the concept: however high the gloss, there is no such thing as textural lack.

Bora performs a bravura analysis of the textural history of the concept of fetishism, including both psychoanalytic and commodity fetishism, that seems to make the displacements of fetishism move, as if at the speed of light, along the displacements of the manufactured or overhighlighted surface. But the narrative-performative density of the other kind of texxture — its ineffaceable historicity — also becomes susceptible to a kind of fetish-value. An example of the latter might occur where the question is one of exoticism, of the palpable and highly acquirable textural record of the cheap, precious work of many foreign hands in the light of many damaged foreign eyes.

Bora's essay also emphasizes that although texture seems to have some kind of definitional grounding with reference to the sense of touch, texture itself is not coextensive with any single sense, but rather tends to be liminally registered "on the border of properties of touch and vision" (101). Indeed, other senses beyond the visual and haptic are involved in the perception of texture, as when we *hear* the brush-brush of corduroy trousers or the crunch of extra-crispy chicken.

If texture involves more than one sense, it is also true that the different properties, and radically divergent modern histories, of different perceptual systems are liable to torque and splay the history of texture as well. The sense of physical touch itself, at least so far, has been remarkably unsusceptible to being amplified by technology. Women who do breast self-examination are occasionally taught to use a film of liquid soap, a square of satiny cloth, or even a pad of thin plastic filled with a layer of water to make the contours of the breast more salient to their fingers. But this minimal sensory enhancement is merely additive compared to the literally exponential enhancements of visual stimulus since Leeuwenhoek and Newton. The narrator of *Middlemarch*, one of the definitive novels of texture, can zoom in a mere two sentences from telescope to microscope (Eliot 83). Once such visual ranges become commonplace the authority of the fingers will never be the same — though their very resistance to amplification may mean that they represent one kind of perceptual gold standard. Indeed, the increasingly divergent physical scales (and the highly differential rates of their change) that characterize the relation between touch and vision in the modern period result in understandings of texture that make it as apt to represent crises and fissures of meaning as metonymic continuities.

Thus, the need to discuss texture across senses brings with it a need to think about texture across different scales. Technologies of travel, for example, as well as of vision emphasize that, although texture has everything to do with scale, there is no one physical scale that intrinsically is the scale of texture. As your plane circles over an airport, texture is what a whole acre of trees can provide. But when you're chopping wood, a single tree may constitute shape or structure within your visual field, whereas texture pertains to the level of the cross-grained fibers of the wood in relation to the sleek bite of the axe.

Furthermore, whatever the scale, one bump on a surface, or even three, won't constitute texture. A repeated pattern like polka dots might, but it depends on how big they are or how close you are: from across the room you might see them as a flat sheet of gray; at a few feet, the dots make a visible texture; through a magnifying glass you'll see an underlying texture of paper or fabric unrelated to the two or three rounded shapes that make a big design. Texture, in short, comprises an array of perceptual data that includes repetition, but whose degree of organization hovers just below the level of shape or structure.

In a challenge to Benjamin's identification of textural salience with bourgeois privacy, William Morris makes a utopian use of these textural properties in his speculative novel *News from Nowhere*, where political equality, communitarian ethics, productive aesthetic pleasure, and psychological equanimity extend unbroken from one to another surface of congruent scale; and the characteristic Morris pattern of equidistant, unforegrounded, unbroken, and perspectiveless ornamentation drawn "from nature" spreads from landscape to architecture to interior design to male and female raiment to the body itself and back again. With their liberatory, elastic aesthetic of texture these characters express "intense and overweening love of the very skin and surface of the earth on which man dwells, such as a lover has in the fair flesh of the woman he loves" (158); conversely, their clothing is ornamented out of "liking to see the coverings of our bodies beautiful like our bodies are—just as a deer's or an otter's skin has been made beautiful from the first" (165).

It is also worth noting how unexpectedly the definition of performativity itself is inflected by the language of texture. The thematics that Austin applies to his taxonomic work on the performative are of a mucky consistency that makes a startling contrast with his dandified fastidious syntax; it is as though the dimensions of true/false (for the constative) and happy/unhappy (for the performative) are always in danger of wiping out along the confounding axis of wet/dry. According to Austin, for all the dry Jack Benny–like hilarity of his style, with his project we are liable to find ourselves "bog[ging], by logical stages, down" (13), or to have "two new keys in our hands, *and*, of course, simultaneously two new skids under our feet" (25). "To feel the firm ground of prejudice slipping away is exhilarating," he writes, "but brings its revenges" (61); "I shall only," he promises later, "give you a run around, or rather a flounder around" (151). Clearly for Austin, taxonomic work with particular sentences is not a rigid, Searlean reification of performativity, but rather the filthy workshop of its creation, criss-crossed with skid marks, full of dichotomies that are "in need, like so many dichotomies, of elimination" (149); it represents the vital, perhaps painful, not-yet-differentiated quick from which the performative emerges.

In ways like these, texture seems like a promising level of attention for shifting the emphasis of some interdisciplinary conversations away from the recent fixation on epistemology (which suggests that performativity/ performance can show us whether or not there are essential truths and how we could, or why we can't, know them) by asking new questions about phenomenology and affect (what motivates performativity and performance, for example, and what individual and collective effects are mobilized in their execution?). The title I've chosen for these essays, *Touching Feeling*, records the intuition that a particular intimacy seems to subsist between textures and emotions. But the same double meaning, tactile plus emotional, is already there in the single word "touching"; equally it's internal to the word "feeling." I am also encouraged in this association by the dubious epithet "touchy-feely," with its implication that even to talk about affect virtually amounts to cutaneous contact.

If anything, the association between touch and affect may be too obvious: its common sense seems to offer too easy support to modern assumptions about the centrality of sexual desire to all human contact and feeling. The post-Romantic "power/knowledge" regime that Foucault analyzes, the one that structures and propagates the repressive hypothesis, follows the Freudian understanding that one physiological drive — sexuality, libido, desire — is the ultimate source, and hence in Foucault's word is seen to embody the "truth," of human motivation, identity, and emotion. In my own first book on sexuality, for example, I drew on this modern consensus in explaining the term "male homosocial desire": "For the most part, I will be using 'desire' in a way analogous to the psychoanalytic use of 'libido'–not for a particular affective state or emotion, but for the affective or social force, the glue, even when its manifestation is hostility or hatred or something less emotively charged, that shapes an important relationship" (Sedgwick, *Between Men* 2). This consensus view does not exclude emotions, but as the quotation suggests, it views emotion primarily as a vehicle or manifestation of an underlying libidinal drive. Excitement, rage, even indifference are seen as more or less equivalent transformations of "desire." The nature or quality of the affect itself, seemingly, is not of much more consequence than the color of the airplane used to speed a person to a destination.

Reducing affect to drive in this way permits a diagrammatic sharpness of thought that may, however, be too impoverishing in qualitative terms. Each essay in *Touching Feeling* tries in some way to offer alternatives to that habitual subordination of affect to drive. Chapter 3 discusses some early stages of Adam Frank's and my encounter with the writing of Silvan Tomkins, the psychologist whose theories underpin most of these approaches.[1] For Tomkins, the difference between the drive system and the affect system is not that one is more rooted in the body than the other; he understands both to be thoroughly embodied, as well as more or less intensively interwoven with cognitive processes. The difference instead is between more specific and more general, more and less constrained: between biologically based systems that are less and more capable of generating complexity or degrees of freedom.[2] Thus, for example, the drives are relatively narrowly constrained in their aims: breathing will not satisfy my hunger, nor will sleeping satisfy my need to excrete waste. The drives are also relatively time-constrained, inasmuch as I need to breathe within the next minute, drink something today, and eat within the next few weeks to sustain life. Most important, their range of objects is also relatively constrained: only a tiny subset of gases satisfy my need to breathe or of liquids my need to drink. In these and several other ways, sexuality is clearly the least constrained (most affectlike) of the drives. "Had Freud not smuggled some of the properties of the affect system into his conception of the drives, his system would have been of much less interest," Tomkins writes, and he also sees Freudian theory as damaged by using sexuality to represent drives in general (*Shame*

49). But to the (limited) degree that sexuality is a drive, it shares the immediate *instrumentality,* the defining orientation toward a specified aim and end
different from itself, that finally distinguishes the drives from the affects.

Short of a complete summary of Tomkins, these dimensions may stand
for the significant differences between affects and drives. Affects have far
greater freedom than drives with respect to, for example, time (anger can
evaporate in seconds but can also motivate a decades-long career of revenge)
and aim (my pleasure in hearing a piece of music can make me want to hear
it repeatedly, listen to other music, or study to become a composer myself).
Especially, however, affects have greater freedom with respect to object, for
unlike the drives, "any affect may have any 'object.' This is the basic source
of complexity of human motivation and behavior" (7). The object of affects
such as anger, enjoyment, excitement, or shame is not proper to the affects
in the same way that air is the object proper to respiration: "There is literally
no kind of object which has not historically been linked to one or another
of the affects. Positive affect has been invested in pain and every kind of
human misery, and negative affect has been experienced as a consequence
of pleasure and every kind of triumph of the human spirit. . . . The same
mechanisms enable [people] to invest any and every aspect of existence with
the magic of excitement and joy or with the dread of fear or shame and distress" (54). Affects can be, and are, attached to things, people, ideas, sensations, relations, activities, ambitions, institutions, and any number of other
things, including other affects. Thus, one can be excited by anger, disgusted
by shame, or surprised by joy.

This freedom of affects also gives them a structural potential not enjoyed by the drive system: in contrast to the instrumentality of drives and
their direct orientation toward an aim different from themselves, the affects
can be autotelic: "There is no strict analog in the affect system for the rewarding effect of drive consummation. It is rather the case that *affect arousal
and reward are identical in the case of positive affects;* what activates positive
affects 'satisfies' " (58; emphasis added). In Tomkins's extended thought experiment about how to create a genuinely human automoton,

> [the machine] would require an affect system. What does this mean in terms
> of a specific program? There must be built into such a machine a number
> of responses which have self-rewarding and self-punishing characteristics.
> This means that these responses are inherently acceptable or inherently un-

acceptable.³ These are essentially aesthetic characteristics of the affective responses—and in one sense no further reducible. Just as the experience of
redness could not be further described to a color-blind man, so the particular
qualities of excitement, joy, fear, sadness, shame, and anger cannot be further described if one is missing the necessary effector and receptor apparatus.
This is not to say that the physical properties of the stimuli and the recep-
tors cannot be further analyzed. This analysis is without limit. It is rather
the phenomenological quality which we are urging has intrinsic rewarding
or punishing characteristics.

If and when the automaton learns English we would require a spontaneous reaction to joy or excitement of the sort "I like this," and to fear and
shame and distress "Whatever this is, I don't care for it." We cannot define
this quality in terms of the immediate behavioral responses to it, since *it is the
gap between these affective responses and instrumental responses which is necessary*
if it is to function like a human motivational response. (42; emphasis added)

It makes sense, then, that Tomkins considers sexuality "the drive in which
the affective component plays the largest role": not only is it "the least im-
perious of all the drives," but it is the only one "in which activation of the
drive even without consummation has a rewarding rather than a punishing
quality. It is much more exciting and rewarding," he understates, "to feel
sexually aroused than to feel hungry or thirsty" (60). Even though sexual
desire is usually oriented toward an aim and object other than itself, it is
much more malleable in its aims and objects than are the other drives, and
also, like the positive affects, has the potential of being autotelic.

The most important commonsensical assumption about drives that
Tomkins shows to be false is that, because they are more immediately tied to
survival, they are therefore experienced more directly, more urgently, and
more robustly than are affects. Common sense holds, that is, that the drive
system is the primary motivator of human behavior, to which the affects
are inevitably secondary. Tomkins shows the opposite to be true: that motivation itself, even the motivation to satisfy biological drives, is the business
of the affect system:

I almost fell out of my chair in surprise and excitement when I suddenly
realized that the panic of one who experiences the suffocation of interruption of his vital air supply has nothing to do with the anoxic drive signal

per se [because gradual loss of oxygen, even when fatal, produces no panic because there is no trigger for the affect of surprise]. . . . It was a short step to see that excitement had nothing per se to do with sexuality or with hunger, and that the apparent urgency of the drive system was borrowed from its co-assembly with appropriate affects as necessary amplifiers. Freud's id suddenly appeared to be a paper tiger since sexuality, as he best knew, was the most finicky of drives, easily rendered impotent by shame or anxiety or boredom or rage. ("Quest" 309)

In short, the drive system cannot be properly understood as a primary structure in which the affects function as subordinate details or supports. In fact, because of their freedom and complexity, "affects may be either much more casual than any drive could be or much more monopolistic. . . . Most of the characteristics which Freud attributed to the Unconscious and to the Id are in fact salient aspects of the affect system. . . . Affects enable both insatiability and extreme lability, fickleness and finickiness" (52).

If texture and affect, touching and feeling seem to belong together, then, it is not because they share a particular delicacy of scale, such as would necessarily call for "close reading" or "thick description." What they have in common is that *at whatever scale they are attended to,* both are irreducibly phenomenological. To describe them primarily in terms of structure is always a qualitative misrepresentation. Attending to psychology and materiality at the level of affect and texture is also to enter a conceptual realm that is not shaped by lack nor by commonsensical dualities of subject versus object or of means versus ends.

Differences among the successive essays in *Touching Feeling* seem to trace several concurrent narratives whose meaning is not evident to me. The sexual interest of the essays, as I've mentioned, seems to decrease, whereas the sense of pedagogy deepens. All the essays are very involved with affect, but the particular affect, shame, whose fascination led me so far into the forest of affect theory let go its hold on me there. By the end of the book, the positive affects (interest-excitement and, especially, enjoyment-joy, in Tomkins's schema) are much more involving. That these are not only the happy but also the autotelic affects seems resonant with this volume's placement of Buddhism. If such narratives can be braided together, what appears will hardly be more linear than the account I tried to compose in *A Dialogue on Love,* where the therapist's notes near the end invoke

SILK WORK — TURNING FABRIC INTO OTHER FABRIC / CHILDHOOD BLANKET WITH THE SATIN BINDING / SKIN HUNGER / BRO'S PILLOW "PIFFO," HIS DROOLING, "MAKING FISHES" ON IT / MAY SAY SOMETHING ABOUT HOW HUNGRY OUR SKIN WAS FOR TOUCH; BUT ALSO ABOUT OUR HAVING THE PERMISSION TO DEVELOP AUTONOMOUS RESOURCES / . . . . TREASURE SCRAPS OF SILK / SOMEHOW THE SILK AND SHIT GO TOGETHER — THE WASTE PRODUCTS, FANTASIES OF SELF SUFFICIENCY, NOT DEPENDENT, SPINNING STRAW INTO GOLD. (206)

JUDITH SCOTT, TEXTILE ARTIST

The photograph on the frontispiece of *Touching Feeling* was the catalyst that impelled me to assemble the book in its present form. It is one of many taken by the California photographer Leon A. Borensztein of Judith Scott (b. 1943) with her work.

The sculpture in this picture is fairly characteristic of Scott's work in its construction: a core assembled from large, heterogeneous materials has been hidden under many wrapped or darned layers of multicolored yarn, cord, ribbon, rope, and other fiber, producing a durable three-dimensional shape, usually oriented along a single axis of length, whose curves and planes are biomorphically resonant and whose scale bears comparison to Scott's own body. The formal achievements that are consistent in her art include her inventive techniques for securing the giant bundles, her subtle building and modulation of complex three-dimensional lines and curves, and her startlingly original use of color, whether bright or muted, which can stretch across a plane, simmer deeply through the multilayered wrapping, or drizzle graphically along an emphatic suture.

All of Scott's work that I've seen on its own has an intense presence, but the subject of this photograph also includes her relation to her completed work, and presumptively also the viewer's relation to the sight of that dyad. For me, to experience a subject-object distance from this image is no more plausible than to envision such a relation between Scott and her work. She and her creation here present themselves to one another with equally expansive welcome. Through their closeness, the sense of sight is seen to dissolve in favor of that of touch. Not only the artist's hands and bare forearms but her face are busy with the transaction of texture. Parents and babies, twins (Scott is a twin), or lovers might commune through such haptic absorption. There is no single way to understand the "besideness" of these two forms, even though one of them was made by the other. The affect that saturates the photo is mysterious, or at least multiple, in quality: besides the obvious tenderness with which Scott embraces the sculpture, her relaxed musculature and bowed head suggest sadness, for example, as perhaps does the abandon with which she allows her features to be squashed against it. The height and breadth of her embrace could suggest either that she is consoling or herself seeks consolation from the sculpture, which is slightly canted toward her while she stands upright on her own feet; the loose-jointed breadth of her embrace can also be read as a sign of her Down syndrome. Yet the jaunty top and bottom points of the rounded shape are only the most visible of the suggestions that this soberly toned black and white photograph is at the same time ablaze with triumph, satisfaction, and relief.

Inevitably, both before and since her recent recognition within the framework of "outsider" art, Scott has been repeatedly diagnosed in terms of lack. Her deafness, the one deficit that went undiagnosed until middle age, led to extreme exaggerations of the severity of her retardation; classed as "ineducable" in childhood, she was warehoused in a crushingly negligent Ohio asylum system for over thirty-five years (MacGregor 49–51; Smith). Even after she emerged as an artist with the support of California's Creative Growth Art Center, her most encouraging and excited teacher, the fiber artist Sylvia Seventy, inexplicably decided that she was color blind (MacGregor 69) and unable to decide for herself when a piece was finished (72). And John MacGregor, the psychoanalytic critic of Art Brut who has been her strongest proponent, is nonetheless compulsive in applying to her the language of emphatic negation: "There is not the slightest possibility that Judith envisions the eventual outcome, the final form, of her work" (33); "Judith was certainly not engaged in the production of works of art" (72); "Judith is completely unaware of the existence of sculpture" (92); "The notion of abstract, non-representational form is a complex idea totally outside of Judith's ability to conceptualize" (109). MacGregor also seems to consider that all of Scott's artistic activity — maybe all her activity, in fact — must be categorized as "unconscious," perhaps because she does not use language (106, 111).

I don't suppose it's necessarily innocuous when a fully fluent, well-rewarded language user, who has never lacked any educational opportunity, fastens with such a strong sense of identification on a photograph, an oeuvre, and a narrative like these of Judith Scott's. Yet oddly, I think my identification with Scott is less as the subject of some kind of privation than as the holder of an obscure treasure, or as a person receptively held by it. The drama of Scott's talent is surely heightened by her awful history, her isolation from language, and what I assume must be frequent cognitive frustrations. But the obvious fullness of her aesthetic consciousness, her stubbornly confident access to autotelic production, her artist's ability to continue asking new, troubling questions of her materials that will be difficult and satisfying for them to answer — these privileges seem to radiate at some angle that is orthogonal to the axis of disability.

Barbara Herrnstein Smith is fond of the notion of the "senile sublime," as she calls it, and I've always been attracted to it, too. She uses it in conversation to describe various more or less intelligible performances by old brilliant people, whether artists, scientists, or intellectuals, where the bare outlines of a creative idiom seem finally to emerge from what had been the obscuring puppy fat of personableness, timeliness, or sometimes even of coherent sense. Who wouldn't find it attractive, the idea of emerging into a senile sublime? I do feel close to Scott in that we evidently share a sensibility in which fibers and textures have particular value, relationally and somehow also ontologically. But in acknowledging the sense of tenderness toward a treasured gift that wants exploring, I suppose I also identify with the very expressive sadness and fatigue in this photograph. Probably one reason Scott's picture was catalytic for this hard-to-articulate book: it conveys an affective and aesthetic fullness that can attach even to experiences of cognitive frustration. In writing this book I've continually felt pressed against the limits of my stupidity, even as I've felt the promising closeness of transmissible gifts.

NOTES

1. So far, I have been following common usage in using "affect" and "emotion" interchangeably. In the rest of this section, however, I focus on "affects" in Tomkins's sense. For Tomkins, a limited number of affects — analogous to the elements of a periodic table — combine to produce what are normally thought of as emotions, which, like the physical substances formed from the elements, are theoretically unlimited in number. See Tomkins, *Shame* 34–74.

2. In this context Tomkins does not use "freedom" in the sense of an individual's volun-

tarity; for his useful discussion of the relation between freedom and complexity, see *Shame* 35–52, which offers some tools for a systems-theory approach to what I referred to above as "the middle ranges of agency."

3. Note that it is the *responses,* not the stimuli, that have inherent affective qualities. This represents an important difference from behaviorists, whose ideas Tomkins had no patience with, although, to twenty-first-century readers, his writing style can make him sound like them.

INTERLUDE, PEDAGOGIC

She resembles a recurrent
Scene from my childhood.
A scene called Mother Has Fainted.
Mother's body
Was larger, now it no longer moved;
Breathed, somehow, as if it no longer breathed.
Her face no longer smiled at us
Or frowned at us. Did anything to us.
Her face was queerly flushed
Or else queerly pale; I am no longer certain.
That it was queer I am certain.
—RANDALL JARRELL, "Hope"

The most dramatic thing that happened to me in the summer of 1991 was when I passed out for television. The TV cameras from the local news shows were there because we were having a demonstration, organized by an Ad Hoc Coalition of Black Lesbians and Gays, with participation from ACT UP–Triangle, against the University of North Carolina's local PBS station, which was refusing to air Marlon Riggs's *Tongues Untied,* the first film on the almost genocidally underrepresented topic of black gay men in the United States. It was a muggy southern summer afternoon by the side of a highway in Research Triangle Park. I had thought I was feeling strong enough for what looked to be a sedate demonstration (no civil disobedience), in spite of several months of chemotherapy that had pretty much decimated my blood cells.

But I guess I'd forgotten or repressed how arduous a thing it is any time a group of people try to project voices and bodies into a space of public protest that has continually to be reinvented from scratch, even though (or because) the protest *function* is so routinized and banalized by the state and media institutions that enable it. You know what local news shows look like, how natural it seems that there should be, now and then, those shots of grim, dispirited people waving signs and moving their mouths, I mean moving our mouths, I mean yelling.

Yet the routinization of that tableau doesn't mean a lack of danger to the people occupying it. Arriving, I flashed onto a very different scene from New England a few winters earlier, when Amherst College, so pliant and responsive in matters curricular, stony and ruthless in matters managerial, had set out to do some (successful) union busting at the quaint Lord Jeffery Amherst Inn. On a ravishing Dickinsonian winter afternoon the concerned faculty—maybe five of us—and students gathered on the town green, holding signs, to silently "witness" the civil disobedience of a dozen union employees who were going to block traffic in front of the Inn and get arrested. The police had a yellow schoolbus there, everything was ready, and a beautiful, thick, silent and silencing snow began to fall. It was one of the first demonstrations I'd been a part of that wasn't a mass demonstration, and my heart, in spite of me, almost burst with exaltation at the spare and indicative Americanness of the scene, like reading Thoreau but also like a movie, at the pageantlike and intimately scaled democratic space of the town commons, at the patience of the highly choreographed police, at what seemed the thrilling symbolic leverage, within a tightly articulated legal discourse and history, of the protesters' most austere speech acts—silence, immobility, refusal—and at, I suppose, the secularized religiosity of my own function of "witnessing" this scene, another silent but apparently dense performative that made standing still with my mouth shut feel like embodying the whole Bill of Rights. It was the snow, profuse, gratuitous, equalizing, theatrically transformative, that seemed most to guarantee the totality and symbolic evenness of this pure, signifying space. It was also, however, the contingency of the snow that, in the slow unfolding of the afternoon, projected heart-stoppingly onto the largest screen the ambiguities about the "symbolic" standing of the protestors' refusals. Would the traffic stop for these anomalous figures in the road? *Could* it? Did they always know whether it could? Were nerves fraying? As protestors got read their rights, handcuffed, bundled off into the icing schoolbus, questions of standing devolved into dangerous questions of footing: it doesn't take much state force, in the twist of a policeman's wrist, in the simple not-thereness or symmetrical refusal of a policeman's arm, to send a handcuffed person crashing to the slippery ground. And it seemed puzzlingly as if the concrete and very contingent dangers of the scene, interfering on the pure symbolic register of civil disobedience, at the same time somehow were of its essence and indeed actually constituted its symbolic and performative power.

That was New England, though, and this was North Carolina, a New South whose stringy and desultory spaces seemed already designed to provide a checkerboard of tedium and violence. Also that was a labor dispute, whose issues were always within referring distance of the great white scouring abstraction Money; this was a fight about blackness, queerness, and (implicitly) AIDS: properties of bodies, some of them our bodies, of bodies that it seemed important to say most people are very willing, and some people murderously eager, to see not exist. I got there late, hugged and kissed the friends and students I hadn't seen in a few weeks, and Brian gave me his sign to carry. I can't remember—I hardly noticed—what was on it, even though when I was a kid I remember that most of the symbolic power of the picket lines I saw used to seem to inhere in the voluntary self-violation, the then almost inconceivable willed assumption of stigma, that seemed to me to be involved in anyone's consenting to go public as a written-upon body, an ambulatory placard—a figure I, as a child, could associate only with the disciplining of children. I wonder now how I related that voluntary stigma to the nondiscretionary stigma of skin color—that is, of skin color other than white—considering how fully, when I was growing up in the 1950s and early 1960s, "protest" itself implied black civil rights protest. It was at some distance from that childhood terror of the written-upon body, though not at an infinite distance, that, already wearing the black "Silence=Death" T-shirt chosen because I thought it would read more graphically from a distance than my white ACT UP–Triangle T-shirt, I gratefully took Brian's placard and commenced wagging it around with energy and satisfaction, as if to animate it with the animation of my own body and make it speak: to the TV cameras, to people in the cars that were passing, to the little line of demonstrators across the road. The heat, the highway, the outdoors seemed to blot up voices and gestures and the chants that we hurled out of our lungs, trying exhaustingly to create a seamless curtain of rage and demand: "We're here, we're queer, and we won't pledge this year"; or better, "Snap! Snap! Snap! What is this racist crap?" There was also a lot of ACT UP's favorite funny chant, which makes me very nervous, a call-and-response borrowed from a heckler at an earlier demonstration of ours: one side rousingly yells "Freedom of speech!" and the other side responds "Shut up!"—"Freedom of speech!" "Shut up!"

The space of the demonstration was riddled, not only with acoustical sinkholes, but with vast unbridgeable gaps of meaning. It was in these gaps, or from out of them, that the force of any public protest might materialize, but into which, as well, it constantly risked dissolving. I think of the way our space was created and de-created, continually, by the raking attentions and sullen withdrawals of, on the one hand, the state troopers—the pathetically young and overdressed white state troopers, who at the same time looked totally out of it in their sweltering uniforms and yet effortlessly, through the same uniforms and because they had guns and radios, commanded all the physical presence and symbolic density that we were struggling to accrue, who made a space of their own ostentatiously apart from the demonstrators, ostentatiously "neutral," untouchable by the force of anything we could shout; but who had also the function of radiating jags of menace in our direction, shards of volatile possibility that boomeranged around in the ether of our expression—and on the other hand, from another direction, the TV cameras, actually a complex of trucks, tripods, portable and stationary machines, and white people to occupy both ends of them: camera people, insolent with implicit dare and promise, to take them for walks along the line of our faces and bodies, and pretty girl and boy reporters to make a foreground to which our angry bodies could serve as background, generating the depth of field, the assurance of perspective and ten-foot-pole distance, for which television news serves as guardian and guarantee.

The uses we had for this news apparatus, as opposed to the uses it had for us, I condensed in my mind under the double formulation "shaming and smuggling." With the force of our words—referentially, that is—our object was to discredit the pretense at representing the public maintained by our local "public" broadcasting station, to shame them into compliance or negotiation on the issue of airing this film. With the force of our bodies, however, and in that sense performatively, our object was not merely to demand representation, representation elsewhere, but ourselves to give, to *be* representation: somehow to smuggle onto the prohibitive airwaves some version of the apparently unrepresentably dangerous and endangered conjunction, queer and black.

Our need to be exemplary bodies sprang from the history of radical denial of exemplary function to black gay bodies at the intersection of two kinds of community that seem so often to carve each other out of perceptual existence: a tacitly racist white gay community for whom a black queer body, however eroticized, might stand as a representation of blackness but could never seem to embody queerness itself, and a more or less openly homophobic African American community by whom the queerness of any black figure must be denied, suppressed, or overridden for that figure to be allowed to function as an embodiment of black identity or struggle.

The ambitions of our group of demonstrators—shaming, smuggling— were distinct, but for either ambition to be effective, they had to be presented as one. The assertion that black queer absence gave the lie to the claims of a representative use of the airwaves could take its point only from the patent availability, indeed the assertive presence of such bodies. The protest function also, however, offered pretext and legitimacy to the presence of such bodies: it seems likely that our protest was the first occasion on which local TV in central North Carolina was constrained to offer images of people explicitly self-classified under the rubrics of black queer identity.

Shaming, smuggling: the two ambitions gesture at, and in a sense can stand for, a tradition of philosophical/linguistic play between constative and performative utterance. Shaming, in this instance constatively: "The inclusive representation you, North Carolina Public Television, have claimed to offer of this society demonstrably excludes a constituent part of it" — a verifiable, referential assertion about something away over there. Smuggling, performatively: "Present! *Ecce homo*" — a self-validating, hence self-referential form of meaning guaranteed by its relation to embodiment.

And yet I can't claim for the twinned ambitions behind this demonstration the supposedly clean distinctions between constative and performative, or between reference and embodiment. Few words, after all, could be more performative in the Austinian sense than "shame": "Shame on you," "For shame," or just "Shame!", the locutions that give sense to the word, do not describe or refer to shame but themselves confer it. At the same time, our "smuggling" activity of embodiment, however self-referential, could boast of no autonomy from the oblique circuits of representation. *At least* because a majority of our smuggling-intent bodies were not themselves black, many of us who had so much need to make a new space for black queer representation were haplessly embroiled in the processes of reference: reference to other bodies standing beside our own, to the words on our placards, to what we could only hope would be the sufficiently substantial sense — if, indeed, even *we* understood it rightly — of our own intent.

After a while I could tell I was feeling tired and dizzy; sensibly, I sat down. There was something so absorbing and so radically heterogeneous about this space of protest that when, next thing I knew, the urgent sound of my name and a slowly dawning sense of disorientation suggested that I seemed very oddly to be stretched out in the dirt — coming to — surfacing violently from the deep pit of another world — with a state trooper taking my pulse and an ambulance already on the way — the gaping, unbridgeable hole left in my own consciousness felt like a mise-en-abîme image of the whole afternoon; not least because the image, a compelling one on which both TV cameras were converging, hindered by protestors who struggled to block their sightlines ("Now *that's* censorship," the TV people rumbled, with some justice) — that image, of a mountainous figure, supine, black-clad, paper-white, weirdly bald (my nice African hat had pitched to a distance), Silence = Death emblazoned, motionless, apparently female, uncannily gravid with meaning (but with what possible meaning? what usable meaning?) was available to everybody there except herself.

> As people arrive, no music, only silence.
> I like such awkward silences, though many resist them,
> especially in my classes. But a lot goes on during them.
> —MICHAEL LYNCH, instructions for his
> memorial service, February 1990

☞ The meaning with which that body was so dense, too dense, was indeed not a usable one (call me the face on the cutting-room floor) in relation to the complexly choreographed performative agendas and effects of that demonstration. Yet I like to brood over the reconstruction of that moment when I fainted partly because, through my absentation, it seems to place me, however briefly, at the center of the work of protest—as though I were Alice Walker's luminous vacuum of a heroine Meridian, say, whose narcoleptic presence/absence seems the perfect condensation of her contagious unconsciousness of fear, her uncanny talent for crystallizing loss and rage as socially embodied defiance and movement.

I wish I had those meridianal traits, but can only wish it; if that sprawling body offered testimony, it was less to a triumphal purposefulness than to a certain magnetic queerness (by magnetic I mean productive of deviance) in the process called demonstration. What felt to me like an almost telescopic condensation of the protest event embodied, as the most radical condensations will, less the power of condensation than of the displacements of meaning that interline it. (Displacements: the white skin of someone to whom black queer invisibility had come to feel—partly through representational work like *Tongues Untied*, partly in the brutalities of every day's paper, partly through transferentially charged interactions with students—like an aching gap in the real; the legible bodily stigmata not of AIDS but of a "female" cancer whose lessons for living powerfully with I found myself, at that time, learning largely from men with AIDS; the defamiliarization and indeed the gaps of de-recognition toward my "own" "female" "white" body, experienced under the pressure of amputation and prosthesis, of drugs, of the gender-imploding experience of female baldness; the way in which, whatever one's privilege, a person living with a grave disease in this particular culture is inducted ever more consciously, ever more needily, yet with ever more profound and transformative revulsion into the manglingly differential world of health care under American capitalism.) It was with joy, with chagrin, with intense discomfort that I was coming to feel such displacements more and more in the condensing and complexly representative space of the classroom as well—a classroom space regularly reconstituted by threat and mourning and by the bareness of the cognitive and performative resistances we were able to mount to them. Finding myself as teacher, as exemplar, as persuader, as reader to be less and less at the center of my own classroom, I was also finding that the voice of a certain abyssal displacement—and mine was certainly not the only such displacement going on in these classrooms—could provide effects that might sometimes wrench the boundaries of discourse around in productive if not always obvious ways.

Chapter 1

SHAME, THEATRICALITY, AND

QUEER PERFORMATIVITY: HENRY JAMES'S

The Art of the Novel

In the couple of weeks after the World Trade Center was destroyed in September 2001, I had a daily repetition of an odd experience, one that was probably shared by many walkers in the same midsouthern latitudes of Manhattan. Turning from a street onto Fifth Avenue, even if I was heading north, I would feel compelled first to look south in the direction of the World Trade Center, now gone. This inexplicably furtive glance was associated with a conscious wish: that my southward vista would again be blocked by the familiar sight of the pre–September 11 twin towers, somehow come back to loom over us in all their complacent ugliness. But, of course, the towers were always still gone. Turning away, shame was what I would feel.

Why shame? I think this was, in effect, one of those situations in which, as Silvan Tomkins puts it, "one is suddenly looked at by one who is strange, or . . . one wishes to look at or commune with another person but suddenly cannot because he is strange, or one expected him to be familiar but he suddenly appears unfamiliar, or one started to smile but found one was smiling at a stranger" (*Shame* 135). Not that an urban vista is quite the same as a loved face, but it isn't quite different, either: the despoiled view was a suddenly toothless face, say, or suddenly preoccupied, or suddenly dead—to say nothing, even, of the historical implications surrounding that particular change of landscape.

These flashes of shame didn't seem particularly related to prohibition or transgression. Beyond that, though it was I who felt the shame, it wasn't especially myself I was ashamed of. It would be closer to say I was ashamed *for* the estranged and denuded skyline; such feelings interlined, of course, the pride, solidarity, and grief that also bound me to the city. The shame had to do, too, with visibility and spectacle—the hapless visibility of the towers' absence now, the shockingly compelling theatricality of their destruction.

Recent work by theorists and psychologists of shame locates the proto-form (eyes down, head averted) of this powerful affect—which appears in infants very early, between the third and seventh month of life, just after the infant has become able to distinguish and recognize the face of its care-giver—at a particular moment in a particular repeated narrative. That is the moment when the circuit of mirroring expressions between the child's face and the caregiver's recognized face (a circuit that, if it can be called a form of primary narcissism, suggests that narcissism from the very first throws itself sociably, dangerously into the gravitational field of the other) is bro-ken: the moment when the adult face fails or refuses to play its part in the continuation of mutual gaze; when, for any one of many reasons, it fails to be recognizable to, or recognizing of, the infant who has been, so to speak, "giving face" based on a faith in the continuity of this circuit. As Michael Franz Basch explains, "The infant's behavioral adaptation is quite totally dependent on maintaining effective communication with the executive and coordinating part of the infant-mother system. The shame-humiliation re-sponse, when it appears, represents the failure or absence of the smile of contact, a reaction to the loss of feedback from others, indicating social isolation and signaling the need for relief from that condition" (765). The protoaffect shame is thus not defined by prohibition (nor, as a result, by repression). Shame floods into being as a moment, a disruptive moment, in a circuit of identity-constituting identificatory communication. Indeed, like a stigma, shame is itself a form of communication. Blazons of shame, the "fallen face" with eyes down and head averted—and, to a lesser extent, the blush—are semaphores of trouble and at the same time of a desire to reconstitute the interpersonal bridge.

But in interrupting identification, shame, too, makes identity. In fact, shame and identity remain in very dynamic relation to one another, at once deconstituting and foundational, because shame is both peculiarly contagious and peculiarly individuating. One of the strangest features of shame, but perhaps also the one that offers the most conceptual leverage for political projects, is the way bad treatment of someone else, bad treatment *by* someone else, someone else's embarrassment, stigma, debility, bad smell, or strange behavior, seemingly having nothing to do with me, can so readily flood me—assuming I'm a shame-prone person—with this sensation whose very suffusiveness seems to delineate my precise, individual outlines in the most isolating way imaginable.

Lecturing on shame, I used to ask listeners to join in a thought experiment, visualizing an unwashed, half-insane man who would wander into the lecture hall mumbling loudly, his speech increasingly accusatory and disjointed, and publicly urinate in the front of the room, then wander out again. I pictured the excruciation of everyone else in the room: each looking down, wishing to be anywhere else yet conscious of the inexorable fate of being exactly there, inside the individual skin of which each was burningly aware; at the same time, though, unable to stanch the hemorrhage of painful identification with the misbehaving man. That's the double movement shame makes: toward painful individuation, toward uncontrollable relationality.

The conventional way of distinguishing shame from guilt is that shame attaches to and sharpens the sense of what one is, whereas guilt attaches to what one does. Although Tomkins is less interested than anthropologists, moralists, or popular psychologists in distinguishing between the two, the implication remains that one *is something* in experiencing shame, though one may or may not have secure hypotheses about what. In the developmental process, shame is now often considered the affect that most defines the space wherein a sense of self will develop ("Shame is to self psychology what anxiety is to ego psychology—the keystone affect" [Broucek 369]). Which I take to mean, not at all that it is the place where identity is most securely attached to essences, but rather that it is the place where the *question* of identity arises most originarily and most relationally.

At the same time, shame both derives from and aims toward sociability. As Basch writes, "The shame-humiliation reaction in infancy of hanging the head and averting the eyes does not mean the child is conscious of rejection, but indicates that effective contact with another person has been broken. . . . Therefore, shame-humiliation throughout life can be thought of as an inability to effectively arouse the other person's positive reactions to one's communications. The exquisite painfulness of that reaction in later life harks back to the earliest period when such a condition is not simply uncomfortable but threatens life itself" (765–66). So that whenever the actor, or the performance artist, or, I could add, the activist in an identity politics, proffers the spectacle of her or his "infantile" narcissism to a spectating eye, the stage is set (so to speak) for either a newly dramatized flooding of the subject by the shame of refused return, or the successful pulsation of the mirroring regard through a narcissistic circuit rendered elliptical (which is to say: necessarily distorted) by the hyperbole of its original cast. As best described by Tomkins, shame effaces itself; shame points and projects; shame turns itself skin side out; shame and pride, shame and dignity, shame and self-display, shame and exhibitionism are different interlinings of the same glove. Shame, it might finally be said, transformational shame, *is performance*. I mean theatrical performance. Performance interlines shame as more than just its result or a way of warding it off, though importantly it is those things. Shame is the affect that mantles the threshold between introversion and extroversion, between absorption and theatricality, between performativity and— performativity.

☞ Henry James undertook the New York edition of his work (a handsome twenty-four-volume consolidation and revision, with new prefaces, of what he saw as his most important novels and stories to date) at the end of a relatively blissful period of literary production ("the major phase")— a blissful period poised, however, between two devastating bouts of melancholia. The first of these scouring depressions was precipitated in 1895 by what James experienced as the obliterative failure of his ambitions as a playwright, being howled off the stage at the premiere of *Guy Domville*. By 1907, though, when the volumes of the New York edition were beginning to appear, James's theatrical self-projection was sufficiently healed that he had actually begun a new round of playwrighting and of negotiations with producers—eventuating, indeed, in performance. The next of James's terrible depressions was triggered, not by humiliation on the stage, but by the failure of the New York edition itself: its total failure to sell and its apparently terminal failure to evoke any recognition from any readership.

When we read the New York edition prefaces, then, we read a series of texts that are in the most active imaginable relation to shame. Marking and indeed exulting in James's recovery from a near-fatal episode of shame in

the theater, the prefaces, gorgeous with the playful spectacle of a productive and almost promiscuously entrusted or "thrown" authorial narcissism,
yet also offer the spectacle of inviting (that is, leaving themselves open to)
what was in fact their and their author's immediate fate: annihilation by
the blankest of nonrecognizing responses from any reader. The prefaces are
way out there, in short, and in more than a couple of senses of out.

In them, at least two different circuits of the hyperbolic narcissism/shame
orbit are being enacted, and in a volatile relation to each other. The first
of these, as I've suggested, is the drama of James's relation to his audience
of readers. In using the term "audience" here, I want to mark James's own
insistent thematization of elements in this writing as specifically theatrical,
with all the implications of excitement, overinvestment, danger, loss, and
melancholia that, as Joseph Litvak has argued in *Caught in the Act,* the theater
by this time held for him. The second and related narcissism/shame circuit
dramatized in the prefaces is the perilous and productive one that extends
between the speaker and his own past. James's most usual gesture in the
prefaces is to figure his relation to the past as the intensely charged relationship between the author of the prefaces and the often much younger man
who wrote the novels and stories to which the prefaces are appended—or
between either of these men and a yet younger figure who represents the
fiction itself.

What undertaking could be more narcissistically exciting or more narcissistically dangerous than that of rereading, revising, and consolidating
one's own "collected works"? If these, or their conjured young author, return one's longing gaze with dead, indifferent, or even distracted eyes, what
limit can there be to the shame (of him, of oneself) so incurred? Equal to
that danger, however, is the danger of one's own failure to recognize or to
desire them or him. As Tomkins writes, "Like disgust, [shame] operates
only after interest or enjoyment has been activated, and inhibits one or the
other or both. The innate activator of shame is the incomplete reduction
of interest or joy. Hence any barrier to further exploration which partially
reduces interest . . . will activate the lowering of the head and eyes in shame
and reduce further exploration or self-exposure" (*Shame* 135). To consider
interest itself a distinct affect and to posit an association between shame and
(the [incomplete] inhibition of) interest makes sense phenomenologically, I
think, about depression, and specifically about the depressions out of which
James had emerged to write his "major novels"—novels that do, indeed,

seem to show the effects of a complicated history of disruptions and prodigal remediations in the ability to take an interest. Into such depressions as
well, however, he was again to be plunged.

The James of the prefaces revels in the same startling metaphor that animates the present-day popular literature of the "inner child": the metaphor
that presents one's relation to one's own past as a relationship, intersubjective as it is intergenerational. And, it might be added, for most people by
definition homoerotic. Often, the younger author is present in these prefaces as a figure in himself, but even more frequently the fictions themselves,
or characters in them, are given his form. One needn't be invested (as pop
psychology is) in a normalizing, hygienic teleology of healing this relationship, in a mawkish overvaluation of the "child" 's access to narrative authority at the expense of that of the "adult," or in a totalizing ambition to
get the two selves permanently merged into one, to find that this figuration opens out a rich landscape of relational positionalities — perhaps especially around issues of shame. James certainly displays no desire to become
once again the young and mystified author of his early productions. To the
contrary, the very distance of these inner self-figurations from the speaking
self of the present is marked, treasured, and in fact eroticized. Their distance (temporal, figured as intersubjective, figured in turn as spatial) seems,
if anything, to constitute the relished internal space of James's absorbed
subjectivity. Yet for all that the distance itself is prized, James's speculation
as to what different outcomes might be evoked by different kinds of over-
ture across the distance — by different sorts of solicitation, different forms
of touch, interest, and love between the less and the more initiated figure —
provides a great deal of the impetus to his theoretical project in these essays.
The speaking self of the prefaces does not attempt to merge with the potentially shaming or shamed figurations of its younger self, younger fictions,
younger heroes; its attempt is to love them. That love is shown to occur
both in spite of shame and, more remarkably, through it.

Not infrequently, as we'll see, the undertaking to reparent, as it were,
or "reissue" the bastard infant of (what is presented as) James's juvenilia is
described simply as male parturition. James also reports finding in himself
"that finer consideration hanging in the parental breast about the maimed
or slighted, the disfigured or defeated, the unlucky or unlikely child — with
this hapless small mortal thought of further as somehow 'compromising' "
(*Art* 80–81). James offers a variety of reasons for being embarrassed by these

waifs of his past, but the persistence with which shame accompanies their repeated conjuration is matched by the persistence with which, in turn, he describes himself as cathecting or eroticizing that very shame as a way of coming into loving relation to queer or "compromising" youth.

In a number of places, for example, James more or less explicitly invokes Frankenstein and all the potential uncanniness of the violently disavowed male birth. But he invokes that uncanniness in order to undo it, or at least do something further with it, by offering the spectacle of—not his refusal—but his eroticized eagerness to recognize his progeny even in its oddness: "The thing done and dismissed has ever, at the best, for the ambitious work-man, a trick of looking dead if not buried, so that he almost throbs with ecstasy when, on an anxious review, the flush of life reappears. It is verily on recognising that flush on a whole side of 'The Awkward Age' that I brand it all, but ever so tenderly, as monstrous" (*Art* 99). It is as if the ecstasy-inducing power of the young creature's "flush of life," which refers to even while evoking the potentially shaming brand of monstrosity, is the reflux of the blush of shame or repudiation the older man in this rewriting doesn't feel. Similarly, James writes about his mortifyingly extravagant miscalcu-lations concerning the length of (what he had imagined as) a short story: "Painfully associated for me has "The Spoils of Poynton" remained, until recent reperusal, with the awkward consequence of that fond error. The subject had emerged . . . all suffused with a flush of meaning; thanks to which irresistible air, as I could but plead in the event, I found myself . . . beguiled and led on." "The thing had 'come,'" he concludes with an undis-guised sensuous pleasure but hardly a simple one, "the flower of conception had bloomed" (124). And he describes his revision of the early fictions both as his (or their?) way of "remaining *unshamed*" and as a process by which they have "all joyously and *blushingly* renewed themselves" (345; emphasis added). What James seems to want here is to remove the blush from its ter-minal place as the betraying blazon of a ruptured narcissistic circuit, and instead to put it in circulation: as the sign of a tenderly strengthened and indeed now "irresistible" bond between the writer of the present and the abashed writer of the past, or between either of them and the queer little *conceptus*.

You can see the displacement at work in this passage from James's most extended description of his process of revision:

Since to get and to keep finished and dismissed work well behind one, and to have as little to say to it and about it as possible, had been for years one's only law, so, during that flat interregnum . . . creeping superstitions as to what it might really have been had time to grow up and flourish. Not least among these rioted doubtless the fond fear that any tidying-up of the un-canny brood, any removal of accumulated dust, any washing of wizened faces, or straightening of grizzled locks, or twitching, to a better effect, of superannuated garments, might let one in, as the phrase is, for expensive renovations. I make use here of the figure of age and infirmity, but in point of fact I had rather viewed the reappearance of the first-born of my progeny . . . as a descent of awkward infants from the nursery to the drawing-room under the kind appeal of enquiring, of possibly interested, visitors. I had accord-ingly taken for granted the common decencies of such a case — the respon-sible glance of some power above from one nursling to another, the rapid flash of an anxious needle, the not imperceptible effect of a certain audible splash of soap-and-water. . . .

"Hands off altogether on the nurse's part!" was . . . strictly conceivable; but only in the light of the truth that it had never taken effect in any fair and stately . . . re-issue of anything. Therefore it was easy to see that any such apologetic suppression as that of the "altogether," any such admission as that of a single dab of the soap, left the door very much ajar. (*Art* 337–38)

The passage that begins by conjuring the uncanniness of an abandoned, stunted, old/young Frankenstein brood (reminiscent of the repudiated or abused children in Dickens, such as Smike and Jenny Wren, whose de-formed bodies stand for developmental narratives at once accelerated and frozen by, among other things, extreme material want) modulates reassur-ingly into the warm, overprotected Christopher Robin coziness of bour-geois Edwardian nursery ritual. The eventuality of the uncanny child's actual exposure to solitude and destitution has been deflected by an invoked domesticity. Invoked with that domesticity, in the now fostered and nur-tured and therefore "childlike" child, is a new, pleasurable form of exhibi-tionistic flirtation with adults that dramatizes the child's very distance from abandonment and repudiation. In the place where the eye of parental care had threatened to be withheld, there is now a bath where even the nurse's attention is supplemented by the overhearing ear of inquiring and inter-ested visitors. And in the place where the fear of solitary exposure has been warded off, there's now the playful nakedness of ablution and a door left "very much ajar" for a little joke about the suppression of the "altogether."

This sanctioned intergenerational flirtation represents a sustained chord in the New York edition. James describes the blandishment of his finished works in tones that are strikingly like the ones with which, in his letters, he has also been addressing Hendrik Anderson, Jocelyn Persse, Hugh Walpole, and the other younger men who at this stage of his life are setting out, with happy success, to attract him. Note in this passage (from the *Ambassadors* preface) that "impudence" is the glamorizing trait James attributes to his stories—impudence that bespeaks not the absence of shame from this scene of flirtation, but rather its pleasurably recirculated afterglow: "[The story] rejoices . . . to seem to offer itself in a light, to seem to know, and with the very last knowledge, what it's about—liable as it yet is at moments to be caught by us with its tongue in its cheek and absolutely no warrant but its splendid impudence. Let us grant then that the impudence is always there— there, so to speak, for grace and effect and *allure;* there, above all, because the Story is just the spoiled child of art, and because, as we are always disappointed when the pampered don't 'play up,' we like it, to that extent, to look all its character. It probably does so, in truth, even when we most flatter ourselves that we negotiate with it by treaty" (*Art* 315). To dramatize the story as *impudent* in relation to its creator is also to dramatize the luxurious distance between this scene and one of *repudiation:* the conceivable shame of a past self, a past production, is being caught up and recirculated through a lambent interpersonal figuration of the intimate, indulged mutual pressure of light differentials of power and knowledge.

James writes about the writing of *The American,* "One would like to woo back such hours of fine precipitation . . . of images so free and confident and ready that they brush questions aside and disport themselves, like the artless schoolboys of Gray's beautiful Ode, in all the ecstasy of the ignorance attending them" (25). (Or boasts of "The Turn of the Screw": "another grain . . . would have spoiled the precious pinch addressed to its end" [170].) Sometimes the solicitude is ultimately frustrated: "I strove in vain . . . to embroil and adorn this young man on whom a hundred ingenious touches are thus lavished" (97). The wooing in these scenes of pederastic revision is not unidirectional, however; even the age differential can be figured quite differently, as when James finds himself, on rereading *The American,* "clinging to my hero as to a tall, protective, good-natured elder brother in a rough place" (39), or says of Lambert Strether, "I rejoiced in the promise of a hero so mature, who would give me thereby the more to bite into" (310). James refers to the protagonist of "The Beast in the Jungle" as "another poor sensitive gentleman, fit indeed to mate with Stransom of 'The Altar [of the Dead],'" adding, "My attested predilection for poor sensitive gentlemen almost embarrasses me as I march!" (246). The predilective yoking of the "I" with the surname of John Marcher, the romantic pairing off of Marcher in turn with the equally "sensitive" bachelor George Stransom, give if anything an excess of gay point to the "almost" embarrassment that is, however, treated, not as a pretext for authorial self-coverture, but as an explicit source of new, performatively induced authorial magnetism.

James, then, in the prefaces is using reparenting or "reissue" as a strategy for dramatizing and integrating shame, in the sense of rendering this potentially paralyzing affect narratively, emotionally, and performatively productive. The reparenting scenario is also, in James's theoretical writing, a pederastic/pedagogical one in which the flush of shame becomes an affecting and eroticized form of mutual display. The writing subject's seductive bond with the unmerged but unrepudiated "inner" child seems, indeed, to be the condition of that subject's having an interiority at all, a spatialized subjectivity that can be characterized by absorption. Or perhaps I should say: it is a condition of his *displaying* the spatialized subjectivity that can be characterized by absorption. For the spectacle of James's performative absorption appears only in relation (though in a most complex and unstable relation) to the setting of his performative theatricality; the narcissism/shame circuit between the writing self and its "inner child" intersects with that other hyperbolic and dangerous narcissistic circuit, figured as theatrical performance, that extends outward between the presented and expressive face and its audience.

I am developing here the hypothesis that James's reflections on performativity will appear most interestingly in his ways of negotiating the intersection between absorption and theatricality, between the subjectivity-generating space defined by the loved but unintegrated "inner child," on the one hand, and on the other hand the frontal space of performance. James works in the prefaces on developing a theoretical vocabulary for distinguishing (in the structure of his novels) between what Austin will provisionally come to call the constative and the performative, and between different senses of performativity. None of this differential vocabulary, however, retains its analytic consistency intact as it gets recruited into the scenarios of the prefaces' performance. Among the diacritical pairings that get more or less mapped onto differentials around performativity—and, that accomplished, get more or less explicitly deconstructed there—are romance versus reality (e.g., *Art* 30–31), substance versus form (e.g., *Art* 115–116), anecdote versus picture (e.g., *Art* 139), anecdotic versus (and note the shift here) developmental (e.g., *Art* 233).

An example of the more or less explicit self-deconstruction of these differentials: each scene of *The Awkward Age*, precisely because it "abides without a moment's deflexion by the principle of the stage-play," is said to "help us ever so happily to see the grave distinction between substance and form in a really wrought work of art signally break down. I hold it impossible to say, before 'The Awkward Age,' where one of these elements ends and the other begins: I have been unable at least myself, on re-examination, to mark any such joint or seam, to see the two *discharged* offices as separate. They are separate before the fact, but the sacrament of execution indissolubly marries them, and the marriage, like any other marriage, has only to be a 'true' one for the scandal of a breach not to show" (*Art* 115–16). Seemingly, the theatrical performativity of *The Awkward Age* is supposed to mesh with its speech act performativity, as its substance is supposed to mesh with its form, as man and wife are supposed to be "indissolubly" unified in the exemplary speech act of marriage. But one hardly has to look to *The Awkward Age* itself (though of course one could), nor need one look ahead to the sly deflations in Austin, to see that the indissoluble unity of marriage offers no very stout guarantee of the stability of this chain of homologies. Bad enough that marriage is a sacrament of *execution;* bad enough that, only a score of words after it has been pronounced indissoluble, marriage turns out to be efficacious not in preventing a breach, not even in preventing the scandal attending a breach, but only, for what it's worth, in keeping the scandal of a breach from showing. But the worst news is that to guarantee even these limited benefits, the marriage "has" ("only") "to be a 'true' one." The Jamesian scare quotes call attention to how weaselly the qualification is. In what sense must a marriage be "a 'true' one" to guarantee that the scandal of a breach not show? Perhaps it must be true in the sense that its parties are "true" to each other, or to their vows, or that the marriage "takes" at some ineffable level—in the sense, that is, of partners' rendering their vows constatively precise descriptions of their behavior. Thus there's no occasion for a breach, and the guarantee is guaranteed unnecessary—that is to say, as a guarantee, meaningless. To bring in the truth qualification at all is to suggest that a speech act may be performatively efficacious only to the degree of (which is to say, only *through*) its constative validity.

The most sustained of the differentials through which James works out the meanings of performativity is the near-ubiquitous opposition between drama itself (or the "scenic") and "picture." The high instability and high mutual torsiveness of the terms of this opposition are occasions for both shame and excitement:

> I haven't the heart now, I confess, to adduce the detail of so many lapsed importances; the explanation of most of which, after all, I take to have been in the crudity of a truth beating full upon me through these reconsiderations, the odd inveteracy with which picture, at almost any turn, is jealous of drama, and drama (though on the whole with greater patience, I think) suspicious of picture. Between them, no doubt, they do much for the theme; yet each baffles insidiously the other's ideal and eats round the edges of its position. (*Art* 298)

> Beautiful exceedingly, for that matter, those occasions or parts of an occasion when the boundary line between picture and scene bears a little the weight of the double pressure. (300)

Characteristically, James's aesthetic asseveration of the beauty of the "double pressure" between picture and scene is embedded in psychological narrative at several textual levels. It adheres to a pederastic relation between characters, and equally again to the one between the author and the anthropomorphized novel, the attaching character. Rereading *The Ambassadors,* James notes there "the exquisite treachery even . . . the straightest execution may ever be trusted to inflict even on the most mature plan" (*Art* 325). He locates this lapse, which is a lapse in authorial technique, a lapse, he says, from the "scenic" into "the non-scenic form" (325), at a particular foundational crux of the novel: the scene in which Strether, whom James (as we've already noted) finds lovable for his maturity, suddenly becomes infatuated with a young man, Chad Newsome. Chad, however, is destined to disappoint in turning out to be quite an ordinary, self-ignorant young heterosexual, incapable of responding to Strether's intensities even as he is incapable of doing real justice to the love he evokes in women. "The exquisite treachery even . . . the straightest . . . may ever be trusted to inflict even on the most mature" is at once something Chad inflicts on Strether, something the novel (or its characters) inflict on James, and something that "picture," as a descriptive or propositional principle of composition, inflicts on "scene" as a performative one. At each level, in a characteristic locution, it represents "deviation (from too fond an original vision)" (325). The author's fond, mature original vision of an uncontaminatedly "scenic" technique suffers the same fate as his mature hero's fond first vision of Chad, and is destined equally to be "diminished . . . compromised . . . despoiled . . . so that, in a word, the whole economy of his author's relation to him has at important points to be redetermined" (325–26). But note again that the treachery is described, however ambiguously, as "exquisite," and the certainty of treachery is something in which one is invited, however ironically, to "trust." It is the very instability among these relations, and in particular, I infer, their ability to *resist* clear representation at any given, single level, that confers value: "The book, however, critically viewed, is touchingly full of these disguised and repaired losses, these insidious recoveries, these intensely redemptive consistencies" (326). In James's theorizing of the novel, consistency is the name, not for any homogeneous purity of the speech act at a given level, but rather for the irreducible, attaching heterogeneity and indeed impurity with which each meets the "touch" of another.

☞ What should also be specified is the imaged sexual zoning and sexual act in which these relations repeatedly dramatize themselves in the prefaces. In a footnote to a previous essay on James, "The Beast in the Closet," I quoted a passage from James's notebooks, written during a visit to California only a few months before he started on the New York edition, which still seems to me the best condensation of what these prefaces press us to recognize as his most characteristic and fecund relation to his own anal eroticism:

> I sit here, after long weeks, at any rate, in front of my arrears, with an inward accumulation of material of which I feel the wealth, and as to which I can only invoke my familiar demon of patience, who always comes, doesn't he?, when I call. He is here with me in front of this cool green Pacific—he sits close and I feel his soft breath, which cools and steadies and inspires, on my cheek. Everything sinks in: nothing is lost; everything abides and fertilizes

and renews its golden promise, making me think with closed eyes of deep and grateful longing when, in the full summer days of L[amb] H[ouse], my long dusty adventure over, I shall be able to [plunge] my hand, my arm, in, deep and far, up to the shoulder—into the heavy bag of remembrance—of suggestion—of imagination—of art—and fish out every little figure and felicity, every little fact and fancy that can be to my purpose. These things are all packed away, now, thicker than I can penetrate, deeper than I can fathom, and there let them rest for the present, in their sacred cool darkness, till I shall let in upon them the mild still light of dear old L[amb] H[ouse]—in which they will begin to gleam and glitter and take form like the gold and jewels of a mine. (*Notebooks* 318)

At the time, I quoted this as a description of "fisting-as-*écriture*" (*Episte-mology* 208); I am sure it is that, but the context of the prefaces brings out two other saliences of this scene of fisting equally strongly—saliences related to each other and, of course, also to the writing process. These involve, first, wealth, and second, parturition. One of the most audible intertexts in the passage is surely "Full fathom five thy father lies," with the emphasis, perhaps, on "five," the five of fingers. The other important intertext seems to be from Book 4 of *The Dunciad*, the passage where Annius describes the Greek coins he has swallowed to protect them from robbers and anticipates their being delivered, in the course of nature, from "the living shrine" of his gut to the man who has bought them from him:

> this our paunch before
> Still bears them, faithful; and that thus I eat,
> Is to refund the Medals with the meat.
> To prove me, Goddess! clear of all design,
> Bid me with Pollio sup, as well as dine:
> There all the Learn'd shall at the labour stand,
> And Douglas lend his soft, obstetric hand. (Pope, book 4, ll. 387–94)

In the context of *The Dunciad*, the obstetric hand feeling for wealth in the rectum seems meant to represent the ultimate in abjection and gross-out, but under the pressure of James's brooding it has clearly undergone a sea change to become a virtually absolute symbol of imaginative value.

Sharply as this thematic emphasis may differ from a received understanding of James's aesthetic proccupations, any reader interested in Henry

James's bowels is, as it turns out, in fine company. "I blush to say," William James writes to Henry in 1869, "that detailed bulletins of your bowels . . . are of the most enthralling interest to me" (*Correspondence* 73). Maybe it seems, to some, an odd site for such captivation, but I would nonetheless argue that to attend passionately or well to much of James's strongest writing is necessarily, as it were already, to be in thrall to what had long been his painful, fussy, immensely productive focus on the sensations, actions and paralyses, accumulations and probings and expulsions of his own lower digestive tract. The recent publication of the two brothers' early correspondence, including pages upon pages about Henry's constipation ("what you term so happily my moving intestinal drama" [138]), begins to offer an objective correlative — startling in its detail and intimacy, if not in its substance — for what had before been inferential readings of the centrality of an anal preoccupation in James's sense of his body, his production, and his pleasure.

Even from these early letters, it is evident that there is no such thing as the *simple* fact of James's constipation: it informs not only his eating, exercise, and medical attendance but also his travel destinations (during a part of his life defined by travel), his reading, his family relations, and the composition and circulation of his writing. The need to discuss his condition with the brother at home, for instance, mobilizes a drama of secret complicity (William: "It makes me sick to think of your life being blighted by this hideous affliction. I will say nothing to the family about it, as they can do you no good, and it will only give them pain" [*Correspondence* 113]) that both mimics Henry's internal blockage and seemingly invokes the atmosphere of a sexual secret. William advises Henry, for instance: "A good plan is for you to write such on separate slips of paper marked private, so that I may then give freely the rest of the letter to Alice to carry about & reread. . . . If you put it in the midst of other matter it prevents the whole letter from circulation. Sur ce, Dieu vous garde" (84). The organizing question in the brothers' long consultation is: What available technology (chemical, electric, thermal, hydraulic, manual) can best be mobilized to reach into and disimpact Henry's bowel? William advises: "Inject . . . as large & hot an enema as you can bear (not get it, more tuo, scalding) of soap suds & oil. . . . — Electricity sometimes has a wonderful effect, applied not in the piddling way you recollect last winter but by a strong galvanic current from the spine to the abdominal muscles, or if the rectum be paralysed one pole put inside the rectum. If I were you I wd. resort to it" (113). And from Henry:

The diet here is good—both simple & palatable. But the only treatment for my complaint is the sitzbath. I was disappointed not to find here some such mechanism (i.e. that injection-douche) as you found at Divonne. (63)

I may actually say that I can't get a passage. My "little squirt" has ceased to have more than a nominal use. The water either remains altogether or comes out as innocent as it entered. For the past ten days I have become quite demoralized & have been frantically dosing myself with pills. But they too are almost useless & I may take a dozen & hardly hear of them. . . . Somehow or other I must take the thing in hand. (105)

What I have called the "crisis" was brought on by taking 2 so-called "antibilious" pills, recommended me at the English druggist's. They failed to relieve me & completely disagreed with me—bringing on a species of abortive diarrhoea. That is I felt the most reiterated & most violent inclination to stool, without being able to effect anything save the passage of a little blood. . . . Of course I sent for the . . . Irish physician. . . . He made me take an injection, of some unknown elements, which completely failed to move me. I repeated it largely—wholly in vain. He left me late in the evening, apparently quite in despair. . . . Several days have now passed. I have seen the doctor repeatedly, as he seems inclined (to what extent as a friend & to what as a doctor &[c] I ignore) to keep me in hand. . . . He examined [my bowels] (as far as he could) by the insertion of his finger (horrid tale!) & says there is no palpable obstruction. . . . I find it hard to make him (as I should anyone who had'n't observed it) at all understand the stubbornness & extent—the length & breadth & depth, of my trouble. (108)

From this intense, acutely unhappy relation of a young writer to a part of his body were also to emerge, however, pleasures and riches. In particular, the valences attaching to digestive accumulation and to manual penetration were to undergo a profound change. Let thirty years elapse, and more, in the career of this deeply imagined erotic and writerly thematic. The early letters' accounts give particular point (the point of distance and imaginative transmutation, as much as the point of similarity) to a passage like the 1905 notebook entry with which I began this section.

By the time of the writing of the prefaces, the images of the obstetric hand, the fisted bowel materialize as if holographically in the convergence of two incongruent spatialities: the spatiality of inside and outside on (as it were) the one hand, and on the other the spatiality of aspects ("aspects—uncanny as the little term might sound" [*Art* 110]), of presented and averted, of face and back. They go together like recto and rectum.

The condensation of the two spatialities, frontal and interior, adheres insistently to invocations of the medal or medallion, perhaps through an association with the *Dunciad* passage quoted above. In the preface to *The Wings of the Dove*, for instance, James suggests that the novel's two plots are the sides of an engraved and fingered coin: "Could I but make my medal hang free, its obverse and its reverse, its face and its back, would beautifully become optional for the spectator. I somehow wanted them correspondingly embossed, wanted them inscribed and figured with an equal salience; yet it was none the less visibly my 'key,' as I have said, that though my regenerate young New Yorker [Milly], and what might depend on her, should form my centre, my circumference was every whit as treatable. . . . Preparatively and, as it were, yearningly—given the whole ground—one begArt in the event, with the outer ring, approaching the centre thus by narrowing circumvallations" (294). To make any sense of how a geography of the concentric, involving a "key" and the penetration of rings inner and outer, supervenes in this passage on a flat, two-sided geography of obverse and reverse virtually requires that obverse and reverse be read as recto and verso—and that "recto" as the (depthless) frontal face be understood as opening freely onto "rectum" as the (penetrable) rear. James writes about *What Maisie Knew* of "that bright hard medal, of so strange an alloy, one face of which is somebody's right and ease and the other somebody's pain and wrong" (143). If indeed "face" and "back" "beautifully become optional for the spectator," that is because recto and verso, the straight or "right" and the "turned" or perverted or "wrong," converge so narrowly onto what is not a mere punning syllable, but rather an anatomical double entendre whose interest and desirability James (and I can only join him in this) appears by this time to have experienced as inexhaustible.

Hard to overstate the importance of "right" and some other words (direct, erect) from the Latin /rect/ in mediating for James between, as it were, recto and verso of the presented and enjoyed body: "For the dramatist always, by the very law of his genius, believes not only in a possible right issue from the rightly-conceived tight place; he does much more than this—he believes, irresistibly, in the necessary, the precious 'tightness' of the place (whatever the issue). . . . So that the point is not in the least what to make of it, but only, very delightfully and very damnably, where to put one's hand on it" (*Art* 311–12). "A possible right issue from the rightly-conceived tight place": a phrase like this one can refer at the same time to the "straight" (proper or conventional) avenue of issue from the "straight" place of conception and to the rectal issue from the rectal place of conception, "strait" only in the sense of pleasurably tight. Whatever the "issue," "nothing is right save as we rightly imagine it."

This family of words, insisted on as in these constructions, positively swarm in James's late writing (the novels as well as the prefaces), as if such syllables enjoyed some privileged access to "the raw essence of fantasy": "This is the charming, the tormenting, the eternal little matter to be made right, in all the weaving of silver threads and tapping on golden nails; and I should take perhaps too fantastic a comfort—I mean were not the comforts of the artist just of the raw essence of fantasy—in any glimpse of such achieved rightnesses" (69). Nor, as we'll see, is the associated invocation of the hand at all less frequent.

Considering that *The Art of the Novel* is taken (when discussed at all) as the purest manifesto for the possibility of organic form and the power of the organizing center of consciousness in fiction, it is striking how much of it constitutes a memorandum of misplaced middles. There is nothing unproblematic about centers or circumferences in any of the prefaces. James speaks of

> a particular vice of the artistic spirit, against which vigilance had been destined from the first to exert itself in vain, and the effect of which was that again and again, perversely, incurably, the centre of my structure would insist on placing itself not, so to speak, in the middle. . . . I urge myself to the candid confession that in very few of my productions, to my eye, has the organic centre succeeded in getting into proper position.
>
> Time after time, then, has the precious waistband or girdle, studded and buckled and placed for brave outward show, practically worked itself, and in spite of desperate remonstrance, or in other words essential counterplotting, to a point perilously near the knees. . . . These productions have in fact, if I may be so bold about it, specious and spurious centres altogether, to make up for the failure of the true. (*Art* 85–86)

"Center" is clearly being used in a multivalent way in passages like these, as much as when it had conjured the impossible orifice by which a flat round medallion opens out into depth. Here it offers a pretext for the comically explicit anthropomorphization of the novel as a body, a body celebrated for its way of being always more than at risk of "perverse" reorganization around a "perilously" displaced and low-down zone. But, confusingly, these spatial metaphors refer to the interrelation among characters' points of view (e.g., as "centers of consciousness") but also (and quite incommensurably) to the relation between the first half and the latter (or, anthropomorphically, the lower and/or back) half of each novel. As when James in the preface to *The Wings of the Dove* diagnostically probes "the latter half, that is the false and deformed half" of the novel, maintaining his "free hand" for "the preliminary cunning quest for the spot where deformity has begun" (302–3). Incoherent as it is, however, the relation between the halves is one whose very perils can be pleasures, and whose pleasures have the rhythm of climax: James celebrates in *The Tragic Muse* "a compactness into which the imagination may cut thick, as into the rich density of wedding-cake. The moral of all which indeed, I fear, is, perhaps too trivially, but that the 'thick,' the false, the dissembling second half of the work before me . . . presents that effort as at the very last a quite convulsive, yet in its way highly agreeable, spasm" (88).

And over the anthropomorphic mapping of these relations there constantly hovers the even more incommensurable image of the theater. "The first half of a fiction insists ever on figuring to me as the stage or theatre for the second half," James writes, for instance, "and I have in general given so much space to making the theatre propitious that my halves have too often proved strangely unequal" (*Art* 86). Or, in a very different kind of mapping: "The novel, as largely practised in English, is the perfect paradise of the loose end. The play consents to the logic of but one way, mathematically right, and with the loose end [a] gross . . . impertinence on its surface" (114).

To trace the ramifications of these images through the prefaces would involve quoting from (literally) every single page of them. A more efficient approach would be, perhaps, to offer something brief in the way of a lexicon of a few of the main words and semantic clusters through which the fisting image works in these prefaces — since the accumulated and digested redolence of particular signifiers is one of the delights James most boasts of enjoying in "my struggle to keep compression rich, if not, better still, to keep accretions compressed" (232).

But in advance of offering this lexicon, I suppose I should say something about what it is to hear these richly accreted, almost alchemically imbued signifiers in this highly sexualized way—and more generally, about the kinds of resistance that the reading I suggest here may offer to a psychoanalytic interpretive project. In her psychoanalytic work on James, Kaja Silverman declares herself (for one particular passage in one particular preface) willing to "risk . . . violating a fundamental tenet of James criticism— the tenet that no matter how luridly suggestive the Master's language, it cannot have a sexual import" ("Too Early" 165). I'm certainly with her on that one—except that Silverman's readiness to hear how very openly sexy James's prefaces are is made possible only by her strange insistence that he couldn't have known they were. James's eroticized relation to his writings and characters, in her reading, is governed by "unconscious desire rather than an organizing consciousness"; "armored against unwanted self-knowledge," James is diagnosed by Silverman as having his "defenses" "securely in place against such an unwelcome discovery" (149). I am very eager that James's sexual language be heard, but that it not be heard with this insulting presumption of the hearer's epistemological privilege—a privilege attached, furthermore, to Silverman's uncritical insistence on viewing sexuality exclusively in terms of repression and self-ignorance. When we tune in to James's language on these frequencies, it is not as superior, privileged eavesdroppers on a sexual narrative hidden from himself; rather, it is as an audience offered the privilege of sharing in his exhibitionistic enjoyment and performance of a sexuality organized around shame. Indeed, it is as an audience desired to do so—which is also happily to say, as an audience desired.

Some terms that particularly clamor for inclusion in this little lexicon— though there could be many more, and indeed, any reader of even these few passages is likely to be able to generate a list of other repeated, magnetic, and often enigmatic signifiers that would need to be added—are FOND/FOUNDATION, ISSUE, ASSIST, FRAGRANT/FLAGRANT, GLOVE or GAGE, HALF, and, as we have already seen, RIGHT and a group of words around /rect/, CENTER/CIRCUMFERENCE, ASPECT, MEDAL. I pick these words out not because they are commonplace "Freudian" signifiers in the conventional phallic mode, a mode that was scarcely James's, but instead because each underwent for him "that mystic, that 'chemical' change . . . the felt fermentation, ever interesting, but flagrantly so in the example before us, that enables the sense originally communicated to make fresh and possibly quite different terms for the new employment there awaiting it" (*Art* 249). Each opens onto — as it condenses — a juncture between the erotic fantasy-localization per se, and some aspect or aspects of its performative dimension.

For example, FOND is one of James's most cherished words, especially when used self-descriptively: whether applied to the young author's "first fond good faith of composition" (13), to the older "fond fabulist" (318), or to the "fond . . . complacency" (21) of a personified fiction. It marks the place of the author's pleasure in dramatizing himself as all but flooded with self-absorbed delusion and embarrassment, but equally with pleasure. When he speaks of himself as having had a "fond idea," you don't know whether you're therefore meant to see it as having been a *bad* idea or whether you're hearing, in James's phrase, the still-current "exhibit" of "an elation possibly presumptuous" (30). But the self-absorbing "fond" marks him, by the same token, as all but flooded with transitive, cathectic energy, the energy of interest, fond *of* . . . someone — in particular, as lovingly and interestedly inclining toward the other, usually younger male figurations in this inter/intrapersonal drama, loving and interested "all sublimely and perhaps a little fatuously" (29). The fatuous "fond" notation of delight and self-delight already notable in the California journal passage is warp and woof of the fabric of the prefaces: "Inclined to retrospect, he fondly takes, under this backward view, his whole unfolding, his process of production, for a thrilling tale" (4).

Or, with a different use of emphasis: "Inclined to *retrospect*, he fondly takes, *under* this *backward* view, his whole unfolding, his process of production, for a thrilling tale." That *fond* is also the French word for bottom may explain its affinity with the "retrospect," the "backward view," even with the "thrilling tale." The fondness of the artist, as James paraphrases it in one preface, may lie in his "willingness to pass mainly for an ass" (*Art* 83).

The association between fondness and the fundament extends, as well, to James's interest in the FOUNDATION, in the highly (and always anthropomorphically) architectural image with which he describes his ambitions for the structure of his works: "Amusement deeply abides, I think, in any artistic attempt the basis and groundwork of which are conscious of a particular firmness. . . . It is the difficulty produced by the loose foundation . . . that breaks the heart. . . . The dramatist strong in the sense of his postulate . . . has verily to *build*, is committed to architecture, to construction at any cost; to driving in deep his vertical supports and laying across and firmly fixing his horizontal, his resting pieces—at the risk of no matter what vibration from the tap of his master-hammer. This makes the active value of his basis immense, enabling him, with his flanks protected, to advance" (*Art* 109). *Fond,* then, is a node where the theatrics of shame, affection, and display are brought together with a compositional principle and at the same time lodged firmly, at the level of the signifier, in a particular zone of the eroticized body. (See also, if this were a completer lexicon, James's quasi-architectural, quasi-anthropomorphic use of the terms ARCH, BRACE, PRESSURE, WEIGHT.) Another thing it makes sense to me to speculate about FOND: that this syllable provides the vibratory bass note in the "fun" that James was so fond of putting in flirtatious scare quotes: "For the infatuated artist, how many copious springs of our never-to-be-slighted 'fun' " (324)! "It all comes back to that, to my and your 'fun' " (345). *Au fond.*

An important pair of pivot words in the prefaces is ISSUE and ASSIST. Each is significantly charged by allusion to the obstetric scene, as when the injunction "Hands off altogether on the nurse's part!" (though "strictly conceivable") is said to render impossible "any fair and stately . . . re-issue of anything" (*Art* 337–38). Each, too, like BROOD and CONCEIVE, which ought rightly to have separate lexicon entries, is also specific to the compositional or dramatic scene. I've remarked on how the reissue cum revision of the books and the, so to speak, reparenting process of the prefaces seem to come together in the signifier *issue.* The "issue" is not only the edition and the child or other emitted matter but the birth canal, the channel by which the issue issues, the "possible right issue from the rightly-conceived tight place" (311). And as with the "backward view" of the fond "retrospect," as also with the novels' "latter" halves, the temporal can be mapped anthropomorphically as the spatial, the past issue becoming the posterior issue: "When it shall come to fitting, historically, anything like all my many small children of fancy with their pair of progenitors, and all my reproductive unions with their inevitable fruit, I shall seem to offer my backward consciousness in the image of a shell charged and recharged by the Fates with some patent and infallible explosive" (178).

Like ISSUE, ASSIST seems to begin by alluding to the scene of birthing; it links the obstetric hand with the applauding one, the childbed with, not publication, but the theater. In the preface to *The Wings of the Dove,* James seems both to assume the attending position of the novel's master physician

Sir Luke Strett, and at the same time, through a chain of suggestive semantic choices, to rewrite Milly Theale's fatal illness as a pregnancy at which "one would have quite honestly to assist": her illness is designated as "the interesting state," with intensities that "quicken" and then "crown"; her part in the matter is "the unsurpassable activity of passionate, of inspired resistance. This last fact was the real issue, for the way grew straight . . ." (289).

But it is less easy to say which sense of "assist," the obstetric or the theatrical, is operative in this account of the play of point of view in *The American:* "At the window of [Newman's] wide, quite sufficiently wide, consciousness we are seated, from that admirable position we 'assist.' He therefore supremely matters; all the rest matters only as he feels it, treats it, meets it. A beautiful infatuation this, always, I think, the intensity of the creative effort to get into the skin of the creature; the act of personal possession of one being by another at its completest. . . . So much remains true then on behalf of my instinct of multiplying the fine touches by which Newman should live and communicate life" (38). "Assist" is in scare quotes here, and it's not easy (it hardly ever is in James) to see why—unless to point to the word's double meaning (obstetric/theatrical), or unless to signal flickeringly, as the scare quotes around "fun" do, that a not quite legitimate French pun is slipping about in the background: in this case, the association between being seated at the window and, "from that admirable position," assisting. *Assister* (attending, as at childbed or theater) and *s'asseoir* (to sit) aren't actually related, even in French, but they do sound alike via the resonant syllable *ass-*. And firm though it may be with an architectural firmness, the unexpectedly dramatic associations of the seat, in particular of the relished ample seat, the "immense" "basis," "wide, quite sufficiently wide," are well attested in the prefaces. At one of the windows, for instance, at which James has done his writing, "a 'great house' . . . gloomed, in dusky brick, as the extent of my view, but with a vast convenient neutrality which I found, soon enough, protective and not inquisitive, so that whatever there was of my sedentary life and regular habits took a sort of local wealth of colour from the special greyish-brown tone of the surface always before me. This surface hung there like the most voluminous of curtains—it masked the very stage of the great theatre of the town. To sit for certain hours at one's desk before it was somehow to occupy in the most suitable way in the world the proportionately ample interests of the mightiest of dramas" (*Art* 212).[1]

One set of associations for all this seated labor has to do with the process of digestion and its products; no feasible amount of quotation could offer a sense of how fully these perfume the language of the prefaces: "[Art] plucks its material . . . in the garden of life — which material elsewhere grown is stale and uneatable. But it has no sooner done this than it has to take account of a process . . . that of the expression, the literal squeezing-out, of value. . . . This is precisely the infusion that, as I submit, completes the strong mixture. . . . It's all a sedentary part" (*Art* 312). The most available language for digestion is that more or less ostensibly of cooking, each "thinkable . . . — so far as thinkable at all — in chemical, almost in mystical terms":

> We can surely account for nothing in the novelist's work that has n't passed through the crucible of his imagination, has n't, in that perpetually simmering cauldron his intellectual *pot-au-feu*, been reduced to savoury fusion. We here figure the morsel, of course, not as boiled to nothing, but as exposed, in return for the taste it gives out, to a new and richer saturation. In this state it is in due course picked out and served, and a meagre esteem will await . . . if it does n't speak most of its late genial medium, the good, the wonderful company it has, as I hint, aesthetically kept. It has entered, in fine, into new relations, it emerges for new ones. Its final savour has been constituted, but its prime identity destroyed. . . . Thus it has become a different and, thanks to a rare alchemy, a better thing. (*Art* 230)

The products of cooking and of digestion seem interchangeable — and equally irresistible — because each is the result of a process of recirculation described as if it could go on endlessly, only adding to the richness of (what James usually calls) the "residuum," the thing "picked," "plucked" (*Art* 155), or, as in the California passage and many others, "fished" out. ("The long pole of memory stirs and rummages the bottom, and we fish up such fragments and relics of the submerged life and the extinct consciousness as tempt us to piece them together" [26].) In the artist's intellectual life, James says, "The 'old' matter is there, re-accepted, re-tasted, exquisitely re-assimilated and re-enjoyed . . . the whole growth of one's 'taste,' as our fathers used to say: a blessed comprehensive name for many of the things deepest in us. The 'taste' of the poet is, at bottom and so far as the poet in him prevails over everything else, his active sense of life: in accordance with which truth to keep one's hand on it is to hold the silver clue to the whole labyrinth of his consciousness. He feels this himself, good man" (339–40).

To trace the career of the word FRAGRANT (possibly including its more explicitly, indeed flamingly performative variant FLAGRANT) through the prefaces would be to get at least somewhere with the digestive plot. One culminating usage:

> The further analysis is for that matter almost always the torch of rapture and victory, as the artist's firm hand grasps and plays it—I mean naturally, of the smothered rapture and the obscure victory, enjoyed and celebrated not in the street but before some innermost shrine; the odds being a hundred to one, in almost any connexion, that it does n't arrive by any easy first process at the *best* residuum of truth. That was the charm, sensibly, of the picture . . . the elements so couldn't but flush, to their very surface, with some deeper depth of irony than the mere obvious. It lurked in the crude postulate like a buried scent; the more the attention hovered the more aware it became of the fragrance. To which I may add that the more I scratched the surface and penetrated, the more potent, to the intellectual nostril, became this virtue. At last, accordingly, the residuum, as I have called it, reached, I was in presence of the red dramatic spark that glowed at the core of my vision and that, as I gently blew upon it, burned higher and clearer. (*Art* 142)

I don't want to make the prefaces sound too much like *The Silence of the Lambs,* but James does have a very graphic way of figuring authorial relations in terms of dermal habitation. As we've seen, he considers "the intensity of the creative effort to get into the skin of the creature" to be "a beautiful infatuation," indeed, "the act of personal possession of one being by another at its completest" (*Art* 37). All the blushing/flushing that marks the skin as a primary organ for both the generation and the contagion of affect seems linked to a fantasy of the skin's being entered—entered specifically by a hand, a hand that touches. Some words James favors for this relation are GLOVE, GAGE, French *gageure:* "That was my problem, so to speak, and my *gageure*—to play the small handful of values really for all they were worth—and to work my . . . particular degree of pressure on the spring of interest" (330–31). Indeed, the glove or gage is, for James, a prime image of *engagement,* of interest, motivation, and cathexis *tout simple*—of the writerly "charm that grows in proportion as the appeal to it tests and stretches and strains it, puts it powerfully to the touch" (111). Even more powerfully, it offers a durable image for the creation (which is to say: the entering of the skin) of personified characters. As when James sees "a tall quiet slim studious young man of admirable type," who offers habitation to a character whom James had before barely so much as imagined: "Owen Wingrave, nebulous and fluid, may only, *at the touch,* have found *himself* in this gentleman; found, that is, a figure and a habit, a form, a face, a fate" (259–60; first emphasis added).

And, of course, the animation of character by reaching a hand up its backside has a theater of its own: in this case, the puppet theater: "No privilege of the teller of tales and the handler of puppets is more delightful, or has more of the suspense and the thrill of a game of difficulty breathlessly played, than just this business of looking for the unseen and the occult, in a scheme half-grasped, by the light or, so to speak, by the clinging scent, of the gage already in hand" (*Art* 311). The scent that clings to glove, to hand, to puppet may not seem particularly inexplicable by this time. It is the smell of shit even as it is the smell of shame. It is the smell of a cherished identity performed through a process of turning inside out.[2]

Clearly, there are more lexicon entries that could be shown to work in comparable ways in the prefaces; I mention only BRISTLE, INTEREST, USE, BASIS, UNCANNY, TREATMENT, STRAIN, EXPRESS, ELASTIC, the HIGH/FREE HAND, HANDSOME, BEAR (v.), CONCEIVE, TOUCHING (adj.), RICH, SPRING (n. and v.), WASTE/WAIST, POSTULATE, PREPOSTEROUS, TURN (n.), PASSAGE, and FORESHORTEN. The variety of these signifiers answers to, among other things, the range of sexual aims, objects, body parts, and bodily fantasies and pleasures clustering however loosely around the fisting phantasmatic: there are flickers of the phallus, the womb, the prostate, as well as the bowel and anus; flickers between steady and climactic rhythms, between insertive and receptive, between accumulation and release, between the allo- and the autoerotic. I hope it's evident enough that the prefaces do respond to this way of reading, "whenever the mind is, as I have said, accessible — accessible, that is, to the finer appeal of accumulated 'good stuff' and to the interest of taking it in hand at all":

> For myself, I am prompted to note, the "taking" has been to my consciousness, through the whole procession of this re-issue, the least part of the affair: under the first touch of the spring my hands were to feel themselves full; so much more did it become a question, on the part of the accumulated good stuff, of seeming insistently to give and give. (*Art* 341)

> The simplest truth about a human entity, a situation, a relation . . . on behalf of which the claim to charmed attention is made, strains ever, under one's

hand, more intensely, *most* intensely, to justify that claim; strains ever, as it were, toward the uttermost end or aim of one's meaning or of its own numerous connexions; struggles at each step, and in defiance of one's raised admonitory finger, fully and completely to express itself. (*Art* 278)

Yet, however richly the text responds to it, this cumulative and accumulative, lexicon-driven reading remains a particular, hence a partial *kind* of reading—not so much because it is organized around "sexuality" as because it is organized around the semantic unit. To say that it is tethered to the semantic and thematic is perhaps also to say that it is unsublimatably (however unstably) tethered to the intensively zoned human body. Hardly the worse for that. Yet, obviously enough, the argumentational momentum of the prefaces is impeded as much as facilitated by a reading that indulges or honors James's investment in the absorptive or (as he generally puts it) the "rich" (or strange) signifier. The clumsy, "fond" rhythm of reading enforced by any semantic absorption or adhesion seems necessarily to constitute a theoretical deviance.

☞ To gesture at a summing up: The thing I least want to be heard as offering here is a "theory of homosexuality." I have none and I want none. When I attempt to do some justice to the specificity, the richness, above all the explicitness of James's particular erotics, it is not with an eye to making him an exemplar of "homosexuality" or even of one "kind" of "homosexuality," though I certainly don't want, either, to make him sound as if he isn't gay. Nonetheless, I do mean to nominate the James of the New York edition prefaces as a kind of prototype of, not "homosexuality," but queerness, or queer performativity. In this usage, "queer performativity" is the name of a strategy for the production of meaning and being, in relation to the affect shame and to the later and related fact of stigma.

I don't know yet what claims may be worth making, ontologically, about the queer performativity I have been describing here. Would it be useful to suggest that some of the associations I've been making with queer performativity might actually be features of all performativity? Or useful, instead, to suggest that the transformational grammar of "Shame on you" may form only part of the performative activity seen as most intimately related to queerness, by people self-identified as queer? The usefulness of thinking about shame in relation to queer performativity, in any event, does not come from its adding any extra certainty to the question of what utterances or acts may be classed as "performative" or what people may be classed as "queer." Least of all does it pretend to define the relation between queerness and same-sex love and desire. What it does, to the contrary, is perhaps offer some psychological, phenomenological, thematic density and motivation to what I described in the introduction as the "torsions" or aberrances between reference and performativity, or indeed between queerness and other ways of experiencing identity and desire.

But I don't, either, want it to sound as though my project has mainly to do with recuperating for deconstruction (or other antiessentialist projects) a queerness drained of specificity or political reference. To the contrary: I suggest that to view performativity in terms of habitual shame and its transformations opens a lot of new doors for thinking about identity politics.

It seems very likely that the structuring of associations and attachments around the affect shame is among the most telling differentials among cultures and times: not that the entire world can be divided between (supposedly primitive) "shame cultures" and (supposedly evolved) "guilt cultures," but rather that, as an affect, shame is a component (and differently a component) of all. Shame, like other affects in Tomkins's usage of the term, is not a discrete intrapsychic structure, but a kind of free radical that (in different people and also in different cultures) attaches to and permanently intensifies or alters the meaning of—of almost anything: a zone of the body, a sensory system, a prohibited or indeed a permitted behavior, another affect such as anger or arousal, a named identity, a script for interpreting other people's behavior toward oneself. Thus, one of the things that anyone's character or personality is is a record of the highly individual histories by which the fleeting emotion of shame has instituted far more durable, structural changes in one's relational and interpretive strategies toward both self and others.

Which means, among other things, that therapeutic or political strategies aimed directly at getting rid of individual or group shame, or undoing it, have something preposterous about them: they may "work"—they certainly have powerful effects—but they can't work in the way they say they work. (I am thinking here of a range of movements that deal with shame variously in the form of, for instance, the communal *dignity* of the civil rights movement; the individuating *pride* of "Black is Beautiful" and gay pride; various forms of nativist *ressentiment;* the menacingly exhibited *abjec-*

tion of the skinhead; the early feminist experiments with the naming and foregrounding of anger as a response to shame; the incest survivors movement's epistemological stress on truth-telling about shame; and, of course, many many others.) The forms taken by shame are not distinct "toxic" parts of a group or individual identity that can be excised; they are instead integral to and residual in the processes by which identity itself is formed. They are available for the work of metamorphosis, reframing, refiguration, *trans*figuration, affective and symbolic loading and deformation, but perhaps all too potent for the work of purgation and deontological closure.

If the structuration of shame differs strongly between cultures, between periods, and between different forms of politics, however, it differs also simply from one person to another within a given culture and time. Some of the infants, children, and adults in whom shame remains the most available mediator of identity are the ones called (a related word) shy. ("Remember the fifties?" Lily Tomlin used to ask. "No one was gay in the fifties; they were just shy.") Queer, I'd suggest, might usefully be thought of as referring in the first place to this group or an overlapping group of infants and children, those whose sense of identity is for some reason tuned most durably to the note of shame. What it is about them (or us) that makes this true remains to be specified. I mean that in the sense that I can't tell you now what it is—it certainly isn't a single thing—but also in the sense that, for them, it remains to be specified, is always belated: the shame-delineated place of identity doesn't determine the consistency or meaning of that identity, and race, gender, class, sexuality, appearance, and abledness are only a few of the defining social constructions that will crystallize there, developing from this originary affect their particular structures of expression, creativity, pleasure, and struggle. I'd venture that queerness in this sense has, at this historical moment, some definitionally very significant overlap, though a vibrantly elastic and temporally convoluted one, with the complex of attributes today condensed as adult or adolescent "gayness." Everyone knows that there are some lesbians and gay men who could never count as queer and other people who vibrate to the chord of queer without having much same-sex eroticism, or without routing their same-sex eroticism through the identity labels lesbian or gay. Yet many of the performative identity vernaculars that seem most recognizably "flushed" (to use James's word) with shame consciousness and shame creativity do cluster intimately around lesbian and gay worldly spaces. To name only a few: butch abjection, femmitude, leather, pride, SM, drag, musicality, fisting, attitude, zines, histrionicism, asceticism, Snap! culture, diva worship, florid religiosity; in a word, *flaming*.

And activism.

Shame interests me politically, then, because it generates and legitimates the place of identity — the question of identity — at the origin of the impulse to the performative, but does so without giving that identity space the standing of an essence. It constitutes it as to-be-constituted, which is also to say, as already there for the (necessary, productive) misconstrual and misrecognition. Shame — living, as it does, on and in the muscles and capillaries of the face — seems to be uniquely contagious from one person to another. And the contagiousness of shame is only facilitated by its anamorphic, protean susceptibility to new expressive grammars.

These facts suggest, I think, that asking good questions about shame and shame/performativity could get us somewhere with a lot of the recalcitrant knots that tie themselves into the guts of identity politics — yet without delegitimating the felt urgency and power of the notion "identity" itself. The dynamics of trashing and of ideological or institutional pogroms, like the dynamics of mourning, are incomprehensible without an understanding of shame. Survivors' guilt and, more generally, the politics of guilt will be better understood when we can see them in some relation to the slippery dynamics of shame. I suggest that the same is true of the politics of solidarity and identification; perhaps those, as well, of humor and humorlessness. I'd also, if parenthetically, want to suggest that shame/performativity may get us a lot further with the cluster of phenomena generally called "camp" than the notion of parody will, and more too than will any opposition between "depth" and "surface." And can anyone suppose that we'll ever figure out what happened around political correctness if we don't see it as, among other things, a highly politicized chain reaction of shame dynamics?

It has been all too easy for the psychologists and the few psychoanalysts working on shame to write it back into the moralisms of the repressive hypothesis: "healthy" or "unhealthy," shame can be seen as good because it preserves privacy and decency, bad because it colludes with self-repression or social repression. Clearly, neither of these valuations is what I'm getting at. I want to say that at least for certain ("queer") people, shame is simply the first, and remains a permanent, structuring fact of identity: one that, as

James's example suggests, has its own, powerfully productive and power fully social metamorphic possibilities.

NOTES

1. Or again, on going back to the magazine where an old story had been published: "I recently had the chance to 'look up' [and note *these* scare quotes], for old sake's sake, that momentary seat of the good-humoured satiric muse — the seats of the muses, even when the merest flutter of one of their robes has been involved, losing no scrap of sanctity for me, I profess, by the accident of my having myself had the honour to offer the visitant the chair" (*Art* 214).

2. That it is thus also the smell of excitement can seem to involve grotesquely inappropriate affect, as the passage I've just quoted from continues: "No dreadful old pursuit of the hidden slave with bloodhounds and the rag of association can ever, for 'excitement,' I judge, have bettered it at its best" (*Art* 311). It is nauseatingly unclear in this sentence whether the "excitement" (note the scare quotes) attaches to the subject position of the escaping slave or of the enslaving pursuer. The way I'm inclined to read this sentence, though I could be quite wrong, ties it back up with the matter of puppetry: James's ostensible reference, I think, with the flippant phrase *"dreadful old* pursuit of the hidden slave"* is not to slavery itself but to the popular forms of theatrical melodrama and audience interpellation based on (for instance) *Uncle Tom's Cabin.* But condensed in the flippancy of this citation are two occasions of shame that were enduring ones for James: first, that he did not enlist to fight in the Civil War, what he describes in another preface as the "deluge of fire and blood and tears" needed to "correct" slavery (*Art* 215), and second, the unattenuated but often fiercely disavowed dependence of his own, rarefied art on popular melodramatic forms and traditions.

Chapter 2

AROUND THE PERFORMATIVE:

PERIPERFORMATIVE VICINITIES IN

NINETEENTH-CENTURY

NARRATIVE

But, in a larger sense, we cannot dedicate —
we cannot consecrate — we cannot hallow this ground.
— ABRAHAM LINCOLN, Gettysburg Address

"But, in a larger sense, we cannot dedicate — we cannot consecrate — we cannot hallow this ground." I begin with this sentence as one of the best-known examples of a kind of utterance, actually very common, that seems worth thinking more about. The utterances I explore in this chapter do not fulfill the conditions that the British philosopher J. L. Austin articulated in his classic description of explicit performative utterances properly so called. In *How to Do Things with Words,* the explicit performative is exemplified in a cluster of sentences in the first-person singular present indicative active, about which, Austin says, "it seems clear that to utter the sentence (in, of course, the appropriate circumstances) is not to *describe* my doing [a thing] . . . or to state that I am doing it: it is to do it" (6). Examples of the Austinian performative include "I promise," "I bet . . . ," "I bequeath . . . ," "I christen . . . ," "I apologize," "I dare you," and "I sentence you. . . ."

The sentences and sentence complexes I discuss in this chapter do not, as I say, fall into this category of utterances. What is distinctive about them, instead, is that they *allude to* explicit performative utterances: not, that is, "we dedicate" or "we hereby consecrate," but we *cannot* dedicate, we *cannot* consecrate. Indeed, it is because they refer to or describe explicit performatives, as much as because they sometimes negate them, that they do not themselves fall into that category: thus, "We get a kick out of dedicating this ground" or "We wish we had consecrated it" are similarly not performative utterances, even though (or, I am suggesting, exactly because) they explicitly refer to explicit performative utterances. I am even going to commit the Austinism of inventing a new name for the kind of utterances I am describing here: I would like to call them periperformatives, signifying that, though not themselves performatives, they are *about* performatives and, more properly, that they cluster *around* performatives.

Why might this be an interesting grouping to make? As I argued in the introduction, there may be value in simply reintroducing the spatiality of concepts that are customarily thought of in temporal terms. Jacques Derrida's and Judith Butler's important discussions of performativity, for example, tend to proceed through analyses of its temporal complexity: iteration, citationality, the "always already," that whole valuable repertoire of conceptual shuttle movements that endlessly weave between the future and the past. By contrast, the localness of the periperformative is lodged in a metaphorics of space. Periperformative utterances aren't just about performative utterances in a referential sense: they cluster around them, they are near them or next to them or crowding against them; they are in the neighborhood of the performative. Like the neighborhoods in real estate ads, periperformative neighborhoods have prestigious centers (the explicit performative utterance) but no very fixed circumferences; yet the prestige of the center extends unevenly, even unpredictably through the rest of the neighborhood.

It seems tempting to use the spatial register as a way of trying to refigure some of the most stubborn of the issues, heretofore articulated only in temporal terms, in philosophical discussions of performativity proper: issues, for example, of intent, of uptake, of the relation of illocution to perlocution. A spatialized and local performativity is also likely to offer some new conceptual tools for moving back and forth between speech act theory and dramaturgical performance; ideally, it might even make room for talking about performative affectivity in a way that would not reintroduce either intentional or descriptive fallacies. It also strikes me that this spatialized, "around the performative" framework might offer some more tensile and nuanced ways than we've had so far of pushing further with the Althusserian concept of interpellation.

Let me start with the Austinian example of "I dare you." "I dare you" gets classified cursorily, along with "defy," "protest," "challenge," in Austin's baggy category of the behabitives, which "include the notion of reaction to other people's behaviour and fortunes and of attitudes and expressions of attitudes to someone else's past conduct or imminent conduct" (160–61). But to do justice to the performative force of "I dare you," as opposed to its arguably *constative* function of expressing "attitudes," requires a disimpaction of the scene, as well as the act, of utterance. To begin with, although "I dare you" ostensibly involves only a singular first and a singular second person, it effectually depends as well on the tacit demarcation of the space of a third-person plural, a "they" of witness — whether or not literally present. In daring you to perform some foolhardy act (or else expose yourself as, shall we say, a wuss), "I" (hypothetically singular) necessarily invoke a consensus of the eyes of others. It is these eyes through which you risk being seen as a wuss; by the same token, it is *as* people who share with me a contempt for wussiness that these others are interpellated, with or without their consent, by the act I have performed in daring you.

Now, these people, supposing them real and present, may or may not in fact have any interest in sanctioning against wussiness. They might, indeed, themselves be wussy and proud of it. They may wish actively to oppose a social order based on contempt for the wuss. They may simply, for one reason or another, not identify with my contempt for wusses. Alternatively, they may be skeptical of my own standing in the ongoing war on wussiness: they may be unwilling to leave the work of its arbitration to me; may wonder if I harbor wussish tendencies myself, perhaps revealed in my unresting need to test the w-quotient of others. For that matter, you yourself, the person dared, may share with them any of these skeptical attitudes on the subject and may additionally doubt, or be uninterested in, *their* authority to classify you on a scale of wussiness.

Thus, "I dare you" invokes the presumption, but only the presumption, of a consensus between speaker and witnesses, and to some extent between all of them and the addressee. The presumption is embodied in the lack of a formulaic negative response to being dared or to being interpellated as witness to a dare: to dare is an explicit performative; to not be dared, to undare oneself or another, is likelier to take the form of a periperformative: I won't take you up on it. Who are you to dare me? Who cares what you dare me to do? The fascinating and powerful class of negative performatives—disavowal, demur, renunciation, deprecation, repudiation, "count me out," giving the lie—is marked, in almost every instance, by the asymmetrical property of being much less prone to becoming conventional than the positive performatives. To disinterpellate from a performative scene will usually require, not another explicit performative nor simply the negative of one, but the nonce, referential act of a periperformative. Negative performatives tend to have a high threshold of initiative. (Thus Dante speaks of refusal—even refusal through cowardice—as something "great.")[1] It requires little presence of mind to find the comfortable formula "I dare you," but a good deal more for the dragooned witness to disinterpellate with "Don't do it on my account."

Nonetheless, such feats are possible, are made possible by the utterance itself, and to that extent it is necessary to understand any instance of "I dare you" as constituting a crisis in the ground or space of authority quite as much as it constitutes a discrete act. For in daring you, in undertaking through any given iteration to reinscribe a framework of presumptive relations more deeply, and thereby to establish more firmly my own authority to manipulate them, I place under stress the consensual nature both of those valuations and of my own authority. To have my dare greeted with a periperformative witnesses' chorus of "Don't accept the dare on our account" would radically alter the social, the political, the interlocutory (I-you-they) space of our encounter. So, in a different way, would your calmly accomplishing the dare and coming back to me, in the space demarcated by the presence of the same witnesses, with the expectation of my accomplishing it in turn.

Or let us join Austin in reverting to his first and most influential, arguably the founding, example of the explicit performative: " 'I do (sc. take this woman to be my lawful wedded wife)' —as uttered in the course of the marriage ceremony" (5). The marriage ceremony is, indeed, so central to the origins of "performativity" (given the strange, disavowed but unattenuated persistence of *the exemplary* in this work) that a more accurate name for *How to Do Things with Words* might have been *How to say (or write) "I do" hundreds of times without winding up any more married than you started out.* This is true both because most of the "I do"s (or "I pronounce thee man and wife"s) in the book are offered as examples of the different ways things can go *wrong* with performative utterances (e.g., "because we are, say, married already, or it is the purser and not the captain who is conducting the ceremony" [16]); but even more because it is as examples they are offered in the first place—hence as, performatively, voided in advance. *How to Do Things with Words* thus performs at least a triple gesture with respect to marriage: installing monogamous heterosexual dyadic church- and state-sanctioned marriage at the definitional center of an entire philosophical edifice, it yet posits as the first heuristic device of that philosophy the class of things (e.g., personal characteristics or object choices) that can preclude or vitiate marriage. And it constructs the philosopher himself, the modern Socrates, as a man—presented as highly comic—whose relation to the marriage vow will be one of compulsive, apparently apotropaic repetition and yet of ultimate exemption.

So, as Felman's work in *The Literary Speech Act* confirms, the weird centrality of the marriage example for performativity in general isn't exactly a sign that this train of thought is foredoomed to stultification in sexual orthodoxy. Austin keeps going back to that formula "first-person singular present indicative active." And the marriage example makes me wonder about the apparently natural way the first-person speaking, acting, and pointing subject gets constituted in marriage through a confident appeal to state authority, through the calm interpellation of others present as "witnesses," and through the logic of the (heterosexual) supplement whereby individual subjective agency is guaranteed by the welding into a cross-gender dyad. The subject of "I do" is an "I" only insofar as he or she assents in becoming part of a sanctioned, cross-gender "we" so constituted in the presence of a "they"; and the I "does," or has agency in the matter, only by ritually mystifying its overidentification with the powers (for which no pronoun obtains) of state and frequently of church.

The marriage example, self-evidently, will strike a queer reader at some more oblique angle or angles. Persons who self-identify as queer will be those whose subjectivity is lodged in refusals or deflections of (or by) the logic of the heterosexual supplement; in far less simple associations attaching to state authority and religious sanction; in far less complacent relation to the witness of others. The emergence of the first person, of the singular, of the active, and of the indicative are all questions rather than presumptions for queer performativity.

Any queer who's struggled to articulate to friends or family why he or she loves them but just *doesn't want to be at their wedding* knows from inside the spatialized dynamic of compulsory witness that the marriage ceremony invokes. Compulsory witness not just in the sense that you aren't allowed to absent yourself, but in the way that a much fuller meaning of "witness" (a fuller one than Austin ever treats) gets activated in this prototypical performative. It is the constitution of a community of witness that makes the marriage; the silence of witness (we don't speak now, we forever hold our peace) that permits it; the bare, negative, potent but undiscretionary speech act of one's physical presence—maybe even *especially* the presence of those people whom the institution of marriage defines itself by excluding—that ratifies and recruits the legitimacy of its privilege.

And to attend, as we have been here, to the spatialized role of witness in constituting the relational vicinity of the speech act: where does that get us but to the topic of marriage itself *as* theater—marriage as a kind of fourth wall or invisible proscenium arch that moves through the world (a heterosexual couple secure in their right to hold hands in the street), continually reorienting around itself the surrounding relations of visibility and spectatorship, of the tacit and the explicit, of the possibility or impossibility of a given person's articulating a given enunciatory position? Marriage isn't always hell, but it is true that *le mariage, c'est les autres:* like a play, marriage exists in and for the eyes of others. One of the most ineradicable folk beliefs of the married seems to be that it is no matter-of-fact thing, but rather a great privilege for anyone else to behold a wedding or a married couple or to be privy to their secrets—including oppressive or abusive secrets, the portable puppet theater of Punch and Judy, but also the showy open secret of the "happy marriage." Like the most conventional definition of a play, marriage is constituted as a spectacle that denies its audience the ability either to look away from it or equally to intervene in it.

Even the epistemology of marital relation continues to be profoundly warped by the force field of the marital proscenium. Acquiring worldly wisdom consists in, among other things, building up a usable repertoire of apothegms along the lines of: Don't expect to be forgiven *ever* if you say to your friend X, "I'm glad you two have broken up; I never liked the way Y treated you anyway" and your friend and Y then get back together, however briefly. But also: Don't expect to know what's happening or going to happen between X and Y on the basis of what X tells you is going on, or even on the basis of lovey-dovey or scarifying scenes that may be getting staged in one way or another "for your benefit." (Not, of course, that any actual benefit accrues to you from them.)

Think of all the Victorian novels whose sexual plot climaxes, not in the moment of adultery, but in the moment when the proscenium arch of the marriage is, however excruciatingly, displaced: when the fact of a marriage's unhappiness ceases to be a pseudosecret or an open secret and becomes a bond of mutuality with someone outside the marriage; when a woman says or intimates something about "her marriage" to a friend or lover that she would not say to her husband. These rearrangements of performative vicinity tend to be the most wracking and epistemologically the "biggest" moments of the marriage novel. Such a text, then, also constitutes an exploration of the possible grounds and performative potential of periperformative refusals, fractures, warpings of the mobile proscenium of marital witness.

The entire plot of Henry James's *The Golden Bowl*, for instance, is structured by an extraordinary periperformative aria uttered by Charlotte Stant to Prince Amerigo, her ex-lover, when she has persuaded him to spend an afternoon alone with her on the eve of his marriage to another woman:

"I don't care what you make of it, and I don't ask anything whatever of you — anything but this. I want to have said it — that's all; I want not to have failed to say it. To see you once and be with you, to be as we are now and as we used to be, for one small hour — or say for two — that's what I have had for weeks in my head. I mean, of course, to get it *before* — before what you're going to do. . . . This is what I've got. This is what I shall always have. This is what I should have missed, of course," she pursued, "if you had chosen to make me miss it. . . . I had to take the risk. Well, you're all I could have hoped. That's what I was to have said. I didn't want simply to get my time with you, but I wanted you to know. I wanted you" — she kept it up, slowly, softly, with a small tremor of voice, but without the least failure of sense or sequence — "I wanted you to understand. I wanted you, that is, to hear. I don't care, I think, whether you understand or not. If I ask nothing of you I don't — I mayn't — ask even so much as that. What you may think of me — that doesn't in the least matter. What I want is that it shall always be with you — so that you'll never be able quite to get rid of it — that I *did*. I won't say that *you* did — you may make as little of that as you like. But that I was here with you where we are and *as* we are — I just saying this. . . . That's all." (93–94)

The ostentatious circularity of Charlotte's periperformative utterance ("I want to have said it — that's all; I want not to have failed to say it . . . that I was here with you where we are and *as* we are — I just saying this") puts it in a complicated relation to the performative utterance of the marriage vow about to occur. Charlotte here forestalls and displaces the Prince's marriage vow but without at all preventing it. Her periperformative is so repetitious and insistent because she can't just fill in the blanks of some preexisting performative convention, but rather must move elaborately athwart it, in creating a nonce one. She parodies certain features of the marriage vow, in particular, the slippery inexplicitness with which, in each case, an act of utterance makes the claim both to represent and to subsume a narrative of unspecified sexual acts ("I *did* [it] . . . I won't say that *you* did [it]"). She also makes the most of a certain pathos ("I don't ask anything whatever of you") in her distance from the presumptuous logic of the heteronormative supplement: the agency of her "I" exactly *isn't* to be guaranteed by another echoing "I do" that will constitute it retroactively within a stable "we." But this insisted-on isolation of the unguaranteed "I" also entails a barely implicit threat of sexual blackmail (*"I won't say* [right now] that you did [it]"). Furthermore, Charlotte places herself firmly in a Gothic tradition (think of *The Monk* or *Frankenstein*) where variant allusions to the marriage vow function as maledictions or curses, moving diagonally through time and space, not preventing marriage but poisoning it, prospectively, retroactively, through some unexpected adhesion of literalness to the supposed-to-be-mobile performative signifier. With this speech, Charlotte Stant has done what she can do — and it's a lot — to install her own "I" as a kind of permanent shunt across the marriage proscenium, mining the threshold of who can or must or can't or mayn't regard the drama of whose life; which "I"s are or are not to be constituted as and by the semipublic, conjugal "we" that means and doesn't mean the power of the state.

I hope my examples from the Gettysburg Address and *The Golden Bowl* will sufficiently have illustrated another point about the neighborhood of the performative: that though it has a center and a periphery, the spatial logic of the periperformative is not a logic of simple attenuation. That is, although the prestige of the neighborhood comes from its proximity to an explicit performative, that prestige, or may I say that rhetorical force, does not diminish along an even gradient from performative center to peri-performative edge. Rather, the rhetorical force rarefies or concentrates in unpredictable clusters, outcrops, geological amalgams. Hence the affinity of the periperformative for the mobile proscenium, the itinerant stage, the displaceable threshold. Hence, too, however, the particular kind of ordinari-ness of the periperformative utterance—about which, as contrasted with the explicit performative, I hope no one will ever agonize over the question of whether a particular sentence is or isn't. If a sentence sounds as though it's probably periperformative, then it's probably periperformative—and many, many sentences of all sorts are so. The periperformative is "ordinary language" under the Wordsworthian or Cavellian understanding that the most ordinary things for language to be are complex, heterogeneous, re-flective, mobile, powerful, and even eloquent.

In fact, one of the decades-long obsessions that motivates this project for me is how the frankly mixed neighborhood defined by, but not limited to, the performative can be the site of powerful energies that often warp, transform, and displace, if they do not overthrow, the supposed authoriz-ing centrality of that same performative. Of course, this chain of argument more than flirts with the jaw-dropping tautology that, to say anything at all—interesting or uninteresting—about performative utterances, it often will be necessary to construct sentences that talk about performative utter-ances. But I am not overly bothered by the obviousness of this. The explicit performative, as Derrida demonstrates, offers itself in the form of transpar-ent self-referentiality and pure self-presence, while its force actually depends on a tacit citation of past and future and an occluded reference to a space beyond itself. The periperformative, by contrast, is openly alloreferential before it is anything else. And I don't think we should assume that we under-stand in advance, as it were by analogy or by simple reversal, what can then be the effects of the sting of self-reference only half-concealed in its tail.[2]

In George Eliot's *Daniel Deronda,* for example, where the crucial peri-performative intervention occurs the evening after the marriage vow rather than the afternoon before it, Lydia Glasher's letter to Gwendolen, like Char-lotte's speech to the Prince in *The Golden Bowl,* circumambulates a wide range of performative acts as it tries to recruit a periperformative force that may challenge the apparently bland, effortless, authorized performative, "I do." Lydia, who has been the mistress of Gwendolen's new husband Grandcourt, writes in a note for Gwendolen enclosed with the Grandcourt family diamonds:

> These diamonds, which were once given with ardent love to Lydia Glasher, she passes on to you. You have broken your word to her, that you might possess what once was hers. Perhaps you think of being happy, as she once was, and of having beautiful children such as hers, who will thrust hers aside. God is too just for that. The man you have married has a withered heart. His best young love was mine; you could not take that from me when you took the rest. It is dead; but I am the grave in which your chance of happiness is buried as well as mine. You had your warning. You have chosen to injure me and my children. He had meant to marry me. He would have married me at last, if you had not broken your word. You will have your punishment. I desire it with all my heart.
>
> . . . Shall you like to stand before your husband with these diamonds on you, and these words of mine in his thoughts and yours? . . . You took him with your eyes open. The willing wrong you have done me will be your curse. (406)

This prose alludes to a great number of explicit performative speech acts: a promise, a curse, a warning, a marriage vow, a commitment to the grave, a deed of gift. In spite of every opportunity and, it would seem, every inducement to do so, however, it strictly refrains from producing any of them in the first-person singular present indicative active form that would signal a performative act. I suppose most readers, remembering *Daniel Deronda* and trying to give an account of Mrs. Glasher's letter, would want to paraphrase it as saying something like "I give you the diamonds, and I curse you"; yet the letter goes to some syntactic lengths to avoid either formulation and to present itself instead in the frankly composite, mock-constative form of the periperformative. It's not easy to say why these periperformatives would here be *more* potent than the performative proper. One reason might be that they dramatize (what Neil Hertz refers to as) the pathos of uncertain agency, rather than occluding it as the explicit performative almost must. Austin himself, after all, tends to treat the speaker's agency as self-evident, as if he or she were all but coextensive—at least, continuous—with the power by which the individual speech act is initiated and authorized and may be enforced. (In the most extreme example, he seems to suggest that war is what happens when individual citizens declare war [40, 156]!) "Actions can only be performed by persons," he writes, "and obviously in our cases [of explicit performatives] the utterer must be the performer" (60). Foucauldian, Marxist, deconstructive, psychoanalytic, and other recent theoretical projects have battered at the self-evidence of that "obviously."[3]

Mrs. Glasher's periperformative solution, on the other hand, requires and solicits no demystifying deconstruction of agency by anyone else. "These diamonds, which were once given with ardent love to Lydia Glasher, she passes on to you": note the passive voice that elides the origin of the diamonds; note the coverture of first person by third person (where the explicit performative requires almost the opposite: the condensation of third-person forces in a first-person utterance); note the inversion in the word order of subject and object, so that the diamonds themselves already seem to acquire an oscillating and uncanny agency; note the double displacement (the diamonds "were given" to Lydia Glasher, but she only "passes" them along to Gwendolen) that foreground the material and legal problematics of how a woman may be said either to own or to transmit property. And such techniques extend throughout the letter.

Like her cognate, Euripides' Medea weaving a poisoned gown for her husband Jason's new bride, Mrs. Glasher requires a materialist *techné* that will visibly, even violently, yoke two differing ontological levels together, that will cement the force of a curse to the physical body of a gift, the gift of a habit, of something to wear, from which the poison will then spread by sheer vicinity. Which is indeed the effect of this gift/curse on Gwendolen:

> She sat for a long while, knowing little more than that she was feeling ill, and that those written words kept repeating themselves in her.
>
> Truly here were poisoned gems, and the poison had entered into this poor young creature.
>
> After that long while, there was a tap at the door and Grandcourt entered, dressed for dinner. The sight of him brought a new nervous shock, and Gwendolen screamed again and again with hysterical violence. He had expected to see her dressed and smiling, ready to be led down. He saw her pallid, shrieking as it seemed with terror, the jewels scattered around her on the floor. Was it a fit of madness?
>
> In some form or other the Furies had crossed his threshold. (407)

The breaching of the marital threshold by the Furies, the invocation by Lydia of Gwendolen "stand[ing] before your husband with these diamonds on you, and these words of mine in his thoughts and yours," attest sufficiently to the powerful spatial warping effected by Lydia's periperformative yoking of the two illocutionary acts—the gift, the curse—in the near vicinity of a third illocutionary act: the marriage vow.

But the compounding of illocutionary reference in Lydia's letter demonstrates a further difference between the explicit performative and the periperformative. The force, the "happiness," the illusion of self-referential transparency in the explicit performative all require that illocution be, if not a simple thing—perhaps it can never be that—then at least always a single thing. If, with an explicit performative, I am promising, then I cannot (at the level of illocution) also be threatening; if my illocution is one of donating, then it is not one of cursing. To be invested in the distinctiveness of the explicit performative requires the banishment of these compounding acts to some level other than the defining one of illocution. They may be counted among the perlocutionary *effects* of my speech act (but then, so might such uncontrollable contingencies as my showering you with spit while speaking, or annoying you by my resemblance to your seventh-grade history teacher). Or the compounding acts may be grouped with the emotions I might feel as I perform the speech act; but that's quite a demotion too, for it is of the essence of the concept of performative acts to *dis*link their force conclusively from the psychological question of what feelings I may experience as I perform them. No, illocution is where the action is, at least where the speech act is, in the vicinity of the performative—and, for the explicit performative, the strict limit seems to be one illocution per utterance.

Perhaps, then, another reason the periperformative does not necessarily represent a diminution in force from the explicit performative to which it refers is that, unlike the explicit performative, it can invoke (if not participate fully in) the force of more than one illocutionary act. And this effect, too, has to do with the spatiality of the periperformative—to the extent that, as the next chapter will discuss, a spatial register has so much more aptitude for analogic representation, in contrast to the on/off, digital representation that seems to go with a temporal register. If the periperformative is the neighborhood of a performative, there might well be another performative neighborhood not so very far off to the north or northwest of this one; as I amble farther from the mother lode of my own neighborhood, my compass needle may also tremble with the added magnetism of another numinous center to which I am thereby nearer.

It also seems to me that the periperformative dimension — and oddly, just insofar as it invokes the spatial and the analogic — also has more aptitude than the explicit performative for registering historical change. By contrast to the performative, the periperformative is the mode in which people may invoke illocutionary acts in the explicit context of other illocutionary acts. Thus, it can also accomplish something toward undoing that fateful reliance of explicit performativity on *the exemplary,* on the single example — which so often has meant, for instance, in the contingency of philosophical and literary practice, the exemplarity of the marriage act itself. Even when, as this chapter itself does, the periperformative insists on perpetuating the prestige of marriage as a defining locus of rhetorical efficacy, it nonetheless has the property of sketching in a differential and multidirectional surround that may change and dramatize its meanings and effects.

I'd like here to look briefly at the dynamics of what must count as one of the most conventional, even while it remains for some readers among the most electrifyingly potent, of Victorian periperformative topoi: that is, the one that yokes together the performative acts and scenes that constitute marriage among British subjects, with the performative acts and scenes thought to characterize the institution of chattel slavery of Africans and their descendants in the New World. It was increasingly true during the final century of legalized slavery that one human being's explicitly performative acts of buying, selling, willing, inheriting, claiming, advertising for, and manumitting another human being created the conditions for a kind of chronic incipiency of crisis in the understanding of performativity tout court, along with every other social, linguistic, and spatial form that presumed an intelligible notion of human ontology and agency. It required local, rhetorical, and specifically periperformative acts, however, to make something of such a chronic incipiency. We can look at one example in moving back and forth across the "black Atlantic" stretch between the literature of American slavery and, as a useful Victorian example, Dickens's *Dombey and Son.* My focus on *Dombey and Son,* specifically, indexes a sense that among the many "marriage as slavery" plots in Victorian novels, the marriage of Paul Dombey Sr. to Edith Dombey is one that successfully deroutinizes this topos, offering an almost titanic demonstration of the explicitly periperformative struggle to displace and remap the theatrical space of marriage.

I have just listed a number of performative acts that structured the month-to-month culture of New World slavery—buying, selling, willing, inheriting, claiming, advertising for, manumitting—yet one of the most striking and, I would venture, damaging of the condensations of nineteenth-century slavery discourse seems to have been the one whereby the scene and act of sale came to exemplify the whole institution of slavery. By the publication of *Dombey and Son* in 1848, the predominant visual iconography of slavery and antislavery for British readers, at any rate, would have shifted from the enslaved man in chains, depicted on Josiah Wedgwood's ubiquitous 1787 cameo "Am I Not a Man and a Brother?", to the displayed and averted nude female slave, already common in Romantic and neoclassical painting but most popularized in Hiram Powers's much-reproduced 1843 sculpture "The Greek Slave." The isolated yet speaking male figure of "Am I Not a Man and a Brother?" wears the signs of his status in his highly visible chains and in his salient black color. His later, unspeaking female counterpart, "The Greek Slave," is indeterminate as to race both because she is neoclassically "Greek" and because she is unpainted sculpture; her tense, averted posture and downcast eyes evoke, not the enduring *status* of slave, but the dramaturgically spatialized and affect-defining *scene* of forced display and the *act* of sale. Indeed, the theater historian Joseph Roach has argued that the spectacle of the sale of slaves came to define not only slavery itself, but an entire consumerist theatrics of urban commercial space by the 1850s: "The centrality of naked flesh signifies the abundant availability of all commodities: *everything* can be put up for sale, and everything can be examined and handled even by those who are 'just looking' " (174).

It's painfully clear that, as a metonymic representation for British citizens of American chattel slavery, there is a lot the matter with this repeatedly invoked scene of the forced display and sale of a woman. The persistent lightening of the skin color of the ascriptively African woman is only one clue to what must be described as the violent and mendacious prurience of such representational sites—not that I mean to imply that prurience is anything very simple as an attribute or relation, either. Part of its mendacity lies in the ostentatiously plangent condensation of years upon generations of wearing labor, an interminable temporality unleavened by hope, a complex spatiality unarticulated by safety, nurture, or the grounds of agency, into the one hyperlegible, hyperrelational, empathetically as well as sexu ally hyperavailable female figure whose coerced consent is, finally, to the nondiscretionary representational labor of scenically embodying for anyone who wants to view her, the most volatile affect of shame.

For Victorian writers preoccupied with the domestic marriage plot, the critical surplus value of this image was available for a variety of periperfor- mative uses. Several years after *Dombey and Son*, in 1853–1855, Thackeray still considered it to have undiminished freshness available for his use in the text and illustrations of *The Newcomes*. At this time in the ugly 1850s, when British public opinion in general grew more sympathetic to slave own- ing and more receptive to scientific racism — when Carlyle republished his pamphlet "Occasional Discourse on the Negro Question" with the word "Negro" in the title changed to "Nigger" — Thackeray too emerged as a Southern apologist who, as Deborah Thomas explains in *Thackeray and Slavery*, considered American slavery the kind of issue that one must care- fully represent both sides of. During Thackeray's American tour of 1853, he not only refused to attend a slave market in Richmond but tried to keep his secretary from doing so as well: not from revulsion, but from the fear of damaging the success of his lecture tour by appearing — through his mere witness of the spectacle — to take a judgmental stance against slavery (D. Thomas 138). Thackeray nonetheless made the most of the force of such images as they reflected corrosively back onto the British scene of marriage: as one of his characters declares, "Rather than have a daughter brought up to the trade [of mercenary marriage in London,] I would bring her down from the woods and sell her in Virginia" (D. Thomas 138).

Like Thackeray in the 1850s, Dickens in the late 1840s writing *Dombey and Son* put a lot of faith in the rhetorical force of such a periperformative yoking of the two illocutionary acts: British marriage and the sale of slaves in the United States. That "Greek Slave" demeanor that dramatizes forced display and coerced consent, in the tense struggle of the dignified carriage with the shamed, averted glance, is the explicit keynote of the character of the beautiful Edith Dombey, the trophy second wife of Mr. Dombey, the novel's eponymous tycoon. "Lovely and graceful in an uncommon degree," Edith nonetheless "spurn[s] her own attractions with her haughty brow and lip, as if they were a badge or livery she hated" (371). Upbraiding her mother on the eve of the marriage for making the match, she is periperformatively explicit in insisting on the comparison:

"You know he has bought me. . . . Or that he will, tomorrow. He has con-sidered of his bargain; he has shown it to his friend; he is even rather proud of it; he thinks that it will suit him, and may be had sufficiently cheap; and he will buy to-morrow. God, that I have lived for this, and that I feel it!"

Compress into one handsome face the conscious self-abasement, and the burning indignation of a hundred women, strong in passion and in pride; and there it hid itself with two white shuddering arms.

. . . "There is no slave in a market: there is no horse in a fair: so shown and offered and examined and paraded, mother, as I have been, for ten shame-ful years," cried Edith, with a burning brow. . . . "The licence of look and touch," she said, with flashing eyes, "have I submitted to it . . . until the last grain of self-respect is dead within me, and I loathe myself?" (371)

Edith already signals, however, that within the scene of coerced consent to marriage, she is making and articulating periperformative choices that cre-ate highly charged thresholds of meaning. Not the less highly charged, in fact all the more so, when Dombey fails to perceive or will not acknowl-edge them:

"You might have been well married," said her mother, "twenty times at least, Edith, if you had given encouragement enough."

"No! Who takes me, refuse that I am, and as I well deserve to be," she an-swered, raising her head, and trembling in her energy of shame and stormy pride, "shall take me, as this man does, with no art of mine put forth to lure him. He sees me at the auction, and he thinks it well to buy me. Let him! When he came to view me—perhaps to bid—he required to see the roll of my accomplishments. I gave it to him. When he would have me show one of them, to justify his purchase to his men, I require of him to say which he demands, and I exhibit it. I will do no more. He makes the purchase of his own will, and with his own sense of its worth, and the power of his money; and I hope it may never disappoint him. *I* have not vaunted and pressed the bargain." (376–77)

Can this marriage be saved?

So far, this is the standard-issue comparison of marriage to slave market. But one of the things that contributes to the force of this element in *Dombey and Son* is that, although Dickens shared the Victorian tropism toward the scene and act of the sale of slaves, he also differed from, say, Thackeray in wanting to attend as well to other acts and contexts involved in slavery. That is to say, he was actually interested in American slavery as an institution and a lived experience, rather than just as a mother lode of rhetorical energy to be mined for British domestic use—though clearly, he was susceptible to the latter solicitation as well. His horror and disgust did not make him silent—certainly complaisance did not—and in *American Notes,* his travel book of 1842, he had (unlike Thackeray) knowingly alienated much of his huge American readership by placing slavery at front and center of his account of American culture. Like the U.S. abolitionists, for example, Dickens there makes a powerful periperformative use of something that had fascinated him: the newspaper advertising for fugitive slaves—advertising that aimed, through the new media of publicity, to withdraw to an infinite distance the physical threshold between being enslaved and being free, but that, periperformatively quoted, also entailed the unintended effect (in the ads' shameless enumeration of the brands, scars, and other mutilations by which fugitives were to be identified) of thrusting ajar the portal of quasi-familial privacy behind which the violence of the slave system had been supposed to shelter unwitnessed.

Surely it isn't accidental, but I don't want to suggest that it is more than congruent—I think it tells us something important about Dickens's "structure of feeling," about the shape of his linguistic and social imagination, more than about his political analytics—that the epic psychomachia of the Dombeys' marriage, too, turns into a vast overarching periperformative struggle over the spatial delineation of performative privacy and witness. Unlike Charlotte Stant and Lydia Glasher, who use their periperformative leverage for reaching into marriages from the outside, Edith is already confined inside the marital space. The outsider determined on thrusting across the Dombeys' conjugal threshold is not a rival woman, but Mr. Carker, Dombey's Iago-like lieutenant, a sleek epicene whose aim, transparent to Edith, is to cuckold and cozen his employer and then publicly ruin his employer's wife.

The tensile elegance of this setup, what gives such ferocious resonance to every periperformative gesture and every slightest displacement of the conjugal proscenium, is that each of the three principals has visible contempt for the other two, yet each also has uses for the others' contempt. And all of them have uses to make of the explicitation of the grounds of marital witness. Dombey displays his power over Edith, and what he imagines to be his power over Carker, in arrogantly pulling Carker, whom he knows Edith despises, into the space of their quarrels, insisting on his presence at these scenes and using him as a punitive go-between. Carker profits by Dombey's blind contempt for him, to wind himself around Edith's secrets—secrets made visible and delicious to him precisely by the spectacle of Edith's having to dissimulate her loathing and fear of him. Edith, meanwhile, trapped at every turn, is trying somehow to get leverage against Dombey from Carker's plots to cuckold him, without either surrendering her person or dignity or revealing her helplessness to Carker; and trying at the same time to conceal from both of them her true motive of protecting the one person she loves, Dombey's neglected and abused daughter Florence.

The pleasure of quoting Dickens threatens to take over my discussion. Here's just the first scene of this plot, a scene after a party:

> "I trust," [Carker] said, "that the fatigues of this delightful evening will not inconvenience Mrs. Dombey to-morrow."
>
> "Mrs. Dombey," said Mr. Dombey, advancing, "has sufficiently spared herself fatigue, to relieve you from any anxiety of that kind. I regret to say, Mrs. Dombey, that I could have wished you had fatigued yourself a little more on this occasion."
>
> She looked at him with a supercilious glance, that it seemed not worth her while to protract, and turned away her eyes without speaking.
>
> "I am sorry, madam," said Mr. Dombey, "that you should not have thought it your duty—"
>
> She looked at him again. . . . "Do you know that there is some one here?" she returned, now looking at him steadily.
>
> "No! Carker! I beg that you do not. I insist that you do not," cried Mr. Dombey, stopping that noiseless gentleman in his withdrawal. "Mr. Carker, madam, as you know, possesses my confidence. He is as well acquainted as myself with the subject on which I speak. . . ."
>
> "I ask you," she repeated, bending her disdainful, steady gaze upon him, "do you know that there is someone here, sir?"
>
> "I must entreat," said Mr. Carker, stepping forward, "I must beg, I must demand, to be released. Slight and unimportant as this difference is—" (494–95)

Yet the next day, Carker presents himself to Edith:

"I have presumed," said Mr. Carker, "to solicit an interview. . . ."

"Perhaps you are charged by Mr. Dombey with some message of re-proof," said Edith. "You possess Mr. Dombey's confidence in such an unusual degree, sir, that you would scarcely surprise me if that were your business."

"I have no message to the lady who sheds a lustre upon his name," said Mr. Carker. "But I entreat that lady, on my own behalf, . . . to reflect upon my perfect helplessness last night, and the impossibility of my avoiding the share that was forced upon me in a very painful occasion. [. . . several para-graphs . . .] But, kindly judge of my breast by your own, and you will forgive my interest in him, if in its excess, it goes at all astray."

What a stab to her proud heart, to sit there, face to face with him, and have him tendering her false oath at the altar again and again for her accep-tance, and pressing it upon her like the dregs of a sickening cup she could not own her loathing of, or turn away from! How shame, remorse, and passion raged within her, when, upright and majestic in her beauty before him, she knew that in her spirit she was down at his feet! (499–501)

Soon even the pretense of marital deference is breached between them, yet the hating tension of their struggle does not lighten. "Sir," Edith is goaded into saying to him at a later meeting,

"Why do you present yourself to me, as you have done, and speak to me of love and duty to my husband, and pretend to think that I am happily mar-ried, and that I honour him? How dare you venture so to affront me, when you know—I do not know it better, sir . . . —that in place of affection be-tween us there is aversion and contempt, and that I despise him hardly less than I despise myself for being his? . . ."

She had asked him why he did this. Had she not been blinded by her pride and wrath, and self-humiliation . . . she would have seen the answer in his face. To bring her to this declaration. (595)

It's too tempting to trace in operatic detail how the "unwinding" (in Dickens's phrase) of the successive "ring[s] of the coil" of Carker's entrap-ment of Edith continues inch by inch through the constantly refined, peri-performative explicitation of the grounds of their contact. As when Carker presumes to explain to her:

"Mr. Dombey is really capable of no more true consideration for you, madam, than for me. The comparison is an extreme one; I intend it to be so; but quite just. Mr. Dombey, in the plenitude of his power, asked me—I had it from his own lips yesterday morning—to be his go-between to you, because he knows I am not agreeable to you, and because he intends that I shall be a punishment for your contumacy; and besides that, because he really does consider, that I, his paid servant, am an ambassador whom it is derogatory to the dignity . . . of his wife, a part of himself, to receive. You may imagine how regardless of me, how obtuse to the possibility of my having any individual sentiment or opinion he is, when he tells me, openly, that I am so employed. You know how perfectly indifferent to your feelings he is, when he threatens you with such a messenger. . . ."

She watched him still attentively. But he watched her too; and he saw that this indication of a knowledge on his part, of something that had passed between herself and her husband, rankled and smarted in her haughty breast, like a poisoned arrow. (597–98)

Edith looks like a sure loser in this game, evidently immobilized in the ritual, paralyzingly conventional, yet nonetheless lethal homosocial crossfire of marital witness with which she is continually raked by both husband and would-be lover. Especially does all seem lost when she actually, literally elopes across the threshold of home and nation to rendezvous finally with Carker in a French hotel. She tells Dombey, "I will hold no place in your house to-morrow, or on any recurrence of to-morrow. I will be exhibited to no one, as the refractory slave you purchased. . . . If I kept my marriage-day, I would keep it as a day of shame" (627).

Yet, eloping, she at last mortally humiliates Dombey and exposes Carker to Dombey's murderous rage. Arriving before Carker at the hotel, moreover, she very deliberately takes control over who will know that the two of them are there together, who will understand that she is a fugitive wife, and —literally—what doors to their suite will be open and what doors closed and which side the keys are on. These arrangements enable Edith, at the supposed moment of adulterous climax, to refuse her body also to Carker. "In every vaunt you make," she finally articulates to him,

"I have my triumph. . . . Boast, and revenge me on him! You know how you came here to-night; you know how you stand cowering there. . . . Boast then and revenge me on yourself! . . . I have thrown my fame and good name to the winds! I shall bear the shame that will attach to me—resolved to know that it attaches falsely — that you know it too — and that he does not, never can, and never shall. I'll die, and make no sign. For this I am here alone with you, at the dead of night. For this I have met you here, in a false name, as your wife. For this, I have been seen here by those men, and left here. Nothing can save you now. . . . Lastly, take my warning! Look to yourself!" she said, and smiled again. "You have been betrayed. . . . It has been made known that you are in this place. . . . If I live, I saw my husband in a carriage in th[is] street to-night!" (728–29)

The *thematics* of slavery in the narrative of the Dombeys' marriage never departs significantly from the scene of the involuntary exhibition and sale of a woman. Yet the periperformative spatial *structure* of the mobile threshold is, I would argue, at least as much a part of Dickens's understanding of U.S. slavery — and correctly so — as of British marriage. The force of the performative utterance, that is, depends crucially on its geographic location; both Carker and Edith, like the perpetrators and resisters of U.S. slavery, count among their sharpest weapons these geographic differentials of performative force. In *American Notes,* for example, Dickens reproduces a U.S. newspaper account with the bland title "Interesting Law-Case": "An interesting case is now on trial in the Supreme Court, arising out of the following facts. A gentleman residing in Maryland had allowed an aged pair of his slaves, substantial though not legal freedom for several years. While thus living, a daughter was born to them, who grew up in the same liberty, until she married a free negro, and went with him to reside in Pennsylvania. They had several children, and lived unmolested until the original owner died, when his heir attempted to regain them; but the magistrate before whom they were brought, decided that he had no jurisdiction in the case. *The owner seized the woman and her children in the night, and carried them to Maryland"* (205; emphasis in the original).

Dickens viewed the mobile threshold, including the threshold of marriage as well as of bondage or emancipation, as a constitutive feature of U.S. slavery. As the Maryland case shows, however, this spatial understanding of performativity itself needs to be supplemented with the complex, *nachträglich* sense of temporality offered by deconstruction.

The braid of these elements is more than dramatized in a narrative like that of Harriet Jacobs. Among the "incidents" recorded in Jacobs's history of her own family and life are the following characteristic ones:

1. Her grandmother was legally manumitted but captured by slavers and resold while traveling to Florida.

2. The grandmother's new owner left the grandmother free in her will, but the executor of the will put her up for auction nonetheless. She was purchased by a friend of her late mistress, who freed her.

3. Jacobs's brother escaped onto a New York–bound ship, which was overtaken by a storm and had to put into a port in the South. Recognized because of a newspaper advertisement, he was returned to the ship in chains. He escaped from the chains and swam to shore, but was pursued, captured, carried back to his master, and eventually sold. He finally escaped successfully to the North.

4. The grandmother "freed" two of her sons by mortgaging her house and purchasing them; their continued freedom, therefore, depended on her remaining clear of further debt.

5. Jacobs falls in love with a free-born black artisan, who proposes to purchase her and presumably, though this isn't explicit, to free her so they can be married, because the marriage of a slave has no legal standing. Her owner refuses to sell her into marriage.

6. Jacobs consents to become the mistress of a white man not her owner. He promises to purchase her and to care for their children but is unable to persuade her owner to sell her.

7. Jacobs escapes, but only after years of local concealment is able to get to the North. Her grandmother purchases her children with money borrowed from their father. Jacobs's attempts to purchase herself from her owner are unavailing.

8. The father of the children, now married to a white woman, "adopts" one of them and has the other "adopted" by his sister-in-law. Even when they go to live in the North, their status is somewhere between that of relatives and slaves.

9. With the passage of the Fugitive Slave Law in 1850, Jacobs, though living in the North, becomes once again subject to the Southern laws regarding slavery.

10. Jacobs's owner dies; his widow and children resolve to recapture her. A Northern friend (Cornelia Willis) offers to purchase her. Jacobs, repudiating the equation of being free with being purchased by "the right person," refuses to be purchased in this way, but the friend persists in her negotiations and, without Jacobs's consent, succeeds in

purchasing her. Jacobs writes of this moment, "My heart was exceed
ingly full. I remembered how my poor father had tried to buy me,
when I was a small child. . . . I remembered how my good old grandmother had laid up her earnings to purchase me in later years, and
how often her plans had been frustrated. . . . But God so orders circumstances as to keep me with my friend Mrs. Bruce. Love, duty,
gratitude, also bind me to her side. It is a privilege to serve her who
pities my oppressed people, and who has bestowed the inestimable
boon of freedom on me and my children" (200–201).

When Harriet Jacobs's brother, the slave John S. Jacobs, traveled north
with his owner Samuel Sawyer in 1838, some friends in New York advised
him about the possibility of escaping while in the North. He made his escape
plan with them and, as he writes,

[The Sawyers] dine[d] at the Astor at three o'clock; at half-past four I was to
be on board the boat for Providence. Being unable to write myself at that
time, and unwilling to leave him in suspense, I got a friend to write as follows: — "Sir — I have left you, not to return; when I have got settled, I will
give you further satisfaction. No longer yours, John S. Jacobs."

This note was to be put into the post-office in time for him to get it the
next morning. I waited on him and his wife at dinner. As the town clock
struck four, I left the room. (280–81)

No longer yours, John S. Jacobs: how coolly the eloping slave performs this
electrifying resurrection of meaning in a formula of inert politesse. He does
so by pushing periperformatively at the proscenium of the ever-shifting theater of human ownership, as condensed in a routinized protestation of loy-
alty like, say, "I beg to remain your obedient servant" — supposed to insulate
its meaning from the plain fact that some human beings were in fact, in
1838, *in some places* and not in others, both legally and effectually owned by
other human beings.

A part of my motive in this chapter has been to explore how one complex and protracted historical crime, the holding of African and African-
descended slaves in the Western Hemisphere, gored its mark (highly dif-
ferentially) on the modes of meaning that were possible for anyone in its
periperformative ambit, whether European or African-descended, and in
the Old World as well as the New. Specifically, I have been supposing that

during the time of slavery, and for an uncircumscribable time after its abolition probably extending beyond the present, the cluster of ostentatiously potent linguistic acts that have been grouped loosely, since J. L. Austin, under the rubric of "performatives" must be understood continuously in relation to the exemplary instance of slavery. They must be understood in this way at least as much as they are understood already by philosophers, linguists, and gender theorists in relation to the exemplary instances of courtship/marriage and of juridical acts in a general sense.

I have been be assuming this, as I say, rather than demonstrating it; it has consituted the dimensional grounding of a discussion that aims to suggest why Austin's quite necessary deprecation of the "descriptive fallacy" needn't and shouldn't have the effect of hiving off a depersonalized understanding of performative force from a psychologized and spatialized understanding of affective force, and that aims to thicken our sense of the relation among explicit performatives, utterances that surround and allude to explicit performatives, and the broader field of the performative effects of language and discourse. I have not undertaken this out of a desire to demonstrate how one continuous skin of tone and theory can be forced to stretch, however thinly, over such disparate ontological situations — citizen and chattel, romantic realism and the bearing of witness, the conventions of courtship-and-adultery and the laws of servitude — but to dramatize a likelihood that such tearing stretches must be attempted even though they may amplify the echo of every ugly incongruity — indeed, even where that homiletic point may not itself be their main one.

NOTES

1. "Il gran rifiuto," in the *Inferno*, III, 60. See also Cavafy's poem, "Che fece . . . il gran rifiuto" (12).

2. Despite the choice of examples throughout the essay, I do not mean to suggest that there is anything inherently antinormative about the highlighting of periperformative utterances, even in the vicinity of marriage. A good example to the contrary would be the extraordinarily heightened periperformative consciousness of Mr. Collins in *Pride and Prejudice*.

3. Though one might add, parenthetically, that in post-Foucauldian theory in particular, it seems clear that the leverage for such a critique is available precisely in the space opened up by the Austinian interest in provisionally distinguishing what is being said from the fact of the saying of it. Foucault writes, for instance, about sexuality: "The

central issue . . . is not to determine whether one says yes or no to sex, whether one formulates prohibitions or permissions, whether one asserts its importance or denies its effects . . . but to account for the fact that it is spoken about. . . . What is at issue, briefly, is the over-all 'discursive fact' " (11). The Foucauldian move is not, of course, identical to Austin's distinction between the (true or false) constatation of an utterance and its performative force: a de-emphasis of yes versus no is not the same as a de-emphasis of true versus false. The two moves are congruently structured, however; they invoke and reward very similar interpretive skills. We might say that both Austin and Foucault train readers to identify and perform the kind of figure/ground reversals analyzed by the Gestalt psychology of the first half of the twentieth century. Austin for instance, abandoning the attempt to distinguish between some utterances that are intrinsically performative and others that are intrinsically constative, finally offers a substitute account, applicable to any utterance, that is couched in terms (such as the curious intransitive verb "to abstract") of perception and attention: "With the constative utterance, we abstract from the illocutionary . . . aspects of the speech act, and we concentrate on the locutionary. . . . With the performative utterance, we attend as much as possible to the illocutionary force of the utterance, and abstract from the dimension of correspondence with facts" (145–46).

Chapter 3

SHAME IN THE CYBERNETIC FOLD:

READING SILVAN TOMKINS

Written with Adam Frank

Here are a few things theory knows today.

Or, to phrase it more fairly, here are a few broad assumptions that shape the heuristic habits and positing procedures of theory today (theory not in the primary theoretical texts, but in the routinizing critical projects of "applied theory"; theory as a broad project that now spans the humanities and extends into history and anthropology; theory after Foucault and Greenblatt, after Freud and Lacan, after Lévi-Strauss, after Derrida, after feminism) when it offers any account of human beings or cultures:

1. The distance of any such account from a biological basis is assumed to correlate near precisely with its potential for doing justice to difference (individual, historical, and cross-cultural), to contingency, to performative force, and to the possibility of change.

2. Human language is assumed to offer the most productive, if not the only possible, model for understanding representation.

3. The bipolar, transitive relations of subject to object, self to other, and active to passive, and the physical sense (sight) understood to correspond most closely to these relations are dominant organizing tropes to the extent that their dismantling as such is framed as both an urgent and an interminable task. This preoccupation extends to

such processes as subjectification, self-fashioning, objectification, and Othering; to the gaze; to the core of selfhood whether considered as a developmental telos or as a dangerous illusion requiring vigilant deconstruction.

4. Correspondingly, the structuralist reliance on symbolization through binary pairings of elements, defined in a diacritical relation to one another and no more than arbitrarily associated with the things symbolized, has not only survived the structuralist moment but, if anything, has been propagated ever more broadly through varied and unresting critique — critique that reproduces and popularizes the *structure*, even as it may complicate an understanding of the *workings*, of the binarisms mentioned above along with such others as presence/absence, lack/plenitude, nature/culture, repression/liberation, and subversive/hegemonic.

In this chapter, we discuss a figure not presently well-known, the U.S. psychologist Silvan Tomkins (1911–1991), who seems implicitly to challenge these habits and procedures — to challenge them not from the vantage of the present but from (what we take to be) a moment shortly before their installation *as* theory. He is also, then, a figure whom such habits and procedures would tend sharply to rebuke. In fact, reading Tomkins's work on affect has consistently involved us in a peculiar double movement: to be responsive to the great interest of his writing seems also, continually, to make graphic the mechanism of what would seem an irresistibly easy discreditation. You don't have to be long out of theory kindergarten to make mincemeat of, let's say, a psychology that depends on the separate existence of eight (only sometimes it's nine) distinct affects hardwired into the human biological system.

Yet we can't convince ourselves that, for instance, the formidably rich phenomenology of emotions in Tomkins is in any accidental or separable relation to his highly suspect scientism. If anything, his scientism seems to interpret as an alternative and far coarser scientism the theory that would find his so easy to dismiss. The scientism of "theory," indeed, can become visible in this light as a different product of almost the same, very particular technological moment as Tomkins's. The fact that one, today, sounds cockamamie and the other virtual common sense, or that one sounds ineluctably dated and the other nearly fresh as print, may reveal less about the transhistorical rightness of "theory" than about the dynamics of consensus formation and cross-disciplinary transmission.

☞ One conjoint of affect effects we experienced on the way to becoming addicted to reading Tomkins: his writing excited and calmed, inspired and contented. Once, one of us fell asleep reading and afterwards explained, "I often get tired when I'm learning a lot." There are many examples of the writing's brash generosity, and in a section on affect differences in different species we find an example of the writer's: "The writer successfully domesticated a somewhat wild kitten, Bambi, which had been terrorized by a couple of dozen older cats, all of whom lived together on a farm. Bambi was a wild little anxiety neurotic with an overwhelming fear of all animals, including man. It proved possible to attenuate both his wildness and his fear by holding him tightly as long as was necessary to burn out the fear response. I continued to hold him tightly after his fear had passed, to habituate him to non-fearful human contact. This was repeated daily for some time and eventually the fear subsided" (*Affect* 1:61).[1]

This could as well describe Tomkins's writing: a potentially terrifying and terrified idea or image is taken up and held for as many paragraphs as are necessary to "burn out the fear response," then for as many more until that idea or image can recur in the text without initially evoking terror. Phrases, sentences, sometimes whole paragraphs repeat; pages are taken up with sentences syntactically resembling one another (epistemically modal nonfactive utterances of the form "It is possible that . . . ," "If . . . may . . . ," "Whether because . . ."), sentences not exemplifying a general principle but sampling—listing the possible. This rich claustral writing nurtures, pacifies, replenishes, then sets the idea in motion again. Bambi isn't the only terrified wild thing in this picture.

During Tomkins's postdoctoral years at Harvard he underwent a seven-year psychoanalysis for which the immediate stimulus was a severe reading block. Severe reading block: a symptom we'd never heard named before, but one has only to hear it named to feel one knows it intimately. *Affect Imagery Consciousness* isn't least affecting for the traces it bears of an intensively problematized verbal process. Tomkins's friend of many decades, Irving Alexander, described to us in an interview how Tomkins wrote, six or seven rapid handwritten lines to a page "like automatic writing," and how sometimes, to his great surprise, after writing a long section, he would discover in a drawer a sheaf of papers that he had written months before that reached the same set of conclusions from a different starting point. If the astonishingly heterogeneous writing of *Affect Imagery Consciousness* often embraces multiple overlapping voices to attenuate terror, it is less to reduce the number of voices than to contain their space of overlap lest it spread over larger sections of the work. Structural repetition is rarely exact, as "may" and "can" and the phrases in which they appear alternate without apparent pattern in a paragraph whose rhythms remind one of Gertrude Stein's, another writer who certainly knows the pleasures of lists:

> If you like to be looked at and I like to look at you, we may achieve an enjoyable interpersonal relationship. If you like to talk and I like to listen to you talk, this can be mutually rewarding. If you like to feel enclosed within a claustrum and I like to put my arms around you, we can both enjoy a particular kind of embrace. If you like to be supported and I like to hold you in my arms, we can enjoy such an embrace. If you like to be kissed and I like to kiss you, we may enjoy each other. If you like to be sucked or bitten and I like to suck or bite you, we may enjoy each other. If you like to have your skin rubbed and I like to do this to you, we can enjoy each other. If you enjoy being hugged and I enjoy hugging you, it can be mutually enjoyable. If you enjoy being dominated and I enjoy controlling you, we may enjoy each other. If you enjoy communicating your experiences and ideas and aspirations and I enjoy being informed about the experiences, ideas, and aspirations of others, we can enjoy each other. If you enjoy telling about the past and I enjoy hearing about the past, we may enjoy each other. If you enjoy speculating about and predicting the future and I enjoy being so informed, we can enjoy each other. If you wish to be like me and I wish to have you imitate me, we can enjoy each other. (*Affect* 1:411)

At least as often as paragraphs permit reader and writer to *do*—here to enjoy, but in other textual places to anger, or become excited or ashamed, or to enter scenes and perform scripts that call on affective as well as perceptual and memory capacities—they permit one to *not do:*

> It is not uncommon that two individuals, both very sociophilic, may be incapable of a sustained social relationship because of varying investments in one or another type of interpersonal interaction. Thus you may crave much

body contact and silent communion and I wish to talk. You wish to stare deeply into my eyes, but I achieve intimacy only in the dark in sexual embrace. You wish to be fed and cared for, and I wish to exhibit myself and be looked at. You wish to be hugged and to have your skin rubbed, and I wish to reveal myself only by discussing my philosophy of life. You wish to reveal yourself through your view of the nature of man, but I can externalize myself only through communicating my passion for the steel and tape of a computer that almost thinks like a man. You wish to communicate your most personal feelings about me, but I can achieve social intimacy only through a commonly shared high opinion about the merits of something quite impersonal, such as a particular theory or branch of knowledge or an automobile. (*Affect* 1:413–14)

☞ We got our first taste of Silvan Tomkins when we were looking for some usable ideas on the topic of shame. In a sodden landscape of moralistic or maudlin idées reçues about what is, to the contrary, the most mercurial of emotions, Tomkins's formulations startle: for their sharpness and daring, their amplitude, and a descriptive level-headedness that in the dispiriting context sounds almost surreal. Tomkins considers shame, along with interest, surprise, joy, anger, fear, distress, disgust, and in his later writing contempt ("dissmell") to be the basic set of affects. He places shame, in fact, at one end of the affect polarity *shame-interest:* suggesting that the pulsations of cathexis around shame, of all things, are what either enable or disenable so basic a function as the ability to be interested in the world: "Like disgust, [shame] operates only after interest or enjoyment has been activated, and inhibits one or the other or both. The innate activator of shame is the incomplete reduction of interest or joy. Hence any barrier to further exploration which partially reduces interest . . . will activate the lowering of the head and eyes in shame and reduce further exploration or self-exposure. . . . Such a barrier might be because one is suddenly looked at by one who is strange, or because one wishes to look at or commune with another person but suddenly cannot because he is strange, or one expected him to be familiar but he suddenly appears unfamiliar, or one started to smile but found one was smiling at a stranger" (*Affect* 2:123).

As I suggested in the introduction, Tomkins's emphasis in this account on *the strange* rather than on the prohibited or disapproved was congenial with a motivating intuition that the phenomenon of shame might offer new ways of short-circuiting the seemingly near inescapable habits of thought that Foucault groups together under the name of the "repressive hypothe-sis."At the same time, the "strange"ness of Tomkins's account also seemed nicely different from the engulfing, near eschatological pathos surround-ing shame in the popular discourse where it is currently most extensively discussed: that of the self-help and recovery movements and the self psy-chology that theoretically underpins them.

Indeed, it was through the filter of self psychology and object-relations psychology that we first encountered Tomkins; to the degree that his work has been popularized, it has been as offering a kind of origin myth (in the shame of the infant) for a genetic narrative of the individuation and filiation of a self. Tomkins's theory of affect originated with his close observations of an infant in 1955, and he was able to locate early expressions of shame at a period (around seven months) before the infant could have any concept of prohibition. As Chapter 1 explains, many developmental psychologists, responding to this finding, now consider shame the affect that most defines the space wherein a sense of self will develop. In the context of an object-relations developmental narrative, this use of Tomkins is valuable as one of the repertoire of ways that such a psychology has of displacing the Freudian emphasis on Oedipality and repression. What it obscures, however, is how sublimely alien Tomkins's own work remains to any project of narrating the emergence of a core self. A reader who undergoes the four volumes of Tomkins's *Affect Imagery Consciousness* feels the alchemy of the contingent involve itself so intimately with identity that Tomkins comes to seem the psychologist one would most like to read face-à-face with Proust. He more than countenances both the Proustian fascination with taxonomies of per-sons *and* the Proustian certainty that the highest interest of such taxonomies is ever in making grounds for disconfirmation and surprise.

Characteristically, in Tomkins these penchants were embodied through extravagant negotiations among the disparate, competing disciplines called psychology in the United States from the 1940s through and beyond the 1960s: experimental, clinical, and applied alike. Applied, in this case, as per-sonality theory: during his many years of teaching at Princeton, Tomkins worked concurrently on the development of personality tests for the Edu-cational Testing Service, for example, and wrote a book on interpreting the Thematic Apperception Test—a book that was, as Irving E. Alexander remarks in his biographical essay, "very well received as an intellectual achievement but I doubt if anyone ever used it in order to learn how to interpret a TAT record" (in Tomkins, *Shame* 253). The presumption of a consolidated core personality that would seem implicit in such a disciplinary location is challenged, however, everywhere in Tomkins's work, and at both the grossest and finest levels, by such another disciplinary mobilization as that of cybernetics and systems theory; or, also pervasively, ethology, neuropsychology, perception and cognition, social psychology, and, as well, a prescient series of rereadings of Freud. Paul Goodman, Gregory Bateson, other fertile polymath figures comparably marked by the American postwar moment, didn't have so broad a center of gravity in (and couldn't, therefore, either, exert the same pressure against) disciplinary psychology: the first publication of Tomkins's theory of affect was in French, in a volume edited by a differently comparable figure, Jacques Lacan.

Sublimely alien, we found this psychology, to the developmental presumption/prescription of a core self; sublimely resistant, we might have added, to such presumption — except that the sublimity lies in an exemplary cartographic distance, not in a dialectical struggle. Even rarer in U.S. psychology of the cold war period is the plain absence, not only of homophobia, but of any hint of a heterosexist teleology.[2] This mostly silent and utterly scrupulous disentanglement is the more compelling for the range and heterogeneity of Tomkins's disciplinary sources: ethology, social psychology, psychoanalysis, and so on are each structured around foundationally heterosexist assumptions, and each differently so. Again, however, Tomkins's achievement seems to result not from a concertedly antihomophobic project (nor from any marked gay interest, for that matter) but rather from, almost simply, finding a different place to begin.

Tomkins's resistance to heterosexist teleologies is founded in the most basic terms of his understanding of affect.[3] As discussed in the introduction, a concomitant of distinguishing in the first place between an affect system and a drive system that it analogically amplifies is that, unlike the drives (e.g., to breathe, to eat), "Any affect may have any 'object.' This is the basic source of complexity of human motivation and behavior" (*Affect* 1:347). Furthermore, in a refusal of the terms of behaviorism, the affect system as a whole "has no single 'output' " (3:66); also unlike the drives, "affective amplification is indifferent to the means-end difference" (3:67). "It is enjoyable to enjoy. It is exciting to be excited. It is terrorizing to be terrorized and angering to be angered. Affect is self-validating with or without any further referent" (3:404). It is these specifications that make affect theory such a useful site for resistance to teleological presumptions of the many sorts historically embedded in the disciplines of psychology.

The force of (what comes to seem) the powerfully gracious "may" of the first of these propositions, "Any affect may have any 'object,'" the "may" that emerges through the volumes as Tomkins's least dispensable locution, accrues at least partly from the highly complex, highly explicit layering of biological and machine models in his understanding of the human being. An early question for him was "Could one design a truly humanoid machine?" But closer reading of a passage discussed in the introduction shows that the concept "machine" was a complex one for Tomkins:

> While pursuing this line of thought, I encountered Wiener's early papers on cybernetics. . . . One could not engage in such a project without the concept of multiple assemblies of varying degrees of independence, dependence, interdependence, and control and transformation of one by another.
>
> It was this general conception which, one day in the late 1940s, resulted in my first understanding of the role of the affect mechanism as a separate but amplifying co-assembly. I almost fell out of my chair in surprise and excitement when I suddenly realized that the panic of one who experiences the suffocation of interruption of his vital air supply has nothing to do with the anoxic drive signal per se [because gradual loss of oxygen, even when fatal, produces no panic]. A human being could be, and often is, terrified about anything under the sun. It was a short step to see that excitement had nothing per se to do with sexuality or with hunger, and that the apparent urgency of the drive system was borrowed from its co-assembly with appropriate affects as necessary amplifiers. Freud's id suddenly appeared to be a paper tiger since sexuality, as he best knew, was the most finicky of drives, easily rendered impotent by shame or anxiety or boredom or rage. ("Quest" 309)

Note a most characteristic analytic structure here. What appears to be a diminution in the power assigned to the sexual drive nonetheless corresponds to a multiplication—a finite and concrete multiplication, it will emerge—of different possibilities for sexual relevance (residing in this case in the distinct negative affects shame, anxiety, boredom, rage). Sexuality is no longer an on/off matter whose two possibilities are labeled Express or Repress. Sexuality *as a drive* remains characterized here by a binary (potent/impotent) model; yet its link to attention, to motivation, or indeed to action occurs only through coassembly with an affect system described as encompassing several more, and more qualitatively different, possibilities than on/off.

We discuss this pattern in the framework of Tomkins's habit of layering digital (on/off) with analog (graduated and/or multiply differentiated) representational models, and we argue for the great conceptual value of this habit. If it seems to "rhyme," structurally, with what we have already referred to as his habit of layering biological with machine or computer models of the human being, we must nonetheless deprecate (as would Tomkins and indeed any systems theorist) the further homology that might identify the machine or computer with digital representation, and the biological organism with analogical representation. The tacit homology machine : digital :: animal : analogical (and concomitant privileging of the machine/digital) is, we argue, a very powerful structuring presumption for current theory and emerges especially strongly as a reflexive antibiologism. But it represents bad engineering and bad biology, and it leads to bad theory. Even supposing information machines and living organisms to be altogether distinct classes, they certainly have in common that each comprises a heterogeneous mixture of digitally structured with analogically structured representational mechanisms. For that matter, the distinction between digital and analog is itself anything but absolute: analogical measurement can be used, as in a thermostat or a neuron, to trigger an on/off switch, whereas patterns or cumulations of on/off switchings may, as in Donald Hebb's 1949 model of neural firing in the brain, result in the formation of complex analogic structures.

In a 1970 paper, "Analog and Digital Communication: On Negation, Signification, and Meaning," Anthony Wilden offers this among the "guiding principles" on the subject:

> The question of the analog and the digital is one of relationship, not one of entities.
>
> Switching from analog to digital [and vice versa] is necessary for communication to cross certain types of boundaries. A great deal of communication — perhaps all communication — undoubtedly involves constant switching of this type.

Digital thought is analytic and two-valued; analog thought is dialectical and many-valued.

A digital system is of a higher level of organization and therefore of a lower logical type than an analog system. The digital system has greater "semiotic freedom," but it is ultimately governed by the rules of the analog relationship between systems, subsystems, and supersystems in nature. (188–89)

Tomkins's theory of affect, reflecting an intellectual moment close to Wilden's in this essay, depends on a number of different kinds of crossing between analog and digital forms of representation. For example, some of the affects he discusses are structured in the following way:

I would account for the difference in affect activation by three variants of a single principle—the density of neural firing. By density I mean the frequency of neural firing per unit of time. My theory posits three discrete classes of activators of affect, each of which further amplifies the sources which activate them. These are stimulation increase, stimulation level, and stimulation decrease.

Thus any stimulus with a relatively sudden onset and a steep increase in the rate of neural firing will innately activate a startle response. As shown in Figure 1, if the rate of neural firing increases less rapidly, fear is activated, and if still less rapidly, then interest is innately activated. In contrast, any sustained increase in the level of neural firing, as with a continued loud noise, would innately activate the cry of distress. If it were sustained and still louder, it would innately activate the anger response. Finally, any sudden decrease in stimulation that reduced the rate of neural firing, as in the sudden reduction of excessive noise, would innately activate the rewarding smile of enjoyment. ("Quest" 317)

May we defer discussion of the fear, distress, and anger that will be triggered in theory-minded readers by the density of occurrence of the word "innate" in this passage? Or, for that matter, the laughter with which scientific readers today may register the reductiveness of the concept "density of neural firing"? What we want to point to is, instead, the way Hebb's understanding of neural firing as a discrete, on/off (hence digital) event triggered by quantifiable (hence analog) stimuli is once again analogically quantified, in Tomkins's graph, over the dimension of time, but in a way that leads

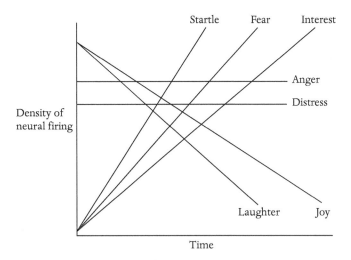

FIGURE I. Graphical representation of a theory of innate activators of affect. From Silvan Tomkins, *Affect, Imagery, Consciousness*, vol. I. Copyright © Springer Publishing Company, Inc., New York 10012. Used by permission.

in turn to the on/off (digital) "activation" of any of several discrete affects. This part of Tomkins's theory could thus be schematized as analog → digital → analog → digital. What that (digitalizing) schema misses, though, is that Tomkins's theory ramifies toward a *many-valued* (and in that sense analogic) understanding of affect: if the on/off of "neural firing" is qualitatively undifferentiated, the on/off of affect activation is qualitatively highly differentiated—among no fewer than seven affects. (Qualitative differentiation is always, in a sense, analogical because, for one thing, to the degree that there are *different* affects, they sustain a claim to be represented, necessarily analogically, via graph or map.) Tomkins writes, "The general advantage of affective arousal to such a broad spectrum of levels and changes of levels of neural firing is to make the individual care about quite different states of affairs *in quite different ways*" ("Quest" 318; emphasis added).

And the "quite different states of affairs," we should add, are never to be understood as purely *external* states: though Tomkins here uses the uncharacteristically simplified example of "a loud noise" to represent a stimulus, in the body of his work density of neural firing is virtually never a direct translation of some external event that could be discretely segregated as "stimulus." Rather, it already itself reflects the complex interleaving of endogenous and exogenous, perceptual, proprioceptive, and interpretive — causes, effects, feedbacks, motives, long-term states such as moods and theories, along with distinct transitory physical or verbal events. Against the behaviorists, Tomkins consistently argues that relevant stimulus for the affect system includes internal as well as external events, concluding firmly that there is no basis, and certainly not the basis internal versus external, for a definitional distinction between response and stimulus. Tomkins reports on one stimulus-response experiment, for example, in a way that quite undoes the presumptive simplicity of the experience of electric shock, which classically had been considered the transparently aversive stimulus par excellence. "One had only to listen to the spontaneous exclamations throughout an experimental series," he writes, "to become aware of the difficulty of evoking one and only one affect by the use of what seems an appropriate stimulus." Simply by recording his subjects' speech at the moment they received electric shocks, he offers a carnivalesque deconstruction in the place of the expected "results." Among the circus of affective responses to the apparently self-identical stimulus: "Feels like when Papa spanked"; "A hundred years ago you'd be sort of a criminal, wouldn't you?"; "If you want a terrorizing pattern you've got it"; "This isn't fair"; "Oh, you rat, cut it out; it's maddening"; "I'm not getting much out of this — I hope you are"; "This experiment is stupid"; "So that's what the shock feels like"; "Afraid it might nauseate me"; "I like the shocks"; "Interesting to get in the hands of a psychologist"; "Is this supposed to make me cautious?"; "I didn't want to be a shock trooper anyway"; "Ouch, that startles you . . . didn't hurt"; "Feels like a sport with a bet on"; "It makes you sort of angry the first time"; "Oh, Lord, I'm falling asleep" (*Affect* 1:193–98).

☞ We remarked earlier that scientifically minded readers would likely balk at the reductiveness of Tomkins's crucial notion of "density of neural firing." Although the notion of neural firing per se seems to be intelligibly used in this work, Tomkins remains (over the years of publication of *Affect Imagery Consciousness*) resistant to the specification of *where* or *in what (presumably functionally specialized) neural locations* this firing is taking place. Although *Affect Imagery Consciousness* otherwise displays quite a lot of interest in brain localization, this one crucial concept, density of neural firing, persists in treating the brain as a homogeneous mass that has, at best, only the potential for developing local qualitative specialization.

This understanding of the brain is, we argue, important for defining Tomkins's (very fruitful) historical relation to what we call the particular moment of the cybernetic fold, roughly from the late 1940s to the mid-1960s. By "cybernetic fold" we mean the moment when scientists' understanding of the brain and other life processes is marked by the concept, the possibility, the *imminence,* of powerful computers, but the actual computational muscle of the new computers isn't available yet. The cybernetic fold, then, is the moment of systems theory—and also, in a directly related but not identical development, the structuralist moment. Indeed, part of our aim is to describe structuralism, not as *that mistaken thing that happened before poststructuralism but fortunately led directly to it,* but rather as part of a rich intellectual ecology, a Gestalt (including systems theory) that allowed it to mean more different and more interesting things than have survived its sleek trajectory into poststructuralism.[4] We argue that the early cybernetic notion of the brain as a homogeneous, differenti*able* but not originally differentiated system is a characteristic and very fruitful emblem of many of the so far unrealized possibilities of this intellectual moment.[5]

The cybernetic fold might be described as a fold between postmodernist and modernist ways of hypothesizing about the brain and mind. The prospect of virtually unlimited computational power gave a new appeal to concepts such as feedback, which had been instrumentally available in mechanical design for over a century, but which, if understood as a continuing feature of many systems, including the biological, would have introduced a quite unassimilable level of complexity to descriptive or predictive calculations. Between the time when it was unthinkable to essay such calculations and the time when it became commonplace to perform them, there intervened a period when they were available to be richly imagined—but were still imagined with a structural elegance, an interest in conceptual economy of means and modeling, that were not destined (and seemingly were not required) to survive the introduction of the actual technology.

The evocative lists that make such a distinctive feature of the writing of *Affect Imagery Consciousness* seem to bear the mark of this moment of technological imagination. With their minimal and apparently nonsignifying grammatical differentiations, the items on the lists gesture toward the possibility of random, virtually infinite permutation, some of it trivial, some of it highly significant; the suggestion of sheer, unlimited extent marks the impress of radical contingency on the possible outcomes. Yet the items on the lists, far from random, are always carefully chosen to open and indicate new vistas, to represent new *kinds* of possible entailments involved in any generalization. They can be read as either undoing or suggesting new taxonomic work. Tomkins's lists probably resemble most the long sentences in Proust where a speculation about someone's motive is couched in a series of long parallel clauses that begin "Whether because . . . ; or because . . . ; or because. . . ." A postmodern syntax that seems to vitiate the very possibility of understanding motive, by pluralizing it as if mechanically, infinitely, seems with the same gesture to proffer semantic tools so irresistibly usable that they bind one ever more imaginatively and profoundly to the local possibilities of an individual psychology. Tomkins's lists invoke the technological juggernaut that would overwhelm and obviate their enumerations; invoking it, however, they also momentarily forestall or displace it. Nor is the issue simplified by how regularly in these volumes Tomkins simply repeats, verbatim, a few of his key examples—perseveration that could suggest a machinelike interchangeability of parts in *Affect Imagery Consciousness* if it didn't more strongly evoke the pathos of blockage and its overcoming, the psychic economies of (what Tomkins calls) "affluence scripts," "perceptual greed," and occasional shaming poverty of resource, that the work offers so many new affordances for understanding.

The epithet "fold" seems applicable to the cybernetic moment partly because systems theory, precisely through its tropism toward the image of an undifferentiated but differentiable ecology, had as one of its great representational strengths an ability to discuss *how things differentiate:* how quantitative differences turn into qualitative ones, how digital and analog representations leapfrog or interleave with one another, what makes the unexpected fault lines between regions of the calculable and the incalculable (destined to evolve into chaos theory), and so forth. Where cognitive psychology has tried to render the mind's processes transparent through and through from the point of view of cognition, where behaviorism has tried to do the same from the point of view of behavioral "outcome," where psychoanalysis has profited from the conceptual elegance of a single bar (repression) between a single continuous "consciousness" and a single "unconscious," Tomkins's affect theory by contrast offers a wealth of sites of productive opacity. The valorization of feedback in systems theory is also, after all, necessarily a valorization of error and blindness as productive of, specifically, *structure.* Think of Frank Rosenblatt's Perceptron (Luger, 516– 28), for example, designed in this early moment to teach itself *how to learn* precisely through a process of trial and error. Its theoretical principles went into supposed obsolescence with the emergence of vastly more powerful computers to reemerge only recently under the rubrics of connectionism and parallel distributed processing. As Tomkins writes, a truly formidable humanlike machine

> would in all probability require a relatively helpless infancy followed by a growing competence through its childhood and adolescence. In short, it would require time in which to learn how to learn through making errors and correcting them. This much is quite clear and is one of the reasons for the limitations of our present automata. Their creators are temperamentally unsuited to create and nurture mechanisms which begin in helplessness, confusion and error. The automaton designer is an overprotective, overdemanding parent who is too pleased with precocity in his creations. As soon as he has been able to translate a human achievement into steel, tape and electricity, he is delighted with the performance of his brain child. Such precocity essentially guarantees a low ceiling to the *learning* ability of his automaton. (*Affect* 1:116)

Tomkins emphasizes that the introduction of opacity and error at the cognitive level alone would not be sufficient even for powerful cognition. About the affect system, he writes, "We have stressed the ambiguity and blindness of this primary motivational system to accentuate what we take to be the necessary price which must be paid by any system which is to spend its major energies in a sea of risk, learning by making errors. The achievement of cognitive power and precision require a motivational system no less plastic and bold. Cognitive strides are limited by the motives which urge them. Cognitive error, which is essential to cognitive learning, can be made only by one capable of committing motivational error, i.e. being wrong about his own wishes, their causes and outcomes" (1:114).[6] Thus it is the inefficiency of the fit between the affect system and the cognitive system—and between either of these and the drive system—that enables learning, development, continuity, differentiation. Freedom, play, affordance, meaning itself derive from the wealth of mutually nontransparent possibilities for being wrong about an object—and, implicatively, about oneself.

☞ But to return to Figure 1. It is important that the many-valuedness of this analogical system refers to *more than two* but also to *finitely many* values or dimensions (as, for instance, on a map: north, south, east, west), though, as in any analogical representation, there may be infinite gradations along the finitely specified dimensions. A common enough and banal enough feature of very many representations. Yet it seems to us that for an affect theory to be structured as this one is by *finitely many (n>2) values* is actually at the heart of the resistance it encounters from, or illumination it can offer to, the current thinking routines of "theory." The resistance occurs because there seems to be some strong adhesion between the specification "finitely many (n>2) values" and that conversation-stopping word *innate*. (Though in Tomkins's work this adhesion proves a spectacularly attenuable one—attenuated, perhaps, precisely by the layering and constant mutual interruption of biological and machine models.) Somehow it's hard to hold on to the concept of eight or thirteen (and yet not infinite) *different kinds of*—of anything important without having a biological model somewhere in the vicinity. This adhesion may well be a historical development: as though some momentum of modernity (call it monotheism? call it the Reformation? call it capitalist rationalization?) has so evacuated the conceptual space between 2 and infinity that it may require the inertial friction of a biologism to even suggest the possibility of reinhabiting that space. We have no interest whatever in minimizing the continuing history of racist, sexist, homophobic, or otherwise abusive biologisms, or the urgency of the exposures of them, that have made the gravamen of so many contemporary projects of critique. At the same time, we fear, with the installation of an *automatic* anti-biologism as the unshifting central tenet of "theory," the loss of conceptual access to an entire thought realm, the analogic realm of finitely many (n>2) values. Access to this realm is important for, among other things, enabling a political vision of difference that might resist both binary homogenization and infinitizing trivialization.[7]

For an example of how affect fares under the recent routines of theory, we could look to a 1992 study by Ann Cvetkovich, *Mixed Feelings: Feminism,*

Mass Culture, and Victorian Sensationalism. We choose this example not because the book is unintelligent or unuseful—it is anything but—but because its achievement seems to depend on an exemplarily clear and expli-
cated relation to the several theoretical currents (psychoanalytic, Marxist,
Foucauldian) that underlie it.[8] It is further unusual only in basing its argument on a theory of affect that it makes an explicit centerpiece of the book.
That central theory, whose goal is "a politics of affect that does not rest on
an essentialist conception of affect" (25), is, however, only very cursorily
specified:

> Like sexuality, affect should be understood as discursively constructed. (30)

> Not only do I assume that the link between sensational events and bodily
> sensations is constructed rather than natural, I also assume that the apparent
> naturalness of bodily sensation or affect is itself a construction. Like sexuality
> and other physical processes, affect is not a pre-discursive entity, a fact that
> is often obscured by the construction of affects or bodily sensations as natu-
> ral. . . . Furthermore, if affective responses are not as natural as they seem
> to be, then the construction of affect as natural might well be part of the
> discursive apparatus that performs the work of what Foucault has described
> as the disciplining of the body. Discipline is powerful precisely because it
> functions as though it were natural rather than imposed. (24–25)

Although Cvetkovich undertakes this inquiry in the name of "theorizing
affect" (the title of an early chapter of the book), it is not immediately clear
why her rather minimal specification that affect is "discursively constructed"
rather than "natural" should claim the status of a theory. Unless, that is, precisely *that* specification is today understood to constitute *anything* as theory.
Rather than broaching or summarizing an actual theory of affect, these sentences instead "theorize affect" in the sense of rounding up affect and herd-
ing it into the big tent of what is already understood to constitute the body of
Theory. The brand on that body is relentlessly legible: "theory" has become
almost simply coextensive with the claim (you can't say it often enough)
It's not natural. An extraordinary claim here presented as self-evident: "The
value [*the* value!] of a theory, like the value of historical analysis, resides in
its ability to challenge assumptions about 'nature' " (43–44).

As suggested in the introduction, this reflexive antibiologism might be
expected to concomit with several habits of argument that will stand in

a seemingly paradoxical relation to the stated principles of Cvetkovich's work:

1. Foucauldian deprecations of "the repressive hypothesis" will be transformed virtually instantaneously into binarized, highly moralistic allegories of the subversive versus the hegemonic, resistance versus power. "If affect is historically constructed, it can then become, as Foucault suggests of sexuality under the rule of the repressive hypothesis, not the mechanism for the liberation of the self but instead the mechanism for the containment and discipline of the self" (31). "If affect can be a source of resistance, it is also . . . a mechanism for power" (40). "Foucault's suggestion that resistance is not exterior to power means that these domains can be both vehicles for resistance *and* vehicles for the imposition of power" (41).

2. A nominal deprecation of the question of essential truth becomes the ground for frequent invocations and detective-like scrutinies of supposed truth claims by others — claims paraphrased and presented in the most absolute terms. One of the pivotal words for Cvetkovich's argument is "guarantee." For example: "The links between personal and social transformation are by no means guaranteed" (1); "The Victorian novel need not be defended in order to guarantee the possibility of social transformation" (41); "Affect . . . cannot be counted on to guarantee a text's subversive tendencies" (34). The ontological options are reduced to guarantee versus no guarantee; even apart from its oddly consumerist sound, this radical coarsening of relations to truth means that the epistemological stress of Cvetkovich's argument, rather than being lightened, is rendered ever more insistent. Characteristically, for instance, she descries after much deductive work that Fredric Jameson's discussion of mass culture is "suspiciously essentialist in its conception of affect" (29). The suspicion resides in the reading eye, not in the read text, but it's a common development, the strange metamorphosis from antiessentialist to ontological private eye.

3. Perhaps most oddly for a "theory of affect," this one has no feelings in it. *Affect* is treated as a unitary category, with a unitary history and unitary politics. There is no theoretical room for any difference between being, say, amused, disgusted, ashamed, and enraged. By

analogy with Foucault's narrative about sexuality, Cvetkovich refers to a modern "history of the construction of affect as meaningful, one evident . . . in the eighteenth-century novels of sensibility and sentimentality and in the emphasis on feelings in Romantic poetry" (30–31). Feelings—but evidently no particular feelings. The sublime, for another example, is described as "the high-culture version of affect" (35) (any particular affects?). And Cvetkovich's implication throughout is that genres are differentiated, not in relation to the *kinds* of affect they may evoke or generate, but more simply by the presence or absence of some reified substance called Affect.

Surely the absence of different affects from this "theory of affect" is no oversight. It represents, instead, a theoretical decision: as if what is presented could not finally be theory if it made any definitional room at all for qualitative differences among affects. Wouldn't it, after all (we imagine the quizzing from any well-drilled graduate seminar), wouldn't it risk essentialism to understand affects as qualitatively different from each other? Yes, it certainly would. In fact, if we are right in hypothesizing that the entire, analogically structured thought realm of *finitely many (n>2) values* is available today only in some relation to biological models, and that the concepts of *the essential, the natural,* and *the biological* have by now become theoretically amalgamated through some historical process,[9] then it makes all the sense in the world that a "theory" structured in the first place around hypervigilant antiessentialism and antinaturalism will stringently require the sacrifice of qualitative differences among, in this case, different affects. The hygiene of current antiessentialism seemingly depends on rigorous adherence to the (erroneously machine-identified) model of digital, on/off representation: insofar as they are "theorized," affects *must* turn into Affect.

Yes, we repeat, at this historical moment any definitional invocation of analogically conceived, qualitative differences, in the form of *finitely many (n>2) values,* does indeed run the risk of reproducing a biologizing essentialism. But that risk is far from being obviated by even the most scrupulous practice of digitalization. The essentialism that adheres to digital models is structured differently from the essentialism of the analog. But, at this moment, it is probably all the more dangerous for that—precisely because, under the current routines of "theory," it is not recognizable as an essentialism. Essence is displaced, under these routines, from the analogic possibility of *finitely multiple qualitative differences* to some prior place where an *undifferentiated* stream of originary matter or energy is being turned (infinitely) ON or OFF. To see the latter as a less "essentialist" metaphorics than the former reflects, we argue, only the habitual privileging of digital models wrongly equated with the machine over analog models wrongly equated with the biological.

For example, although Cvetkovich doesn't discuss the scientific understandings of affect that tacitly underpin her argument, her "theory of affect" is highly congruent with a particular theory of emotion that has become widely accepted with the spread of cognitive psychology. Indeed, her use of this theory without citation would seem to testify to its having become part of the "commonsense" consensus of current theory. It also represents, as it happens, the current (though still contested) common sense of cognitive science, as reflected by its completely uncritical reproduction in the 1987 *Oxford Companion to the Mind:*

> The single most important contribution [to the study of emotion] . . . was made by Stanley Schachter. . . . He postulated that only a general state of visceral arousal was necessary for the experience of emotion: i.e. that different emotional experiences arise out of the same visceral background. Next he assumed that, given a state of visceral arousal, an individual will describe his feelings in terms of the cognitions (thoughts, past experiences, environmental signals) available at the time. . . . Visceral arousal was seen as a necessary condition for emotional experience, but the quality of the emotion depended on cognitive, perceptual evaluations of the external world and the internal state. . . . Current wisdom would suggest that any discrepancy, any interruption of expectations or of intended actions, produces undifferentiated visceral (autonomic) arousal. The *quale* of the subsequent emotion will then depend on the ongoing cognitive evaluation (meaning analysis, appraisal) of the current state of affairs. . . . [Emotions] are not necessarily remnants of our pre-sapient past, but rather they are important characteristics of an active, searching, and thinking human being. Novelty, discrepancy, and interruption generate visceral responses, while our cognitive system interprets the world as threatening, elating, frightening, or joyful. The human world is full of emotions not because we are animals at heart, but rather because it is still full of signals that elate or threaten, and replete with events and people that produce discrepancies and interruptions. (Gregory 219–20)

It's easy to see what makes this theory of affect seem so congenial to "theory." "Discrepancies and interruptions" in an undifferentiated flow of "arousal" have a reassuringly mechanical, Morse code–like sound: no danger whatever, here, of encountering the fallacy that a representation might bear any nonarbitrary relation to the thing represented. Furthermore, the space for discursive social construction of affect seems guaranteed by the notation that (because we are not "animals at heart") the raw material of our arousal is infinitely malleable by a fully acculturated cognitive faculty.

If anything, we anticipate that this account will sound *so* unexceptionable to critical theory readers that it might be useful to remark that it does retain (to say no worse) a certain counterintuitive force. So ask yourself this: How long does it take you after being awakened in the night by (a) a sudden loud noise or (b) gradual sexual arousal to cognitively "analyze" and "appraise" "the current state of affairs" well enough to assign the appropriate *quale* to your emotion? That is, what is the temporal lag from the moment of sleep interruption to the ("subsequent") moment when you can judge whether what you're experiencing is luxuriation or terror?

No, it doesn't take either of us very long, either.

But regardless of whether this cognitive account of emotion is *true*, what we want to emphasize is that it is not *less essentialist* than an account, like Tomkins's, that locates in the body some important part of the difference among different emotions. "Undifferentiated visceral arousal" is in no sense *less biologically based* than differentiated arousal, for all the *Oxford Companion*'s anti-Darwinist eagerness to disassociate Homo sapiens from "our presapient past." The implied biology is, however, different: it is far more thoroughly imbued with a Cartesian mind/body dualism. In fact, "undifferentiated visceral arousal" suggests a markedly homogeneous, lumpish, and recalcitrant bodily essence, one peculiarly unarticulated by structures or processes involving information, feedback, and representation. Those are all attributed, instead, to a distinct, disembodied, and temporally segregated "cognition." For all its antibehaviorist intention, such an account depends implicitly on the strict behaviorist segregation of stimulus from response, even as it propagates that conceptual segregation as humanist common sense.

It would be plausible to see a variety of twentieth-century theoretical languages as attempts, congruent with this one, to detoxify the excesses of body, thought, and feeling by reducing the multiple essentialist risks of analog representation to the single, unavowedly essentialist *certainty* of one or another on/off switch. We don't want to minimize the importance, productiveness, or even what can be the amazing subtlety of thought that takes this form. But it's still like a scanner or copier that can reproduce any work of art in 256,000 shades of gray. However infinitesimally subtle its discriminations may be, there are crucial knowledges it simply cannot transmit unless it is equipped to deal with the coarsely reductive possibility that red is different from yellow is different again from blue.

The antibiologism of current theory assumes, as we've said, that it's the distance of any theory from a biological (or, by mistaken implication, an analog) basis that alone can make the possibility of doing any justice "to difference (individual, historical, and cross-cultural), to contingency, to performative force, and to the possibility of change." Yet there is no reason to believe that the necessarily analog models of the color wheel or, say, the periodic table of the elements constrain an understanding of difference, contingency, performative force, or the possibility of change. Indeed, we've been arguing that they may be irreplaceably crucial for access to certain important ranges of difference. There is not a choice waiting to be made, in evaluating theoretical models, between essentialism and no essentialism. If there's a choice it is between differently structured residual essentialisms. But why be limited to the digital model of the choice? A repertoire of risk, a color wheel of different risks, a periodic table of the infinitely recombinable elements of the affect system, a complex, multilayered phyllo dough of the analog and the digital: these are the models that Tomkins's work makes us eager to deploy.

☞ If, as Tomkins describes it, the lowering of the eyelids, the lowering of the eyes, the hanging of the head is the attitude of shame, it may also be that of reading: reading maps, magazines, novels, comics, and heavy volumes of psychology if not billboards and traffic signs. We (those of us for whom reading was or is a crucial form of interaction with the world) know the force-field creating power of this attitude, the kind of skin that sheer textual attention can weave around a reading body: a noisy bus station or airplane can be excluded from consciousness, an impossible ongoing scene refused, a dull classroom monologue ignored. And none of these is wholly compassed by a certain pernicious understanding of reading as escape. Escape from what? The "real world," ostensibly, the "responsibility" of "acting" or "performing" in that world. Yet this reading posture registers as extroversion at least as much as introversion, as public as it does private: all a reader need do to transform this "inner life" experience to an audible performance is begin reading aloud. Even this may not be necessary: Freud refers our sometime fascination with the sight of a child entirely caught up with playing to "primary narcissism," as if something about sustained and intense engagement simply *is* theatrical, trances themselves entrancing. The additional skin shimmering as if shrink-wrapped around a body-and-book, or body-and-playing/working environment, sharply and sheerly delineates the conjunction or composition, making figural not escape or detachment but attention, interest.

How does the affect shame motivate a theoretical project such as the present one? It is striking that in Tomkins's writing, shame is the exemplary affect for theory. Indeed, the notion of "theory" first emerges in volume 2 of *Affect Imagery Consciousness* around the section "Production of a Total Affect-Shame Bind by Apparently Innocuous and Well-intentioned Parental Action," a "vignette" featuring as "our hero" "a child who is destined to have every affect totally bound by shame" (2:228). Tomkins hypothesizes a set of excruciating scenes in which a child is shamed out of expressing his excitement, distress, anger, fear, disgust, and even shame; through increasingly skilled compression, summarizing, naming, and ordering, our hero elaborates these scenes into a shame theory. Cognitive and affective (for Tomkins, these mechanisms involve many kinds of interdependent transformations),[10] an affect theory has two components: "First, it includes an examination of all incoming information for its relevance to a particular affect, in this case, shame and contempt. This is the cognitive antenna of shame. Second, it includes a set of strategies for coping with a variety of shame and contempt contingencies, to avoid shame if possible or to attenuate its impact if it cannot be avoided" (2:319–20). The stronger the shame theory, the more expensive it is for the person who holds it ("Affect theory must be effective to be weak"),[11] and the more its antennae make "the shame-relevant aspects of any situation . . . become figural in competition with other affect-relevant aspects of the same situation" (2:231); that is, the more often the theorist misrecognizes, imagines, sees, or seizes upon—shame.

But why is shame the example here? Why is the concept of "affect theory," meant to be quite general in its definition as "a simplified and powerful summary of a larger set of affect experiences" (*Affect* 2:230), first developed in chapters on humiliation? In the section called "Shame from Shame Theory" directly following the vignette above, Tomkins lists several possible alternative theories, each of which would, in the same situation, arouse distress, fear, or enjoyment; but shame's exemplary status makes us believe that, for Tomkins, not only shame but also theory come from shame theory. One reason this may be true is because shame and theory are partially analogous at a certain level of digitalization. Wilden writes: "A gestalt is formed by the decision to digitalize a specific difference, so as to form a *distinction* between figure and ground. There is in effect a decision — which may be neural, or conscious, or unconscious, or habitual, or learned, or novel — to introduce a particular boundary or frame into an analog continuum" (174).

Any theory, to be a theory — to at least partially or temporarily specify a domain — requires or produces figure/ground relations, the function of what Tomkins calls the "cognitive antenna" of a theory. Shame, along with contempt ("dissmell") and disgust, is unlike the other six affects of Tomkins's graphical representation of a theory of innate activators of affect (Figure 1) and is not in fact included in this graph. Whereas each of the others — startle, fear, interest, anger, distress, and joy — is activated by a certain "frequency of neural firing per unit time" represented by a straight line of some (positive, negative, or zero) slope, shame, like disgust and contempt, is activated by the drawing of a boundary line or barrier, the "introduc[tion] of a particular boundary or frame into an analog continuum." That is, shame involves a Gestalt, the duck to interest's (or enjoyment's) rabbit.

Without positive affect, there can be no shame: only a scene that offers you enjoyment or engages your interest can make you blush. Similarly, only something you thought might delight or satisfy can disgust. Both these affects produce bodily knowledges: disgust, as when spitting out bad-tasting food, recognizes the difference between inside and outside the body and what should and should not be let in; shame, as precarious hyperreflexivity of the surface of the body, can turn one inside out — or outside in. Wilden writes: "In order for a system to be open to an environment . . . the system must be capable of punctuating itself as distinct from that environment so as to select messages within it" (174). Shame is one of those affects whose digitalizing mechanism works to "punctuat[e the system] as distinct." Perhaps along with contempt and disgust, it can be a switch point for the individuation of imaging systems, of consciousnesses, of bodies, of theories, of selves — an individuation that decides not necessarily an identity, but a figuration, distinction, or mark of punctuation. And unlike contempt or disgust, shame is characterized by its failure ever to renounce its object cathexis, its relation to the desire for pleasure as well as the need to avoid pain.

☞ What does it mean to fall in love with a writer? What does it mean, for that matter — or maybe we should ask, what else could it mean — to cathect in a similar way a theoretical moment not one's own? Our editorial work on Tomkins represents only a part of a project whose dimensions keep changing under our hands. Some of what we're up to is the ordinary literary-critical lover's discourse: we want to propagate among readers nodes of reception for what we take to be an unfamiliar and highly exciting set of moves and tonalities. As people who fall in love with someone wish at the same time to exhibit themselves to others as *being loved,* we've also longed to do something we haven't been able even to begin here: to show how perfectly Tomkins understands *us;* to unveil a text spangled with unpathologizing, at the same time unteleologizing reflections on "the depressive," on claustrophilia, on the teacher's transference: on the rich life of everyday theories, and how expensively theories turn into Theory.

We have been very conscious of wishing to defer a certain moment of accounting, not only out of protectiveness for Tomkins, but out of a sense that, if the deferral proved possible, the terms of that accounting might be richly altered. We have deferred, specifically, the confrontation between any cross-cultural perspective and Tomkins's hypothesis that there is a kind of affective table of the elements, comprising nine components, infinitely recombinable but rooted in the human body in nine distinctive and irreducible ways. At some level we have not demanded even of ourselves that we ascertain whether we believe this hypothesis to be true; we have felt that there was so much to learn first by observing the autonomic nervous system of a routinized dismissal of it in the terms of today's Theory. The moralistic hygiene by which any reader of today is unchallengeably entitled to condescend to the thought of any moment in the past (maybe *especially* the recent past) is globally available to anyone who masters the application of two or three discrediting questions. How provisional, by contrast, how difficult to reconstruct and how exorbitantly specialized of use, are the tools that in any given case would allow one to ask: What was it possible to think or do at a certain moment of the past that it no longer is? And how are those possibilities to be found, unfolded, allowed to move and draw air and seek new voices and uses, in the very different disciplinary ecology of even a few decades distance?

We see Tomkins, like Freud, as a disciplinarily excessive figure in psychology, a writer of heterogeneous energies whose most extraordinary insights had to be interlined with self-ignorance, involved in contradiction, and inextricably interleaved with the speculative science of his time. He is also, therefore, like Freud, a figure through whose work a lot of sharply different, competing, and often conflicting interpretive paths require to be cleared. That history of readings of Freud has made an important intellectual adventure for the twentieth century; it continues to be exciting to introduce Tomkins's work, invigorating and fruitful as we find it, to readers skilled by that history.

NOTES

1. Citations from Tomkins's original, four-volume *Affect Imagery Consciousness* are cited to Affect.

2. An uncharacteristically explicit example:

> The mouth which sucks cannot cry. If the mouth is combined with sexuality it will produce an oral interest in sucking, biting, or swallowing parts of the body of the other or the whole body and in being sucked, bitten or swallowed and incorporated by the other. There can be no doubt that such wishes are common. . . . It is not, as Freud suggested, necessarily restricted to the foreplay and subordinated to the later adult modes of sexual communion. Many normal adults rather utilize genital interpenetration as a way of heightening the oral incorporative wish or the earliest claustral wish. Sexual intercourse, as we shall see, lends itself as a vehicle to every variety of investment of social affect. Clearly it is one of the prime avenues by which the adult may re-experience being physically close to another person, to being held and supported, to having the skin stimulated, to clinging, to being enveloped and enveloping, to becoming united so that the distinction and distance between the self and other is for the moment transcended. . . . For Freud, the earlier modes of communion seemed basically infantile. He could tolerate their appearance in adult genitality only insofar as they were restricted to the foreplay and subordinated to an adult recognition of and concern for the love object as independent of the self. Implicit in his theory is a hidden value judgment that early communion is helpless,

dependent, greedy and blind to the separateness of the love object, and as such to be transcended in development and to be perverse if it is not. (Tomkins, *Affect* 1:420–21)

3. Founded in them, but hardly guaranteed by them: it is sobering to see how effortlessly, in the absence of Tomkins's own care, the heterosexist teleology can make itself at home even in work explicitly based on his. An example is Donald L. Nathanson's *Shame and Pride*, dedicated to Tomkins, which includes such passages as the two following, inconceivable in Tomkins's writing:

> Just as most life forms can be divided into groups by their gender, mature individuals tend to form couples because of these sexual differences. Inherent in the system that causes us to be different on the basis of gender is also the force that creates attraction. . . . Sex refers to the passionate attraction between opposites, to the active process that begins as the coupling of male and female, unites them in sexual intercourse, and results in procreation and the maintenance of the species. (260)

> There are adults whose inner lives are the screaming face of an Edvard Munch painting, the hell of Picasso's *Guernica*, the nightmarish agitation of Leonard Bernstein's *Age of Anxiety*. These are the tortured men who sought surcease in the bath houses that served as homosexual brothels but died horribly of AIDS. (426)

4. On this, see Vincent Descombes's suggestion that structuralism loses its most interesting defining features almost at the very moment that it becomes attached to literary study (85–87).

5. A useful study of this moment is Heims, *The Cybernetics Group*.

6. Computers designed according to such protocols "would be much more interesting than our present computers, but they would also have certain disadvantages. They would be capable of not computing for the designer for long periods of time when other computers were sending messages to them; when they were afraid of overly severe fluctuations in their sources of electricity; when having tried unsuccessfully to solve then insoluble problems, they became depressed; or when they became manic with overweening false confidence. In short, they would represent not the disembodied intelligence of an auxiliary brain but a mechanical intelligence intimately wed to the automaton's own complex purposes" (Tomkins, *Affect* 1:119).

7. Benedict Anderson, for example, writing in 1965, describes the complex devolutions between many-valued and two-valued systems of meaning in Javanese culture. He describes the "real legitimation for widely contrasting social and psychological types" offered by the "rich variety of concrete models" in the ancient, popular, and pervasive *wayang* mythology (26) and analyzes the mechanisms by which this range of *finitely many (n>2)* models can tend to get abstracted into a chain of binarisms under the pressure of monotheism, nationalism, commercial urbanism, and the competing formal structures of film.

This chapter's discussion of the voided space in contemporary thought between 2 and infinity is partly an attempt to work further on issues raised by Axiom 1, "People are different from each other," in Sedgwick, *Epistemology*, 22-27.

8. Why, we've been asked, use a first book as our sole example in articulating this argument, rather than refer by name (and, of course, the names might be legion and include Sedgwick) to other theorists more rankly steeped in these routines of theory, and indeed more directly responsible for their popularization? We persist in this gracelessness for two reasons. First, we envisioned for this chapter a Gestalt strategy of involving readers in a sudden perceptual reorganization and unexpected self-recognition — private in the first place — concerning some critical practices that might in this way be effectively defamiliarized; if we had designated a number of theorists about whom many readers will already have assigned themselves a parti pris, our strategy would have had no chance of success. Second, however, it makes sense to look at Cvetkovich's book — among the many other ways one might look at it — precisely *as* a first book, originating in a dissertation, as, that is, a rite de passage whose conventions can best dramatize the economy of transmissibility (across academic generations as well as across disciplines) that is our subject here.

9. We emphasize: through a *historical* process. In Plato, for example, the essential, the biological, and the natural are very far from being assumed to be equivalent. This point was made to us by Timothy Gould. An important unpacking of these terms is performed in Halley, "Sexual Orientation and the Politics of Biology."

10. "The distinction we have drawn between the cognitive half and the motivational half must be considered to be a fragile distinction between transformation and amplification as a specialized type of tranformation. Cognitions coassembled with affects become hot and urgent. Affects coassembled with cognitions become better informed and smarter. . . . Amplification without transformation would be blind; transformation without amplification would be weak" (Tomkins, *Affect* 4:7).

11. Tomkins suggests that the measure of a theory's strength is not how well it avoids negative affect or finds positive affect, but the size and topology of the domain that it organizes and its methods of determining that domain. His recurrent example of a weak theory is one that allows many of us to cross streets often without fear: those sets of actions summed up in the phrase "Look both ways before you cross" that enable an individual to act as if afraid so as to avoid the actual experience of fear — "affect acting at a distance" (*Affect* 2:320). What is weak about this theory is its restricted domain, perhaps initially understood to include only walking across the street where one first learned the rule as a child, analogically expanded to include walking across other streets or streetlike passages, then expanded more to include riding a bicycle or driving a car. Consider the case where this weak theory gets strong: "If the individual cannot find the rules whereby he can cross the street without feeling anxious [because of a series of unfortunate accidents, say], then his avoidance strategies will necessarily become more and more diffuse. Under these conditions the individual might be forced,

first, to avoid all busy streets and then to go out only late at night when traffic was light; finally, he would remain inside, and if his house were to be hit by a car, he would have to seek refuge in a deeper shelter" (*Affect* 2:324).

A strong theory is not more successful than a weak theory at "preventing the experience of negative affect," here fear; in this case, quite the opposite. Both the cognitive antennae of the theory and the preventive strategies have changed. This individual has learned to count many more things as a street: this strong fear theorist is always ready to draw the line that expands his theory's domain.

"Digital distinctions introduce GAPS into continuums . . . whereas analog differences . . . FILL continuums," writes Wilden (186), and this helps to specify one difference between weak and strong theories. A weak theory's domain can be thought of as pockets of terrains each in analogic relation to the others and expandable only by textured analogy. A strong theory's domain is more digital: more highly organized and expandable by analogies evacuated of certain qualities. If a weak theory encounters some terrain unlike any it has ever tripped over — if it can't understand this terrain as significantly similar or resemblant enough to one or more in its domain — it will throw up its hands, shrug its shoulders, remain dumb: "The analog does not possess the syntax necessary to say 'No' or to say anything involving 'not,' one can REFUSE or REJECT in the analog, but one cannot DENY or NEGATE" (Wilden 163). A strong theory always has something to say, about anything, because it can always say No.

Chapter 4

PARANOID READING AND REPARATIVE READING,

OR, YOU'RE SO PARANOID, YOU PROBABLY THINK

THIS ESSAY IS ABOUT YOU

Sometime back in the middle of the first decade of the AIDS epidemic, I was picking the brains of a friend of mine, the activist scholar Cindy Patton, about the probable natural history of HIV. This was at a time when speculation was ubiquitous about whether the virus had been deliberately engineered or spread, whether HIV represented a plot or experiment by the U.S. military that had gotten out of control, or perhaps that was behaving exactly as it was meant to. After hearing a lot from her about the geography and economics of the global traffic in blood products, I finally, with some eagerness, asked Patton what she thought of these sinister rumors about the virus's origin. "Any of the early steps in its spread could have been either accidental or deliberate," she said. "But I just have trouble getting interested in that. I mean, even suppose we were sure of every element of a conspiracy: that the lives of Africans and African Americans are worthless in the eyes of the United States; that gay men and drug users are held cheap where they aren't actively hated; that the military deliberately researches ways to kill noncombatants whom it sees as enemies; that people in power look calmly on the likelihood of catastrophic environmental and population changes. Supposing we were ever so sure of all those things—what would we know then that we don't already know?"

In the years since that conversation, I've brooded a lot over this response of Patton's. Aside from a certain congenial, stony pessimism, I think what I've found enabling about it is that it suggests the possibility of unpacking, of disentangling from their impacted and overdetermined historical relation to each other some of the separate elements of the intellectual baggage that many of us carry around under a label such as "the hermeneutics of suspicion." Patton's comment suggests that for someone to have an unmystified, angry view of large and genuinely systemic oppressions does not intrinsically or necessarily enjoin that person to any specific train of epistemological or narrative consequences. To know that the origin or spread of HIV *realistically might* have resulted from a state-assisted conspiracy—such knowledge is, it turns out, separable from the question of whether the energies of a given AIDS activist intellectual or group might best be used in the tracing and exposure of such a possible plot. They might, but then again, they might not. Though ethically very fraught, the choice is not self-evident; whether or not to undertake this highly compelling tracing-and-exposure project represents a strategic and local decision, not necessarily a categorical imperative. Patton's response to me seemed to open a space for moving from the rather fixated question Is a particular piece of knowledge true, and how can we know? to the further questions: What does knowledge *do*—the pursuit of it, the having and exposing of it, the receiving again of knowledge of what one already knows? *How*, in short, is knowledge performative, and how best does one move among its causes and effects?

I suppose this ought to seem quite an unremarkable epiphany: that knowledge *does* rather than simply *is* it is by now very routine to discover. Yet it seems that a lot of the real force of such discoveries has been blunted through the habitual practices of the same forms of critical theory that have given such broad currency to the formulae themselves. In particular, it is possible that the very productive critical habits embodied in what Paul Ricoeur memorably called the "hermeneutics of suspicion"—widespread critical habits indeed, perhaps by now nearly synonymous with criticism itself—may have had an unintentionally stultifying side effect: they may have made it less rather than more possible to unpack the local, contingent relations between any given piece of knowledge and its narrative/epistemological entailments for the seeker, knower, or teller.

Ricoeur introduced the category of the hermeneutics of suspicion to describe the position of Marx, Nietzsche, Freud, and their intellectual offspring in a context that also included such alternative disciplinary hermeneutics as the philological and theological "hermeneutics of recovery of meaning." His intent in offering the former of these formulations was descriptive and taxonomic rather than imperative. In the context of recent U.S. critical theory, however, where Marx, Nietzsche, and Freud by themselves are taken as constituting a pretty sufficient genealogy for the mainstream of New Historicist, deconstructive, feminist, queer, and psychoanalytic criticism, to apply a hermeneutics of suspicion is, I believe, widely understood as a mandatory injunction rather than a possibility among other possibilities. The phrase now has something like the sacred status of Fredric Jameson's "Always historicize" — and, like that one, it fits oddly into its new position in the tablets of the Law. *Always* historicize? What could have less to do with historicizing than the commanding, atemporal adverb "always"? It reminds me of the bumper stickers that instruct people in other cars to "Question Authority." Excellent advice, perhaps wasted on anyone who does whatever they're ordered to do by a strip of paper glued to an automobile! The imperative framing will do funny things to a hermeneutics of suspicion.

Not surprisingly, the methodological centrality of suspicion to current critical practice has involved a concomitant privileging of the concept of paranoia. In the last paragraphs of Freud's essay on the paranoid Dr. Schreber, there is discussion of what Freud considers a "striking similarity" between Schreber's systematic persecutory delusion and Freud's own theory. Freud was indeed later to generalize, famously, that "the delusions of paranoiacs have an unpalatable external similarity and internal kinship to the systems of our philosophers" — among whom he included himself (12:79, 17:271). For all his slyness, it may be true that the putative congruence between paranoia and theory was unpalatable to Freud; if so, however, it is no longer viewed as unpalatable. The articulation of such a congruence may have been inevitable, at any rate; as Ricoeur notes, "For Marx, Nietzsche, and Freud, the fundamental category of consciousness is the relation hidden-shown or, if you prefer, simulated-manifested. . . . Thus the distinguishing characteristic of Marx, Freud, and Nietzsche is the general hypothesis concerning both the process of false consciousness and the method of deciphering. The two go together, since the man of suspicion carries out in reverse the work of falsification of the man of guile" (33–34).

The man of suspicion double-bluffing the man of guile: in the hands of thinkers after Freud, paranoia has by now candidly become less a diagnosis than a prescription. In a world where no one need be delusional to find evidence of systemic oppression, to theorize out of anything *but* a paranoid critical stance has come to seem naïve, pious, or complaisant. I myself have no wish to return to the use of "paranoid" as a pathologizing diagnosis, but it seems to me a great loss when paranoid inquiry comes to seem entirely coextensive with critical theoretical inquiry rather than being viewed as one kind of cognitive/affective theoretical practice among other, alternative kinds.

Even aside from the prestige that now attaches to a hermeneutics of suspicion in critical theory as a whole, queer studies in particular has had a distinctive history of intimacy with the paranoid imperative. Freud, of course, traced every instance of paranoia to the repression of specifically same-sex desire, whether in women or in men. The traditional, homophobic psychoanalytic use that has generally been made of Freud's association has been to pathologize homosexuals as paranoid or to consider paranoia a distinctively homosexual disease. In *Homosexual Desire,* however, a 1972 book translated into English in 1978, Guy Hocquenghem returned to Freud's formulations to draw from them a conclusion that would not reproduce this damaging non sequitur. If paranoia reflects the *repression* of same-sex desire, Hocquenghem reasoned, then paranoia is a uniquely privileged site for illuminating not homosexuality itself, as in the Freudian tradition, but rather precisely the mechanisms of homophobic and heterosexist enforcement against it. What is illuminated by an understanding of paranoia is not how homosexuality works, but how homophobia and heterosexism work—in short, if one understands these oppressions to be systemic, how the world works.

Paranoia thus became by the mid-1980s a privileged *object* of antihomophobic theory. How did it spread so quickly from that status to being its uniquely sanctioned *methodology?* I have been looking back into my own writing of the 1980s as well as that of some other critics, trying to retrace that transition—one that seems worthy of remark now but seemed at the time, I think, the most natural move in the world. Part of the explanation lies in a property of paranoia itself. Simply put, paranoia tends to be contagious; more specifically, paranoia is drawn toward and tends to construct symmetrical relations, in particular, symmetrical epistemologies. As Leo Bersani writes, "To inspire interest is to be guaranteed a paranoid reading, just as we must inevitably be suspicious of the interpretations we inspire. Paranoia is an inescapable interpretive doubling of presence" (188). It sets a thief (and, if necessary, becomes one) to catch a thief; it mobilizes guile against suspicion, suspicion against guile; "it takes one to know one." A paranoid friend, who believes I am reading her mind, knows this from reading mine; also a suspicious writer, she is always turning up at crime scenes of plagiarism, indifferently as perpetrator or as victim; a litigious colleague as well, she not only imagines me to be as familiar with the laws of libel as she is, but eventually makes me become so. (All these examples, by the way, are fictitious.)

Given that paranoia seems to have a peculiarly intimate relation to the phobic dynamics around homosexuality, then, it may have been structurally inevitable that the reading practices that became most available and fruitful in antihomophobic work would often in turn have been paranoid ones. There must have been historical as well as structural reasons for this development, however, because it is less easy to account on structural terms for the frequent privileging of paranoid methodologies in recent nonqueer critical projects such as feminist theory, psychoanalytic theory, deconstruction, Marxist criticism, or the New Historicism. One recent discussion of paranoia invokes "a popular maxim of the late 1960s: 'Just because you're paranoid doesn't mean they're *not* out to get you'" (Adams 15). In fact, it seems quite plausible that some version of this axiom (perhaps "Even a paranoid can have enemies," uttered by Henry Kissinger) is so indelibly inscribed in the brains of baby boomers that it offers us the continuing illusion of possessing a special insight into the epistemologies of enmity. My impression, again, is that we are liable to produce this constative formulation as fiercely as if it had a self-evident imperative force: the notation that even paranoid people have enemies is wielded as if its absolutely necessary corollary were the injunction "so *you can never be paranoid enough.*"

But the truth value of the original axiom, assuming it to *be* true, doesn't actually make a paranoid imperative self-evident. Learning that "just because you're paranoid doesn't mean you don't have enemies," somebody might deduce that being paranoid is not an effective way to get rid of enemies. Rather than concluding "so you can never be paranoid enough," this person might instead be moved to reflect "but then, just because you have enemies doesn't mean you have to be paranoid." That is to say, once again: for someone to have an unmystified view of systemic oppressions does not *intrinsically* or *necessarily* enjoin that person to any specific train of epistemological or narrative consequences. To be other than paranoid (and of course, we'll need to define this term much more carefully), to practice other than paranoid forms of knowing does *not,* in itself, entail a denial of the reality or gravity of enmity or oppression.

How are we to understand paranoia in such a way as to situate it as one kind of epistemological practice among other, alternative ones? Besides Freud's, the most usable formulations for this purpose would seem to be those of Melanie Klein and (to the extent that paranoia represents an affective as well as cognitive mode) Silvan Tomkins. In Klein, I find particularly congenial her use of the concept of *positions*—the schizoid/paranoid position, the depressive position—as opposed to, for example, normatively ordered *stages,* stable *structures,* or diagnostic *personality types.* As Hinshelwood writes in his *Dictionary of Kleinian Thought,* "The term 'position' describes the characteristic posture that the ego takes up with respect to its objects. . . . [Klein] wanted to convey, with the idea of position, a much more flexible to-and-fro process between one and the other than is normally meant by regression to fixation points in the developmental phases" (394). The flexible to-and-fro movement implicit in Kleinian *positions* will be useful for my discussion of paranoid and reparative critical *practices,* not as theoretical ideologies (and certainly not as stable personality types of critics), but as changing and heterogeneous relational stances.

The greatest interest of Klein's concept lies, it seems to me, in her seeing the paranoid position always in the oscillatory context of a very different possible one: the depressive position. For Klein's infant or adult, the paranoid position—understandably marked by hatred, envy, and anxiety—is a position of terrible alertness to the dangers posed by the hateful and envious part-objects that one defensively projects into, carves out of, and ingests from the world around one. By contrast, the depressive position is an anxiety-mitigating achievement that the infant or adult only sometimes, and often only briefly, succeeds in inhabiting: this is the position from which it is possible in turn to use one's own resources to assemble or "repair" the murderous part-objects into something like a whole—though, I would emphasize, *not necessarily like any preexisting whole.* Once assembled to one's own specifications, the more satisfying object is available both to be identified with and to offer one nourishment and comfort in turn. Among Klein's names for the reparative process is love.

Given the instability and mutual inscription built into the Kleinian notion of positions, I am also, in the present project, interested in doing justice to the powerful reparative practices that, I am convinced, infuse self-avowedly paranoid critical projects, as well as in the paranoid exigencies that are often necessary for nonparanoid knowing and utterance. For example, Patton's calm response to me about the origins of HIV drew on a lot of research, her own and other people's, much of which required being paranoiacally structured.

For convenience's sake, I borrow my critical examples as I proceed from two influential studies of the past decade, one roughly psychoanalytic and the other roughly New Historicist—but I do so for more than the sake of convenience, as both are books (Judith Butler's *Gender Trouble* and D. A. Miller's *The Novel and the Police*) whose centrality to the development of my own thought, and that of the critical movements that most interest me, are examples of their remarkable force and exemplarity. Each, as well, is interestingly located in a tacit or ostensibly marginal, but in hindsight originary and authorizing relation to different strains of queer theory. Finally, I draw a sense of permission from the fact that neither book is any longer very representative of the most recent work of either author, so that observations about the reading practices of either book may, I hope, escape being glued as if allegorically to the name of the author.

I would like to begin by setting outside the scope of this discussion any overlap between paranoia per se on the one hand, and on the other hand the states variously called dementia praecox (by Kraepelin), schizophrenia (by Bleuler), or, more generally, delusionality or psychosis. As Laplanche and Pontalis note, the history of psychiatry has attempted various mappings of this overlap: "Kraepelin differentiates clearly between paranoia on the one hand and the paranoid form of dementia praecox on the other; Bleuler treats paranoia as a sub-category of dementia praecox, or the group of schizophrenias; as for Freud, he is quite prepared to see certain so-called paranoid forms of dementia praecox brought under the head of paranoia. . . . [For example, Schreber's] case of 'paranoid dementia' is essentially a paranoia proper [and therefore not a form of schizophrenia] in Freud's eyes" (297). In Klein's later writings, meanwhile, the occurrence of psychoticlike mental events is seen as universal in both children and adults, so that mechanisms such as paranoia have a clear ontological priority over diagnostic categories such as dementia. The reason I want to insist in advance on this move is, once again, to try to hypothetically disentangle the question of truth value from the question of performative effect.

I am saying that the main reasons for questioning paranoid practices are other than the possibility that their suspicions can be delusional or simply wrong. Concomitantly, some of the main reasons for practicing paranoid strategies may be other than the possibility that they offer unique access to true knowledge. They represent *a* way, among other ways, of seeking, finding, and organizing knowledge. Paranoia knows some things well and others poorly.

I'd like to undertake now something like a composite sketch of what I mean by paranoia in this connection — not as a tool of differential *diagnosis,* but as a tool for better seeing differentials of practice. My main headings are:

Paranoia is *anticipatory.*
Paranoia is *reflexive* and *mimetic.*
Paranoia is *a strong theory.*
Paranoia is a theory of *negative affects.*
Paranoia places its faith in *exposure.*

PARANOIA IS ANTICIPATORY

That paranoia is anticipatory is clear from every account and theory of the phenomenon. The first imperative of paranoia is *There must be no bad surprises,* and indeed, the aversion to surprise seems to be what cements the intimacy between paranoia and knowledge per se, including both epistemophilia and skepticism. D. A. Miller notes in *The Novel and the Police,* "Surprise . . . is precisely what the paranoid seeks to eliminate, but it is also what, in the event, he survives by reading as a frightening incentive: he can never be paranoid enough" (164).

The unidirectionally future-oriented vigilance of paranoia generates, paradoxically, a complex relation to temporality that burrows both backward and forward: because there must be no bad surprises, and because learning of the possibility of a bad surprise would itself constitute a bad surprise, paranoia requires that bad news be always already known. As Miller's analysis also suggests, the temporal progress and regress of paranoia are, in principle, infinite. Hence perhaps, I suggest, Butler's repeated and scouringly thorough demonstrations in *Gender Trouble* that there can have been no moment prior to the imposition of the totalizing Law of gender difference; hence her unresting vigilance for traces in other theorists' writing of nostalgia for such an impossible prior moment. No time could be too early for one's having-already-known, for its having-already-been-inevitable, that something bad would happen. And no loss could be too far in the future to need to be preemptively discounted.

In noting, as I have already, the contagious tropism of paranoia toward symmetrical epistemologies, I have relied on the double senses of paranoia as reflexive and mimetic. Paranoia seems to require being imitated to be understood, and it, in turn, seems to understand only by imitation. Paranoia proposes both *Anything you can do (to me) I can do worse*, and *Anything you can do (to me) I can do first*—to myself. In *The Novel and the Police*, Miller is much more explicit than Freud in embracing the twin propositions that one understands paranoia only by oneself practicing paranoid knowing, and that the way paranoia has of understanding anything is by imitating and embodying it. That paranoia refuses to be only *either* a way of knowing *or* a thing known, but is characterized by an insistent tropism toward occupying both positions, is wittily dramatized from the opening page of this definitive study of paranoia: a foreword titled "But Officer . . ." begins with an always-already-second-guessing sentence about how "Even the blandest (or bluffest) 'scholarly work' fears getting into trouble," including trouble "with the adversaries whose particular attacks it keeps busy anticipating" (vii). As the book's final paragraph notes about *David Copperfield*, Miller too "everywhere intimates a . . . pattern in which the subject constitutes himself 'against' discipline by assuming that discipline in his own name" (220) or even his own body (191).

It seems no wonder, then, that paranoia, once the topic is broached in a nondiagnostic context, seems to grow like a crystal in a hypersaturated solution, blotting out any sense of the possibility of alternative ways of understanding *or* things to understand. I will say more later about some implications of the status of paranoia as, in this sense, inevitably a "strong theory." What may be even more important is how severely the mimeticism of paranoia circumscribes its potential as a medium of political or cultural struggle. As I pointed out in a 1986 essay (in which my implicit reference was, as it happens, to one of the essays later collected in *The Novel and the Police*), "The problem here is not simply that paranoia is a form of love, for—in a certain language—what is not? The problem is rather that, of all forms of love, paranoia is the most ascetic, *the love that demands least from its object.* . . . The gorgeous narrative work done by the Foucauldian paranoid, transforming the simultaneous chaoses of institutions into a consecutive, drop-dead-elegant diagram of spiralling escapes and recaptures, is also the paranoid subject's proffer of himself and his cognitive talent, now ready for anything *it* can present in the way of blandishment or violence, to an order-of-things *morcelé* that had until then lacked *only* narratibility, a body, cognition" (*Coherence* xi).

At the risk of being awfully reductive, I suggest that this anticipatory, mimetic mechanism may also shed light on a striking feature of recent feminist and queer uses of psychoanalysis. Lacan aside, few actual psychoanalysts would dream of being as rigorously insistent as are many oppositional theorists—of whom Butler is very far from the most single-minded—in asserting the inexorable, irreducible, uncircumnavigable, omnipresent centrality, at *every* psychic juncture, of the facts (however factitious) of "sexual difference" and "the phallus." From such often tautological work, it would be hard to learn that—from Freud onward, including, for example, the later writings of Melanie Klein—the history of psychoanalytic thought offers richly divergent, heterogeneous tools for thinking about aspects of personhood, consciousness, affect, filiation, social dynamics, and sexuality that, though relevant to the experience of gender and queerness, are often not centrally organized around "sexual difference" at all. Not that they are necessarily prior to "sexual difference": they may simply be conceptualized as somewhere to the side of it, tangentially or contingently related or even rather unrelated to it.

Seemingly, the reservoir of such thought and speculation could make an important resource for theorists committed to thinking about human lives otherwise than through the prejudicious gender reifications that are common in psychoanalysis as in other projects of modern philosophy and science. What has happened instead, I think, is something like the following. First, through what might be called a process of vigilant scanning, feminists and queers have rightly understood that no topic or area of psychoanalytic thought can be declared a priori immune to the influence of such gender reifications. Second, however—and, it seems to me, unnecessarily and often damagingly—the lack of such a priori immunity, the absence of any guaranteed nonprejudicial point of beginning for feminist thought within psychoanalysis has led to the widespread adoption by some thinkers of an anticipatory mimetic strategy whereby a certain, stylized violence of sexual differentiation must always be *presumed* or *self-assumed* — even, where necessary, imposed — simply on the ground that it can never be finally *ruled out*. (I don't want to suggest, in using the word "mimetic," that these uses of psychoanalytic gender categories need be either uncritical of or identical to the originals. Butler, among others, has taught us a much less deadening use of "mimetic.") But, for example, in this post-Lacanian tradition, psychoanalytic thought that is not in the first place centrally organized around phallic "sexual difference" must seemingly be translated, with however distorting results, into that language before it can be put to any other theoretical use. The contingent possibilities of thinking otherwise than through "sexual difference" are subordinated to the paranoid imperative that, if the violence of such gender reification cannot be definitively halted in advance, it must at least never arrive on any conceptual scene *as a surprise*. In a paranoid view, it is more dangerous for such reification ever to be unanticipated than often to be unchallenged.

PARANOIA IS A STRONG THEORY

It is for reasons like these that, in the work of Silvan Tomkins, paranoia is offered as the example par excellence of what Tomkins refers to as "strong affect theory" — in this case, a strong humiliation or humiliation-fear theory. As Chapter 3 explains, Tomkins's use of the term "strong theory" — indeed, his use of the term "theory" at all — has something of a double valence. He goes beyond Freud's reflection on possible *similarities between,* say, paranoia and theory; by Tomkins's account, which is strongly marked by early cybernetics' interest in feedback processes, all people's cognitive/affective lives are organized according to alternative, changing, strategic, and hypothetical affect theories. As a result, there would be from the start no ontological difference between the theorizing acts of a Freud and those of, say, one of his analysands. Tomkins does not suggest that there is no metalevel of reflection in Freud's theory, but that affect itself, ordinary affect, while irreducibly corporeal, is also centrally shaped, through the feedback process, by its access to just such theoretical metalevels. In Tomkins, there is no distance at all between affect theory in the sense of the important explicit theorizing some scientists and philosophers do around affects, and affect theory in the sense of the largely tacit theorizing all people do in experiencing and trying to deal with their own and others' affects.

To call paranoia a strong theory is, then, at the same time to congratulate it as a big achievement (it's a strong theory rather as, for Harold Bloom, Milton is a strong poet) but also to classify it. It is one kind of affect theory among other possible kinds, and by Tomkins's account, a number of interrelated affect theories of different kinds and strengths are likely to constitute the mental life of any individual. Most pointedly, the contrast of strong theory in Tomkins is with weak theory, and the contrast is not in every respect to the advantage of the strong kind. The reach and reductiveness of strong theory—that is, its conceptual economy or elegance—involve both assets and deficits. What characterizes strong theory in Tomkins is not, after all, how well it avoids negative affect or finds positive affect, but the size and topology of the domain that it organizes. "Any theory of wide generality," he writes,

> is capable of accounting for a wide spectrum of phenomena which appear to be very remote, one from the other, and from a common source. This is a commonly accepted criterion by which the explanatory power of any scientific theory can be evaluated. To the extent to which the theory can account only for "near" phenomena, it is a weak theory, little better than a description of the phenomena which it purports to explain. As it orders more and more remote phenomena to a single formulation, its power grows. . . . A humiliation theory is strong to the extent to which it enables more and more experiences to be accounted for as instances of humiliating experiences on the one hand, or to the extent to which it enables more and more anticipation of such contingencies before they actually happen. (*Affect* 2:433-34)

As this account suggests, far from becoming stronger through obviating or alleviating humiliation, a humiliation theory becomes stronger exactly insofar as it fails to do so. Tomkins's conclusion is not that all strong theory is ineffective—indeed, it may grow to be only too effective—but that "*affect theory must be effective to be weak*": "We can now see more clearly that although a restricted and weak theory may not always successfully protect the individual against negative affect, it is difficult for it to remain weak unless it does so. Conversely, a negative affect theory gains in strength, paradoxically, by virtue of the continuing failures of its strategies to afford protection through successful avoidance of the experience of negative affect. . . .

It is the repeated and apparently uncontrollable spread of the experience of negative affect which prompts the increasing strength of the ideo-affective organization which we have called a strong affect theory" (2:323–24).

An affect theory is, among other things, a mode of *selective* scanning and amplification; for this reason, any affect theory risks being somewhat tautological, but because of its wide reach and rigorous exclusiveness, a strong theory risks being strongly tautological:

> We have said that there is over-organization in monopolistic humiliation theory. By this we mean not only that there is excessive integration between sub-systems which are normally more independent, but also that each sub-system is over-specialized in the interests of minimizing the experience of humiliation. . . . The entire cognitive apparatus is in a constant state of alert for possibilities, imminent or remote, ambiguous or clear.
>
> Like any highly organized effort at detection, as little as possible is left to chance. The radar antennae are placed wherever it seems possible the enemy may attack. Intelligence officers may monitor even unlikely conversations if there is an outside chance something relevant may be detected or if there is a chance that two independent bits of information taken together may give indication of the enemy's intentions. . . . But above all there is a highly organized way of interpreting information so that what is possibly relevant can be quickly abstracted and magnified, and the rest discarded. (*Affect* 2:433)

This is how it happens that an explanatory structure that a reader may see as tautological, in that it can't help or can't stop or can't do anything other than prove the very same assumptions with which it began, may be experienced by the practitioner as a triumphant advance toward truth and vindication.

More usually, however, the roles in this drama are more mixed or more widely distributed. I don't suppose that too many readers—nor, for that matter, perhaps the author—would be too surprised to hear it noted that the main argument or strong theory of *The Novel and the Police* is entirely circular: everything can be understood as an aspect of the carceral, therefore the carceral is everywhere. But who reads *The Novel and the Police* to find out whether its main argument is true? In this case, as also frequently in the case of the tautologies of "sexual difference," the very breadth of reach that makes the theory strong also offers the space—of which Miller's book takes every advantage—for a wealth of tonal nuance, attitude, worldly observation, performative paradox, aggression, tenderness, wit, inventive reading, obiter dicta, and writerly panache. These rewards are so local and frequent that one might want to say that a plethora of only loosely related weak theories has been invited to shelter in the hypertrophied embrace of the book's overarching strong theory. In many ways, such an arrangement is all to the good—suggestive, pleasurable, and highly productive; an insistence that everything means one thing somehow permits a sharpened sense of all the ways there are of meaning it. But one need not read an infinite number of students' and other critics' derivative rephrasings of the book's grimly strong theory to see, as well, some limitations of this unarticulated relation between strong and weak theories. As strong theory, and as a locus of reflexive mimeticism, paranoia is nothing if not teachable. The powerfully ranging and reductive force of strong theory can make tautological thinking hard to identify even as it makes it compelling and near inevitable; the result is that both writers and readers can damagingly misrecognize whether and where real conceptual work is getting done, and precisely what that work might be.

PARANOIA IS A THEORY OF NEGATIVE AFFECTS

While Tomkins distinguishes among a number of qualitatively different affects, he also for some purposes groups affects together loosely as either positive or negative. In these terms, paranoia is characterized not only by being a strong theory as opposed to a weak one, but by being a strong theory of a negative affect. This proves important in terms of the overarching affective goals Tomkins sees as potentially conflicting with each other in each individual: he distinguishes in the first place between the general goal of seeking to minimize negative affect and that of seeking to maximize positive affect. (The other, respectively more sophisticated goals he identifies are that affect inhibition be minimized and that the power to achieve the preceding three goals be maximized.) In most practices—in most lives—there are small and subtle (though cumulatively powerful) negotiations between and among these goals, but the mushrooming, self-confirming strength of a monopolistic strategy of anticipating negative affect can have, according to Tomkins, the effect of entirely blocking the potentially operative goal of seeking positive affect. "The only sense in which [the paranoid] may strive for positive affect at all is for the shield which it promises against humiliation," he writes. "To take seriously the strategy of *maximizing* positive affect, rather than simply enjoying it when the occasion arises, is entirely out of the question" (*Affect* 2:458–59).

Similarly, in Klein's writings from the 1940s and 1950s, it again represents an actual achievement—a distinct, often risky positional shift—for an infant or adult to move toward a sustained *seeking of pleasure* (through the reparative strategies of the depressive position), rather than continue to pursue the self-reinforcing because self-defeating strategies for *forestalling pain* offered by the paranoid/schizoid position. It's probably more usual for discussions of the depressive position in Klein to emphasize that that position inaugurates ethical possibility—in the form of a guilty, empathetic view of the other as at once good, damaged, integral, and requiring and eliciting love and care. Such ethical possibility, however, is founded on and coextensive with the subject's movement toward what Foucault calls "care of the self," the often very fragile concern to provide the self with pleasure and nourishment in an environment that is perceived as not particularly offering them.

Klein's and Tomkins's conceptual moves here are more sophisticated and, in an important way, less tendentious than the corresponding assumptions in Freud. To begin with, Freud subsumes pleasure seeking and pain avoidance together under the rubric of the supposedly primordial "pleasure principle," as though the two motives could not themselves radically differ.[1] Second, it is the pain-forestalling strategy alone in Freud that (as anxiety) gets extended forward into the developmental achievement of the "reality principle." This leaves pleasure seeking as an always presumable, unexaminable, inexhaustible underground wellspring of supposedly "natural" motive, one that presents only the question of how to keep its irrepressible ebullitions under control. Perhaps even more problematically, this Freudian schema silently installs the anxious paranoid imperative, the impossibility but also the supposed necessity of forestalling pain and surprise, as "reality"—as the only and inevitable mode, motive, content, and proof of true knowledge.

In Freud, then, there would be no room—except as an example of self-delusion—for the Proustian epistemology whereby the narrator of *À la recherche*, who feels in the last volume "jostling each other within me a whole host of truths concerning human passions and character and conduct," recognizes them *as* truths insofar as "*the perception of [them] caused me joy*" (6:303; emphasis added). In the paranoid Freudian epistemology, it is implausible enough to suppose that truth could be even an accidental occasion of joy, inconceivable to imagine joy as a guarantor of truth. Indeed, from any point of view it is circular, or something, to suppose that one's pleasure at knowing something could be taken as evidence of the truth of the knowledge. But a strong theory of positive affect, such as Proust's narrator seems to move toward in *Time Regained*, is no *more* tautological than the strong theory of negative affect represented by, for example, his paranoia in *The Captive*. (Indeed, to the extent that the pursuit of positive affect is far less likely to result in the formation of very strong theory, it may tend rather less toward tautology.) Allow each theory its own, different prime motive, at any rate—the anticipation of pain in one case, the provision of pleasure in the other—and neither can be called more realistic than the other. It's not even necessarily true that the two make different judgments of "reality": it isn't that one is pessimistic and sees the glass as half empty, while the other is optimistic and sees it as half full. In a world full of loss, pain, and oppression, both epistemologies are likely to be based on deep pessimism: the reparative motive of seeking pleasure, after all, arrives, by Klein's account, only with the achievement of a depressive position. But what each looks for—which is again to say, the motive each has *for looking*—is bound to differ widely. Of the two, however, it is only paranoid knowledge that has so thorough a practice of disavowing its affective motive and force and masquerading as the very stuff of truth.

PARANOIA PLACES ITS FAITH IN EXPOSURE

Whatever account it may give of its own motivation, paranoia is characterized by placing, in practice, an extraordinary stress on the efficacy of knowledge per se—knowledge in the form of exposure. Maybe that's why paranoid knowing is so inescapably narrative. Like the deinstitutionalized person on the street who, betrayed and plotted against by everyone else in the city, still urges on you the finger-worn dossier bristling with his precious correspondence, paranoia for all its vaunted suspicion acts as though its work would be accomplished if only it could finally, this time, somehow get its story truly known. That a fully initiated listener could still remain indifferent or inimical, or might have no help to offer, is hardly treated as a possibility.

It's strange that a hermeneutics of suspicion would appear so trusting about the effects of exposure, but Nietzsche (through the genealogy of morals), Marx (through the theory of ideology), and Freud (through the theory of ideals and illusions) already represent, in Ricoeur's phrase, "convergent procedures of demystification" (34) and therefore a seeming faith, inexplicable in their own terms, in the effects of such a proceeding. In the influential final pages of *Gender Trouble,* for example, Butler offers a programmatic argument in favor of demystification as "the normative focus for gay and lesbian practice" (124), with such claims as that "drag implicitly *reveals* the imitative structure of gender itself" (137); "we see sex and gender *denaturalized* by means of a performance" (138); "gender parody *reveals* that the original identity . . . is an imitation" (138); "gender performance will *enact and reveal* the performativity of gender itself" (139); "parodic repetition . . . *exposes* the phantasmatic effect of abiding identity" (141); "the parodic repetition of gender *exposes* . . . the illusion of gender identity" (146); and "hyperbolic exhibitions of 'the natural' . . . *reveal* its fundamentally phantasmatic status" (147) as well as "*exposing* its fundamental unnaturalness" (149; all emphases added).

What marks the paranoid impulse in these pages is, I would say, less even the stress on reflexive mimesis than the seeming faith in exposure. The arch-suspicious author of *The Novel and the Police* also speaks, in this case, for the protocols of many less interesting recent critics when he offers to provide "the 'flash' of increased visibility necessary to render modern discipline a problem in its own right" (D. A. Miller, ix)—as though to make something visible as a problem were, if not a mere hop, skip, and jump away from getting it solved, at least self-evidently a step in that direction. In this respect at least, though not in every one, Miller in *The Novel and the Police* writes as an exemplary New Historicist. For, to a startling extent, the articulations of New Historicist scholarship rely on the prestige of a single, overarching narrative: exposing and problematizing hidden violences in the genealogy of the modern liberal subject.

With the passage of time since the New Historicism was new, it's becoming easier to see the ways that such a paranoid project of exposure may be more historically specific than it seems. "The modern liberal subject": by now it seems, or ought to seem, anything but an obvious choice as the unique terminus ad quem of historical narrative. Where *are* all these supposed modern liberal subjects? I daily encounter graduate students who are dab hands at unveiling the hidden historical violences that underlie a secular, universalist liberal humanism. Yet these students' sentient years, unlike the formative years of their teachers, have been spent entirely in a xenophobic Reagan-Bush-Clinton-Bush America where "liberal" is, if anything, a taboo category and where "secular humanism" is routinely treated as a marginal religious sect, while a vast majority of the population claims to engage in direct intercourse with multiple invisible entities such as angels, Satan, and God.

Furthermore, the force of any interpretive project of *unveiling hidden violence* would seem to depend on a cultural context, like the one assumed in Foucault's early works, in which violence would be deprecated and hence hidden in the first place. Why bother exposing the ruses of power in a country where, at any given moment, 40 percent of young black men are enmeshed in the penal system? In the United States and internationally, while there is plenty of hidden violence that requires exposure there is also, and increasingly, an ethos where forms of violence that are hypervisible from the start may be offered as an exemplary spectacle rather than remain to be unveiled as a scandalous secret. Human rights controversy around, for example, torture and disappearances in Argentina or the use of mass rape as part of ethnic cleansing in Bosnia marks, not an unveiling of practices that had been hidden or naturalized, but a wrestle of different frameworks *of* visibility. That is, violence that was *from the beginning* exemplary and spectacular, pointedly addressed, meant to serve as a public warning or terror to members of a particular community is combated by efforts to *displace and redirect* (as well as simply expand) its aperture of visibility.

A further problem with these critical practices: What does a hermeneutics of suspicion and exposure have to say to social formations in which visibility itself constitutes much of the violence? The point of the reinstatement of chain gangs in several Southern states is less that convicts be required to perform hard labor than that they be required to do so under the gaze of the public, and the enthusiasm for Singapore-style justice that was popularly expressed in the United States around the caning of Michael Fay revealed a growing feeling that well-publicized shaming stigma is just what the doctor ordered for recalcitrant youth. Here is one remarkable index of historical change: it used to be opponents of capital punishment who argued that, if practiced at all, executions should be done in public so as to shame state and spectators by the airing of previously hidden judicial violence. Today it is no longer opponents but death penalty cheerleaders, flushed with triumphal ambitions, who consider that the proper place for executions is on television. What price now the cultural critics' hard-won skill at making visible, behind permissive appearances, the hidden traces of oppression and persecution?

The paranoid trust in exposure seemingly depends, in addition, on an infinite reservoir of naïveté in those who make up the audience for these unveilings. What is the basis for assuming that it will surprise or disturb, never mind motivate, anyone to learn that a given social manifestation is artificial, self-contradictory, imitative, phantasmatic, or even violent? As Peter Sloterdijk points out, cynicism or "enlightened false consciousness"—false consciousness that knows itself to be false, "its falseness already reflexively buffered"—already represents "the universally widespread way in which enlightened people see to it that they are not taken for suckers" (5). How television-starved would someone have to be to find it shocking that ideologies contradict themselves, that simulacra don't have originals, or that gender representations are artificial? My own guess is that such popular cynicism, though undoubtedly widespread, is only one among the heterogeneous, competing theories that constitute the mental ecology of most people. Some exposés, some demystifications, some bearings of witness do have great effectual force (though often of an unanticipated kind). Many that are just as true and convincing have none at all, however, and as long as that is so, we must admit that the efficacy and directionality of such acts reside somewhere else than in their relation to knowledge per se.

Writing in 1988—that is, after two full terms of Reaganism in the United States—D. A. Miller proposes to follow Foucault in demystifying "the intensive and continuous 'pastoral' care that liberal society proposes to take of each and every one of its charges" (viii). As if! I'm a lot less worried about being pathologized by my therapist than about my vanishing mental health coverage—and that's given the great good luck of having health insurance at all. Since the beginning of the tax revolt, the government of the United States—and, increasingly, those of other so-called liberal democracies—has been positively rushing to divest itself of answerability for care to its charges, with no other institutions proposing to fill the gap.

This development, however, is the last thing anyone could have expected from reading New Historicist prose, which constitutes a full genealogy of the secular welfare state that peaked in the 1960s and 1970s, along with a watertight proof of why things must become more and more like that forever. No one can blame a writer in the 1980s for not having foreseen the effects of the Republicans' 1994 Contract with America. But if, as Miller says, "Surprise . . . is precisely what the paranoid seeks to eliminate," it must be admitted that, as a form of paranoia, the New Historicism fails spectacularly. While its general tenor of "things are bad and getting worse" is immune to refutation, any more specific predictive value — and as a result, arguably, any value for making oppositional strategy — has been nil. Such accelerating failure to anticipate change is, moreover, as I've discussed, entirely in the nature of the paranoid process, whose sphere of influence (like that of the New Historicism itself) only expands as each unanticipated disaster seems to demonstrate more conclusively that, guess what, *you can never be paranoid enough.*

To look from a present day vantage at Richard Hofstadter's immensely influential 1963 essay "The Paranoid Style in American Politics" is to see the extent of a powerful discursive change. Hofstadter's essay is a prime expression of the complacent, coercive liberal consensus that practically begs for the kind of paranoid demystification in which, for example, D. A. Miller educates his readers. Its style is mechanically even-handed: Hofstadter finds paranoia on both left and right: among abolitionists, anti-Masons and anti-Catholics and anti-Mormons, nativists and populists and those who believe in conspiracies of bankers or munitions makers; in anyone who doubts that JFK was killed by a lone gunman, "in the popular left-wing press, in the contemporary American right wing, and on both sides of the race controversy today" (9). Although these categories seem to cover a lot of people, there remains nonetheless a presumptive "we" — apparently still practically everyone — who can agree to view such extremes from a calm, understanding, and encompassing middle ground, where "we" can all agree that, for example, though "innumerable decisions of . . . the cold war can be faulted," they represent "simply the mistakes of well-meaning men" (36). Hofstadter has no trouble admitting that paranoid people or movements can perceive true things, though "a distorted style is . . . a possible signal that may alert us to a distorted judgment, just as in art an ugly style is a cue to fundamental defects of taste" (6):

> A few simple and relatively non-controversial examples may make [the distinction between content and style] wholly clear. Shortly after the assassination of President Kennedy, a great deal of publicity was given to a bill . . .

to tighten federal controls over the sale of firearms through the mail. When hearings were being held on the measure, three men drove 2,500 miles to Washington from Bagdad, Arizona, to testify against it. Now there are arguments against the Dodd bill which, however unpersuasive one may find them, have the color of conventional political reasoning. But one of the Arizonans opposed it with what might be considered representative paranoid arguments, insisting that it was "a further attempt by a subversive power to make us part of one world socialistic government" and that it threatened to "create chaos" that would help "our enemies" to seize power. (5)

I won't deny that a person could get nostalgic for a time when paranoid gun lobby rhetoric sounded just plain nutty—a "simple and relatively noncontroversial" example of "distorted judgment"—rather than representing the almost uncontested platform of a dominant political party. But the spectacular datedness of Hofstadter's example isn't only an index of how far the American political center has shifted toward the right since 1963. It's also a sign of how normative such paranoid thinking has become at every point in the political spectrum. In a funny way, I feel closer today to that paranoid Arizonan than I do to Hofstadter—even though, or do I mean because, I also assume that the Arizonan is a homophobic white-supremacist Christian Identity militia member who would as soon blow me away as look at me. Peter Sloterdijk does not make explicit that the wised-up popular cynicism or "enlightened false consciousness" that he considers now to be near ubiquitous is, specifically, paranoid in structure. But that conclusion seems inescapable. Arguably, such narrow-gauge, everyday, rather incoherent cynicism is what paranoia looks like when it functions as weak theory rather than strong theory. To keep arriving on this hyperdemystified, paranoid scene with the "news" of a hermeneutics of suspicion, at any rate, is a far different act from what such exposures would have been in the 1960s.

☞ Subversive and demystifying parody, suspicious archaeologies of the present, the detection of hidden patterns of violence and their exposure: as I have been arguing, these infinitely doable and teachable protocols of unveiling have become the common currency of cultural and historicist studies. If there is an obvious danger in the triumphalism of a paranoid hermeneutics, it is that the broad consensual sweep of such methodological assumptions, the current near professionwide agreement about what constitutes narrative or explanation or adequate historicization may, if it persists unquestioned, unintentionally impoverish the gene pool of literary-critical perspectives and skills. The trouble with a shallow gene pool, of course, is its diminished ability to respond to environmental (e.g., political) change.

Another, perhaps more nearly accurate way of describing the present paranoid consensus, however, is that rather than entirely displacing, it may simply have required a certain disarticulation, disavowal, and misrecognition of other ways of knowing, ways less oriented around suspicion, that are actually being practiced, often by the same theorists and as part of the same projects. The monopolistic program of paranoid knowing systematically disallows any explicit recourse to reparative motives, no sooner to be articulated than subject to methodical uprooting. Reparative motives, once they become explicit, are inadmissible in paranoid theory both because they are about pleasure ("merely aesthetic") and because they are frankly ameliorative ("merely reformist").[2] What makes pleasure and amelioration so "mere"? Only the exclusiveness of paranoia's faith in demystifying exposure: only its cruel and contemptuous assumption that the one thing lacking for global revolution, explosion of gender roles, or whatever, is people's (that is, other people's) having the painful effects of their oppression, poverty, or deludedness sufficiently exacerbated to make the pain conscious (as if otherwise it wouldn't have been) and intolerable (as if intolerable situations were famous for generating excellent solutions).

Such ugly prescriptions are not seriously offered by most paranoid theory, but a lot of contemporary theory is nonetheless regularly *structured as if* by them. The kind of aporia we have already discussed in *The Novel and the Police,* where readers are impelled through a grimly monolithic structure of strong paranoid theory by successive engagement with quite varied, often apparently keenly pleasure-oriented, smaller-scale writerly and intellectual solicitations, appears in a lot of other good criticism as well. I certainly recognize it as characterizing a fair amount of my own writing. Does it matter when such projects misdescribe themselves or are misrecognized by readers? I wouldn't suggest that the force of any powerful writing can ever attain complete transparency to itself, or is likely to account for itself very adequately at the constative level of the writing. But suppose one takes seriously the notion, like the one articulated by Tomkins but also like other available ones, that everyday theory qualitatively affects everyday knowledge and experience; and suppose that one doesn't want to draw much ontological distinction between academic theory and everyday theory; and suppose that one has a lot of concern for the quality of other people's and one's own practices of knowing and experiencing. In these cases, it would make sense—if one had the choice—not to cultivate the necessity of a systematic, self-accelerating split between what one is doing and the reasons one does it.

While paranoid theoretical proceedings both depend on and reinforce the structural dominance of monopolistic "strong theory," there may also be benefit in exploring the extremely varied, dynamic, and historically contingent ways that strong theoretical constructs interact with weak ones in the ecology of knowing—an exploration that obviously can't proceed without a respectful interest in weak as well as strong theoretical acts. Tomkins offers far more models for approaching such a project than I've been able to summarize. But the history of literary criticism can also be viewed as a repertoire of alternative models for allowing strong and weak theory to interdigitate. What could better represent "weak theory, little better than a description of the phenomena which it purports to explain," than the devalued and near obsolescent New Critical skill of imaginative close reading?[3] But what was already true in Empson and Burke is true in a different way today: there are important phenomenological and theoretical tasks that can be accomplished only through local theories and nonce taxonomies; the potentially innumerable mechanisms of their relation to stronger theories remain matters of art and speculative thought.

Paranoia, as I have pointed out, represents not only a strong affect theory but a strong *negative* affect theory. The question of the strength of a given theory (or that of the relations between strong and weak theory) may be orthogonal to the question of its affective *quale,* and each may be capable of exploration by different means. A strong theory (i.e., a wide-ranging and reductive one) that was not mainly organized around anticipating, identifying, and warding off the negative affect of humiliation would resemble paranoia in some respects but differ from it in others. I think, for example, that that might be a fair characterization of the preceding section of the present chapter. Because even the specification of paranoia as a theory of negative affect leaves open the distinctions between or among negative affects, there is the additional opportunity of experimenting with a vocabulary that will do justice to a wide affective range. Again, not only with the negative affects: it can also be reifying and, indeed, coercive to have only one, totalizing model of positive affect always in the same featured position. A disturbingly large amount of theory seems explicitly to undertake the proliferation of only one affect, or maybe two, of whatever kind—whether ecstasy, sublimity, self-shattering, *jouissance*, suspicion, abjection, knowingness, horror, grim satisfaction, or righteous indignation. It's like the old joke: "Comes the revolution, Comrade, everyone gets to eat roast beef every day." "But Comrade, I don't like roast beef." "Comes the revolution, Comrade, you'll like roast beef." Comes the revolution, Comrade, you'll be tickled pink by those deconstructive jokes; you'll faint from ennui every minute you're not smashing the state apparatus; you'll definitely want hot sex twenty to thirty times a day. You'll be mournful *and* militant. You'll never want to tell Deleuze and Guattari, "Not tonight, dears, I have a headache."

To recognize in paranoia a distinctively rigid relation to temporality, at once anticipatory and retroactive, averse above all to surprise, is also to glimpse the lineaments of other possibilities. Here, perhaps, Klein is of more help than Tomkins: to read from a reparative position is to surrender the knowing, anxious paranoid determination that no horror, however apparently unthinkable, shall ever come to the reader *as new;* to a reparatively positioned reader, it can seem realistic and necessary to experience surprise. Because there can be terrible surprises, however, there can also be good ones. Hope, often a fracturing, even a traumatic thing to experience, is among the energies by which the reparatively positioned reader tries to organize the fragments and part-objects she encounters or creates.[4] Because the reader has room to realize that the future may be different from the present, it is also possible for her to entertain such profoundly painful, profoundly relieving, ethically crucial possibilities as that the past, in turn, could have happened differently from the way it actually did.[5]

Where does this argument leave projects of queer reading, in particular? With the relative deemphasis of the question of "sexual difference" and sexual "sameness," and with the possibility of moving from a Freudian, homophobia-centered understanding of paranoia to other understandings of it, like Klein's or Tomkins's, that are not particularly Oedipal and are less drive-oriented than affect-oriented, I am also suggesting that the mutual inscription of queer thought with the topic of paranoia may be less necessary, less definitional, less completely constitutive than earlier writing on it, very much including my own, has assumed. A more ecological view of paranoia wouldn't offer the same transhistorical, almost automatic conceptual privileging of gay/lesbian issues that is offered by a Freudian view.

On the other hand, I think it will leave us in a vastly better position to do justice to a wealth of characteristic, culturally central practices, many of which can well be called reparative, that emerge from queer experience but become invisible or illegible under a paranoid optic. As Joseph Litvak writes, for example (in a personal communication, 1996),

> It seems to me that the importance of "mistakes" in queer reading and writing . . . has a lot to do with loosening the traumatic, inevitable-seeming connection between mistakes and humiliation. What I mean is that, if a lot of queer energy, say around adolescence, goes into what Barthes calles "le vouloir-être-intelligent" (as in "If I have to be miserable, at least let me be brainier than everybody else"), accounting in large part for paranoia's enormous prestige as the very signature of smartness (a smartness that smarts), a lot of queer energy, later on, goes into . . . practices aimed at taking the terror out of error, at making the making of mistakes sexy, creative, even cognitively powerful. Doesn't reading queer mean learning, among other things, that mistakes can be good rather than bad surprises?

It's appropriate, I think, that these insights would be contingent developments rather than definitional or transhistorical ones: they aren't things that would inevitably inhere in the experience of every woman-loving woman or man-loving man, say. For if, as I've shown, a paranoid reading practice is closely tied to a notion of the inevitable, there are other features of queer reading that can attune it exquisitely to a heartbeat of contingency.

The dogged, defensive narrative stiffness of a paranoid temporality, after all, in which yesterday can't be allowed to have differed from today and tomorrow must be even more so, takes its shape from a generational narrative that's characterized by a distinctly Oedipal regularity and repetitiveness: it happened to my father's father, it happened to my father, it is happening to me, it will happen to my son, and it will happen to my son's son. But isn't it a feature of queer possibility—only a contingent feature, but a real one, and one that in turn strengthens the force of contingency itself—that our generational relations don't always proceed in this lockstep?

Think of the epiphanic, extravagantly reparative final volume of Proust, in which the narrator, after a long withdrawal from society, goes to a party where he at first thinks everyone is sporting elaborate costumes pretending to be ancient, then realizes that they *are* old, and so is he — and is then assailed, in half a dozen distinct mnemonic shocks, by a climactic series of joy-inducing "truths" about the relation of writing to time. The narrator never says so, but isn't it worth pointing out that the complete temporal disorientation that initiates him into this revelatory space would have been impossible in a heterosexual *père de famille,* in one who had meanwhile been embodying, in the form of inexorably "progressing" identities and roles, the regular arrival of children and grandchildren?

> And now I began to understand what old age was — old age, which perhaps of all the realities is the one of which we preserve for longest in our life a purely abstract conception, looking at calendars, dating our letters, seeing our friends marry and then in their turn the children of our friends, and yet, either from fear or from sloth, not understanding what all this means, until the day when we behold an unknown silhouette . . . which teaches us that we are living in a new world; until the day when a grandson of a woman we once knew, a young man whom instinctively we treat as a contemporary of ours, smiles as though we were making fun of him because it seems that we are old enough to be his grandfather — and I began to understand too what death meant and love and the joys of the spiritual life, the usefulness of suffering, a vocation, etc. (6:354–55)

A more recent contingency, in the brutal foreshortening of so many queer life spans, has deroutinized the temporality of many of us in ways that only intensify this effect. I'm thinking, as I say this, of three very queer friendships I have. One of my friends is sixty; the other two are both thirty, and I, at forty-five, am exactly in the middle. All four of us are academics, and we have in common a lot of interests, energies, and ambitions; we have each had, as well, variously intense activist investments. In a "normal" generational narrative, our identifications with each other would be aligned with an expectation that in another fifteen years, I'd be situated comparably to where my sixty-year-old friend is, while my thirty-year-old friends would be situated comparably to where I am.

But we are all aware that the grounds of such friendships today are likely to differ from that model. They do so in inner cities, and for people subject to racist violence, and for people deprived of health care, and for people in dangerous industries, and for many others; they do so for my friends and me. Specifically, living with advanced breast cancer, I have little chance of ever being the age my older friend is now. My friends who are thirty are equally unlikely ever to experience my present, middle age: one is living with an advanced cancer caused by a massive environmental trauma (basically, he grew up on top of a toxic waste site); the other is living with HIV. The friend who is a very healthy sixty is much the likeliest of us to be living fifteen years from now.

It's hard to say, hard even to know, how these relationships are different from those shared by people of different ages on a landscape whose perspectival lines converge on a common disappearing-point. I'm sure ours are more intensely motivated: whatever else we know, we know there isn't time to bullshit. But what it means to identify with each other must also be very different. On this scene, an older person doesn't love a younger as someone who will someday be where she now is, or vice versa. No one is, so to speak, passing on the family name; there's a sense in which our life narratives will barely overlap. There's another sense in which they slide up more intimately alongside one another than can any lives that are moving forward according to the regular schedule of the generations. It is one another immediately, one another as the present fullness of a becoming whose arc may extend no further, whom we each must learn best to apprehend, fulfill, and bear company.

At a textual level, it seems to me that related practices of reparative knowing may lie, barely recognized and little explored, at the heart of many histories of gay, lesbian, and queer intertextuality. The queer-identified practice of camp, for example, may be seriously misrecognized when it is viewed, as Butler and others view it, through paranoid lenses. As we've seen, camp is most often understood as uniquely appropriate to the projects of parody, denaturalization, demystification, and mocking exposure of the elements and assumptions of a dominant culture. And the degree to which camping is motivated by love seems often to be understood mainly as the degree of its self-hating complicity with an oppressive status quo. By this account, the x-ray gaze of the paranoid impulse in camp sees through to an unfleshed skeleton of the culture; the paranoid aesthetic on view here is one of minimalist elegance and conceptual economy.

The desire of a reparative impulse, on the other hand, is additive and accretive. Its fear, a realistic one, is that the culture surrounding it is inadequate or inimical to its nurture; it wants to assemble and confer plenitude on an object that will then have resources to offer to an inchoate self. To view camp as, among other things, the communal, historically dense exploration of a variety of reparative practices is to do better justice to many of the defining elements of classic camp performance: the startling, juicy displays of excess erudition, for example; the passionate, often hilarious antiquarianism, the prodigal production of alternative historiographies; the "over"-attachment to fragmentary, marginal, waste or leftover products; the rich, highly interruptive affective variety; the irrepressible fascination with ventriloquistic experimentation; the disorienting juxtapositions of present with past, and popular with high culture.[6] As in the writing of D. A. Miller, a glue of surplus beauty, surplus stylistic investment, unexplained upwellings of threat, contempt, and longing cements together and animates the amalgam of powerful part-objects in such work as that of Ronald Firbank, Djuna Barnes, Joseph Cornell, Kenneth Anger, Charles Ludlam, Jack Smith, John Waters, and Holly Hughes.

The very mention of these names, some of them attaching to almost legendarily "paranoid" personalities, confirms, too, Klein's insistence that it is not people but mutable positions — or, I would want to say, practices — that can be divided between the paranoid and the reparative; it is sometimes the most paranoid-tending people who are able to, and need to, develop and disseminate the richest reparative practices. And if the paranoid or the depressive positions operate on a smaller scale than the level of individual typology, they operate also on a larger: that of shared histories, emergent communities, and the weaving of intertextual discourse.

Like Proust, the reparative reader "helps himself again and again"; it is not only important but *possible* to find ways of attending to such reparative motives and positionalities. The vocabulary for articulating any reader's reparative motive toward a text or a culture has long been so sappy, aestheticizing, defensive, anti-intellectual, or reactionary that it's no wonder few critics are willing to describe their acquaintance with such motives. The prohibitive problem, however, has been in the limitations of present theoretical vocabularies rather than in the reparative motive itself. No less acute than a paranoid position, no less realistic, no less attached to a project of survival, and neither less nor more delusional or fantasmatic, the reparative reading position undertakes a different range of affects, ambitions, and risks. What we can best learn from such practices are, perhaps, the many ways selves and communities succeed in extracting sustenance from the objects of a culture—even of a culture whose avowed desire has often been not to sustain them.

1. Laplanche and Pontalis, in their entry under "Pleasure Principle," show that Freud was long aware of this problem. They paraphrase: "Must we therefore be content with a purely economic definition and accept that pleasure and unpleasure are nothing more than the translation of quantitative changes into qualitative terms? And what then is the precise correlation between these two aspects, the qualitative and the quantitative? Little by little, Freud came to lay considerable emphasis on the great difficulty encountered in the attempt to provide a simple answer to this question" (323). In Chapter 3, Adam Frank and I describe Tomkins's work on affect in terms that try to respond to this way of posing the problem.

2. The barely implicit sneer with which Leo Bersani wields the term "redemption" throughout *The Culture of Redemption* might be one good example of the latter kind of usage—except that Bersani's revulsion seems to attach, not quite to the notion that things could be ameliorated, but rather to the pious reification of Art as the appointed agent of such change.

3. Thanks to Tyler Curtain for pointing this out to me.

4. I am thinking here of Timothy Gould's interpretation (in a personal communication, 1994) of Emily Dickinson's poem that begins " 'Hope' is the thing with feathers—/ That perches in the soul—" (116, poem no. 254). Gould suggests that the symptoms of fluttering hope are rather like those of posttraumatic stress disorder, with the difference that the apparently absent cause of perturbation lies in the future, rather than in the past.

5. I don't mean to hypostatize, here, "the way it actually did" happen, or to deny how constructed a thing this "actually did" may be—within certain constraints. The realm of what *might have happened but didn't* is, however, ordinarily even wider and less constrained, and it seems conceptually important that the two not be collapsed; otherwise, the entire possibility of things' *happening differently* can be lost.

6. Michael Moon's *A Small Boy and Others* is one book that conveys this richer sense of queer culture.

Chapter 5

PEDAGOGY OF BUDDHISM

What does it mean when our cats bring small, wounded animals into the house? Most people interpret these deposits as offerings or gifts, however inaptly chosen, meant to please or propitiate us, the cats' humans. But according to the anthropologist Elizabeth Marshall Thomas, "Cats may be assuming the role of educator when they bring prey indoors to their human owners. . . . A mother cat starts teaching her kittens from the moment they start following her. . . . Later she gives them hands-on practice by flipping victims in their direction, exactly as a cat does in play. Mother cats even bring [wounded] prey back to their nests or dens so that their homebound kittens can practice, especially if the prey is of manageable size. So perhaps cats who release living prey in our houses are trying to give us some practice, to hone our hunting skills" (105).

For persons involved with cats or pedagogy, Thomas's supposition here may be unsettling in several ways. First there is the narcissistic wound. Where we had thought to be powerful or admired, quasi-parental figures to our cats, we are cast instead in the role of clumsy newborns requiring special education. Worse, we have not even learned from this education. With all the cat's careful stage management, we seem especially stupid in having failed to so much as recognize the scene as one of pedagogy. Is it true that we can learn only when we are aware we are being taught? How have we so confused the illocutionary acts of gift giving and teaching? A further speech act problem here involves imitation: the cat assumed (but how could we know?) that its own movements were templates for our mimicry, rather than meant to be made room for or graciously accepted by us. A gesture intended to evoke a symmetrical response has instead evoked a complementary one.

Then again, even if we had recognized the cat's project as pedagogical, it's possible we would not have responded appropriately by "honing our hunting skills" on the broken, twitching prey. Possibly we do not want to learn the lesson our cat is teaching. Here, in an affective register, is another mistake about mimesis: the cat's assumption that we identify with it strongly enough to want to act more like it (e.g., eat live rodents). For a human educator, the cat's unsuccessful pedagogy resonates with plenty of everyday nightmares. There are students who view their teachers' hard work as a servile offering in their honor—a distasteful one to boot. There are other students who accept the proffered formulations gratefully, as a gift, but without thinking to mimic the process of their production. No doubt this describes a common impasse faced by psychoanalysts and psychotherapists as well. Teaching privileged undergraduates, I sometimes had a chilling intimation that while I relied on their wish to mirror me and my skills and knowledge, they were motivated instead by seeing me as a cautionary figure: what might become of them if they weren't cool enough, sleek enough, adaptable enough to escape from the thicket of academia into the corporate world.

And beside the frustrations of the feline pedagogue are the more sobering ones of the stupid human owner. It's so often too late when we finally recognize the "resistance" (mouse flipping) of a student/patient as a form of pedagogy aimed at us and inviting our mimesis. We may wonder afterwards whether and how we could have managed to turn into the particular teacher/therapist needed by each one. Perhaps their implication has been: Try it my way—if you're going to teach me. Or even: I have something more important to teach you than you have to teach me.

☞ Among the relations of near-miss pedagogy I discuss in this chapter, obviously the foundational one transpires between Asia and Euro-America on the subject of Buddhism itself. Over the past two decades, even as the long-standing presence of Buddhist elements in U.S. culture has become explosively visible, critical scholarship has explored the vast, systemic misunderstandings and cross-purposes that seem to underlie this trans-Pacific pedagogy. An "American Buddhist" reader of the critical scholarship might well be chastened to learn in how many, crucial, near invisible ways her access to the Asian texts, practices, and understandings has been compromised by the history of their transmission to the West. Donald Lopez, for example, summarizes his exemplary anthology of critical essays by declaring that what has become available to modern Western readers is only a "hypostatized object, called 'Buddhism,'" which, "because it had been created by Europe, could also be controlled by it" (7). Among the distortions manifest in such hypostatization have been a narrative of decline that delegitimates the modern and the vernacular in Buddhist studies; an eagerness to attribute Western roots to Asian Buddhist representation; histories of complicity with nativist and colonialist projects in Japan as well as fascist ones in Italy; arrogant and ignorant claims, such as Jung's, to speak for an exotic Oriental psyche; and a double-binding enlistment of Asian Buddhists in the incompatible roles of informant and guru to scholars from the West.

What is the force of such very critical findings? How and to whom do they matter? Common sense suggests that their impact will fall on nonacademic students of Buddhism more lightly than on scholars in the field. Not only are these exacting studies (most of them published by university presses) less accessible to nonscholars, but the prime motives for reading them are also likely to differ. To put it crudely, academic scholars of Buddhism are vocationally aimed at finding a path, however asymptotic, toward a knowledge of their subject(s) that would be ever less distorted by ignorance, imperialist presumption, and wishful thinking, or by characteristic thought patterns of Western culture. On the other hand, the attachment of the nonacademic reader to the truth value of readings on Buddhism may rest on a good deal more pragmatic base. The question Is this (account) accurate or misleading? may give way for these readers to the question Will this (practice) work or won't it?

The historical place and moment in which the latter question is asked are distinctive ones appropriately described in terms of pluralistic, free market–like forces within essentially secular societies (see Berger). More recently, the somewhat stigmatizing rubrics of "self-help," "New Age," and "therapy-like" have suggested an even less respectable market-niche specification for popularized Buddhist teachings aimed at non-Asian consumers. It is from that niche that the present chapter emerges, reflecting a nonspecialist educator's five-year engagement with English-language "Buddhist" literature ranging from mass-market to scholarly. My first, self-helping motive for that engagement was frankly soteriological, prompted by receiving in middle age a diagnosis of metastatic cancer. As this chapter shows, however, my interest in the Buddhist literature of death and dying proved inextricable as well from an identification with pedagogical passions and antinomies that recur throughout the Mahayana traditions.

The dominant scholarly topos, and indeed, often the self-description, for Western popularizations of Buddhist thought is *adaptation,* whether such adaptation is hailed or decried. It implies that an Asian original is adapting or being adapted for the essentially different habits, sensibilities, Weltanschauung of the West. By the same token, a common defense of adaptational practices is that Buddhism has often, historically, been changed by, as much as it has changed, the varied cultures encountered in its peripatetic history.

This chapter, by focusing on pedagogy as both topic and relation, attempts something different from such a defense: it suggests that *adaptation* is not the only model for Western encounters with popularized Buddhist teachings. Adaptation emphasizes how an original is being altered, modified, fitted for a different use, maybe even decentered, drawn out of an earlier orbit by the gravitational pull of an alien body. To a certain degree the aptness of this topos is undeniable. Furthermore, there is plenty of Buddhist scriptural warrant for it: the Pali canon, sutras, and Jataka stories all contain examples — very privileged ones — of teachings that have been radically adapted to their auditors' varied capacities and frames of reference.

In this chapter, however, I want to try out more, different resources from the great treasury of Buddhist phenomenologies of learning and teaching. What if, for example, an equally canonical topos such as *recognition/realization* describes some dynamics of Western Buddhist popularization better than does the one-directional topos of adaptation? Certainly, it is better suited to the subjectivity and the epistemological concerns of those who consume these popularizations.

A subsidiary aim of this chapter is to illustrate some consequences of what is by now a truism about Asian religious thought: that it has "arrived" and been influential in Western thought in many forms through many different encounters over many centuries. Thus, by now a Buddhist encounter with "Western culture" must also be understood as an encounter with a palimpsest of Asian currents and influences (and vice versa). For example, Americans often shop for Buddhist books on the self-help shelves in popular bookstores. But if the marketing rubric of self-help has an almost alarmingly American sound, isn't that at least in part because it harkens so directly to the early nineteenth-century impulse of Emerson's "Self-Reliance" and Whitman's "Song of Myself"? An impulse, that is, already consciously involved in direct and indirect interchange with Buddhist and Hindu teaching?

☞ The first book I encountered in my Buddhist exploration, and one that probably, in some unexamined ways, still structures my involvement with Buddhism as a topic, was Sogyal Rinpoche's best-selling popularization, *The Tibetan Book of Living and Dying*. Constructed as an extended gloss on the so-called *Tibetan Book of the Dead*, it offers more broadly a beginner's introduction to Tibetan Buddhism and makes the still wider claim (on the back cover of the paperback) to be "a manual for life and death . . . the definitive new spiritual classic for our times."

More than Zen Buddhism or Theravada meditation—other Buddhist traditions that achieved widespread popularity among non-Asian Americans in the twentieth century—Tibetan Buddhism risks seeming inextricable from the cultural circumstances and history of its Asian development. Perhaps the closer focus on meditation in the other traditions gives them an illusion of transparency and universal accessibility that Tibetan Buddhism lacks. Perhaps the relative geographic accessibility of Japan and Southeast Asia leaves Tibetan Buddhism more densely entangled (in Western eyes) with the local, with opacities of language, custom, history, "belief," in short (as the earlier Buddhologists would have it), of "superstition." The Dalai Lama regularly avows, all over the world, "My religion is kindness." But to move beyond that seemingly pellucid introduction is promptly to encounter practices and cosmologies whose weirdness—from a Western point of view—can seem near irreducible.

How does Sogyal negotiate the danger of losing readers in this cultural gap? The opening paragraph of the preface is narratively arresting:

> I was born in Tibet, and I was six months old when I entered the monastery of my master Jamyang Khyentse Chöki Lodrö, in the province of Kham.

In Tibet we have a unique tradition of finding the reincarnations of great masters who have passed away. They are chosen young and given a special education to train them to become the teachers of the future. I was given the name Sogyal, even though it was only later that my master recognized me as the incarnation of Tertön Sogyal, a renowned mystic who was one of his own teachers and a master of the Thirteenth Dalai Lama.

My master, Jamyang Khyentse, was tall for a Tibetan, and he always seemed to stand a good head above others in a crowd. He had silver hair, cut very short, and kind eyes that glowed with humor. His ears were long, like those of the Buddha. (xi)

This fairytale-like opening plunges a reader disorientingly into an unfamiliar system of analogues and incarnations. Strategically, however, the reader's point of view is simultaneously attached to the more radical disorientation of the six-month-old (his parents unmentioned) who "entered the monastery," acquired a "master," and underwent obscure processes of being found or "chosen" before he could either walk or talk.

The rest of the preface follows a similar strategy of parallel initiations. As readers we get information such as, "In Tibet it was never enough simply to have the name of an incarnation, you always had to earn respect, through your learning and through your spiritual practice" (xi). At the same time, another element of the authorial voice represents a child trying to make sense of its confusing surroundings and status: "I was a naughty child. . . . The next time I fled to hide, my tutor came into the room, did three prostrations to my master, and dragged me out. I remember thinking, as I was hauled out of the room, how strange it was that he did not seem to be afraid of my master" (xii). The strangeness encountered by the child seems to belong both to his unusual tulku status and, at the same time, to a more general strangeness (or givenness) that a world presents to anyone unversed in it — Western reader or Tibetan child.

Sogyal Rinpoche's preface, then, offers a past tense in which a child is acculturated by fits and starts alongside an implicit present tense in which a reader is. Sogyal's ingenuous diction and sentence structure laminate the two together. But the double initiation also proceeds under two other, overarching aegises. One is a distinctive emotional tonality, that of gratitude mixed with tenderness. The other, to which that tonality attaches, is the continuing influence of "my master." "Everyone called him *Rinpoche,* 'the

Precious One,' which is the title given to a master, and when he was present no other teacher would be addressed in that way. His presence was so impressive that many affectionately called him 'the Primordial Buddha' " (xiii). In the narrator's childhood he is a sensory presence: "Usually I slept next to my master, on a small bed at the foot of his own. One sound I shall never forget is the clicking of the beads of his *mala*, his Buddhist rosary, as he whispered his prayers. When I went to sleep he would be there, sitting and practicing; and when I awoke in the morning he would already be awake and sitting and practicing again, overflowing with blessing and power. As I opened my eyes and saw him, I would be filled with a warm and cozy happiness. He had such an air of peace about him" (xiii). Equally, extending beyond his death to the present tense of the reader's initiation, "Jamyang Khyentse is the ground of my life, and the inspiration of this book. He was the incarnation of a master who had transformed the practice of Buddhism in our country" (xi). "I have heard that my master said that I would help continue his work, and certainly he always treated me like his own son. I feel that what I have been able to achieve now in my work, and the audience I have been able to reach, is a ripening of the blessing he gave me" (xii). And the preface ends: "I pray this book will transmit something of his great wisdom and compassion to the world, and, through it, you too, wherever you are, can come into the presence of his wisdom mind and find a living connection with him" (xiv).

Although there remain many details in the preface that will puzzle a reader unfamiliar with Tibetan Buddhist traditions, its simple language will already have involved readers in a series of complex, affectively steeped pedagogical relations. The mobility of teacher-student positioning is embodied first in Sogyal himself, who begins the preface as an infant and ends it as a teacher — but without apparent change in the quality of his dependence on his "master." Indeed, along the way he has been "recognized" as an incarnation of his master's own teacher. Which of them, then, will be the reader's master? Apparently some process of ventriloquism/impregnation between them assures that there is no need to choose, indeed no way of discriminating, between Sogyal Rinpoche the student/teacher and that master Rinpoche in whose radiant presence no one else can be one. In fact, "For me he was the Buddha, of that there was no question in my mind. And everyone else recognized it as well" (xiii).

This teaching situation, evidently, thrives on personality and intimate emotional relation. At the same time, it functions as a mysteriously powerful solvent of individual identity.

The dissolution of identity is a commonplace about "Buddhism," to be sure. But in fact, Sogyal's preface has said little about Buddhism per se and nothing at all about its tenets. Rather than into "Buddhism," a reader who begins this book is, by means of her disorientation, interpellated into a rich yet dissolvent relationality of pedagogy itself. In this world it is as though relation *could only be* pedagogical—and for *that* reason, radically transindividual. "Whenever I share that atmosphere of my master with others, they can sense the same profound feeling it aroused in me. What then did Jamyang Khyentse inspire in me? An unshakable confidence in the teachings, and a conviction in the central and dramatic importance of the master" (xiii).

☞ Admittedly, it's easy to make the case that pedagogical relation is substantively central to Vajrayana Buddhism, or "lamaism" as nineteenth-century Europe called it, based on the exceptional prominence given to the lama/guru as initiatory teacher. Not only Vajrayana but the whole of Mahayana Buddhism, however, is radically self-defined in pedagogical terms. What the Mahayana (greater vehicle) is "greater" than, after all, are the shravaka-yana and the pratyeka-yana: the "lesser" vehicles whose perfected beings, the nonteaching shravakas (auditors) and pratyekas (solitary awakened ones), are students or autodidacts only, who achieve nirvana for their own sake alone.

The Mahayana ideal, by direct contrast, attaches to the bodhisattva, "one who aspires to the attainment of Buddhahood and devotes himself to altruistic deeds, especially deeds that cause others to attain enlightenment" (Chang 471). Thus, like shravakas and pratyekas the bodhisattva too remains a student and aspirant, advised to "be the pupil of everyone all the time" (Śāntideva 40). For the bodhisattva, however, the pedagogical imperative of occasioning others' enlightenment takes priority even over one's own spiritual advancement: a bodhisattva defers entering nirvana until after all other sentient beings have learned to do so. Thomas Cleary's translation of bodhisattva as "enlightening being" (2), therefore, with its double reference to enlightening others and growing more enlightened oneself, seems an apt way to express this central condensation, which does more to identify the bodhisattva's positional axes as pedagogical ones than to specify his or her placement on these axes. Furthermore, any person's commitment to Mahayana Buddhism involves a location in the bodhisattva dimensions; the "bodhisattva path" along the plane formed by these axes is not reserved for the spiritually advanced. The defining figure of Mahayana Buddhism, the bodhisattva in turn is defined almost simply as a being whose commitment to pedagogical relationality approaches the horizon of eternity.

Although (or because) self-evident, it may also be worth emphasizing that, like Plato's dialogues, the vastly more voluminous Buddhist sutras in fact comprise nothing but a series of dramatized scenes of instruction. Further, among the multitudinous forms and levels of beings that populate the sutras—asuras, bodhisattvas and Bodhisattva-Mahasattvas, brahmas, devas and devaputras, dragons, gandharvas, garudas, gods, householders, magically produced beings, monks, Nonreturners and Once-returners, pratyekas, rsis, Śakras, śramanas and Śrāvakas, Stream-enterers, yaksas— none wishes for anything more precious than to receive Dharma teachings. In Mahayana scriptures, scenes of teaching and learning are universally desired ends as much as they are instrumental means.

☞ In 1844, when Elizabeth Palmer Peabody published in *The Dial* the first translation from a sutra into the English language, her immediate readership comprised a group of her Boston-area Transcendentalist friends. The selection she chose from Eugène Burnouf's French translation of the Lotus Sutra, while sharing the emphasis of that sutra on the ultimate unity of Buddhist teachings, nonetheless distinguishes carefully among the vehicles of Buddhism. Her care may rather have mystified her readers, given that at that point the most scholarly among them barely distinguished between Brahman and Buddhist. Peabody, however, took the trouble of explaining to them in footnotes that, for example, a Pratyeka-Buddha "is a kind of selfish Buddha, who possesses science without endeavoring to spread it" ("Preaching" 393).

But this discrimination is itself in the service of a paean to the nondiscriminating amplitude of the Buddha's pedagogy. "I explain the law to creatures, after having recognized their inclinations," he says in Peabody's selection, "I proportion my language to the subject and the strength of each":

It is, O Kâçyapa, as if a cloud, raising itself above the universe, covered it entirely, hiding all the earth. . . . Spreading in an uniform manner an immense mass of water, and resplendent with the lightning which escape from its sides, it makes the earth rejoice. And the medicinal plants which have burst from the surface of this earth, the herbs, the bushes, the kings of the forest, little and great trees; the different seeds, and every thing which makes verdure; all the vegetables which are found in the mountains, in the caverns, and in the groves; the herbs, the bushes, the trees, this cloud fills them with joy, it spreads joy upon the dry earth, and it moistens the medicinal plants; and this homogeneous water of the cloud, the herbs and the bushes pump up, every one according to its force and its object. . . . Absorbing the water of the cloud by their trunks, their twigs, their bark, their branches, their boughs, their leaves, the great medicinal plants put forth flowers and fruits. Each one according to its strength, according to its destination, and conformably to the nature of the germ whence it springs, produces a distinct fruit, and nevertheless there is one homogeneous water like that which fell from the cloud. So, O Kâçyapa, the Buddha comes into the world, like a cloud which covers the universe . . . and teaches the true doctrine to creatures. ("Preaching" 398–99)

Presumably, the resonance of such a passage for Transcendental readers would not come from its promise of "true doctrine," but from its focus on a difficult problematic already internal to their Romantic preoccupation with *Bildung:* how a mode of teaching could nurture the individual fates as well as the common needs of those receiving it.

For if ever there was a group as mad for pedagogy as the dramatis personae of the sutras, it must have been the Transcendentalists. With the exception of Thoreau, each of them seemed to attach her or his most vital hope to some practice of viva voce pedagogy—and in each case to one that, independent of university or church credentialing, actively deprecated the claim of authority in favor of that of experiential demand. Also as in the world of the sutras, but much more unusual in the West, the range of these practices—from the Temple School to Margaret Fuller's Conversations to the Concord School of Philosophy—involved people from toddlers to the aged, with no particular phase singled out as uniquely appropriate for education. Thus, that aspect of the Mahayana ideal that refuses to differentiate at the level of identity between teacher and learner coincided with their ideal. Even when adults taught young children, as Elizabeth Peabody wrote in *Record of a School*, a detailed account of Bronson Alcott's short-lived Temple School, "a teacher never should forget that the mind he is directing, may be on a larger scale than his own; that its sensibilities may be deeper, tenderer, wider; that its imagination may be infinitely more rapid; that its intellectual power of proportioning and reasoning may be more powerful; and he should ever have the humility to feel himself at times in the place of the child, and the magnanimity to teach him how to defend himself against his own (i.e. the teacher's) influence" (19–20). Bronson Alcott also followed the principle, "To teach, endeavouring to preserve the understanding from implicit belief" (318). Another of his self-injunctions: "To teach, treating pupils with uniform familiarity, and patience, and with the greatest kindness, tenderness, and respect" (319).

In the Transcendentalists' formal and informal educational manifestos there is no reference to actual Asian practices of teaching; even their basis in a familiarity with Asian scriptures is very attenuated. In the 1830s the Hindu and Buddhist interests of the Transcendentalists were overwhelmingly mediated by those of European Romanticism. Yet the forms taken by German and British scholarly interest in Asia in this period were pedagogically imagined in a different sense. Comparative methods in both philology and religion had resulted in a view of India, in particular, as the maternal origin or "cradle" of Greek, Christian, and indeed all European language and religion (Halbfass 61).

Thus, Peabody's reference is to Orientalist philology as well as domestic sentiment when she writes: "There is nothing in true education which has not its germ in the maternal sentiment; and every mother would find more of the spiritual philosophy in her own affections, if her mind would but read her heart. . . . When an inadequate philosophy, long prevailing, has adulterated in many different ways, the natural language of the heart and imagination, it is especially necessary to newly wash, in the 'undefiled wells' of feeling and thought, whence language first arose, those strong and forcible mother-words which grew out of the philosophy of innate ideas, and which, since its decline, have been obscured and kicked aside as unregarded 'pebbles, in the dusty wheel-ruts of custom'" (*Record* 181–82). She enacts a similar double narrative of spiritual ontogeny and phylogeny in remarking: "The first stage of true religion, perhaps, is necessarily pantheism.

And babyhood is the right time for pantheism. It will die out, and give place to Christian theism, as individuality is realized" (183).

Although she conventionally describes contemporary Asia as crushed by superannuated "institutions and idols that have degraded the race below men" (*Record* 187), and in spite of her more than nominal Christian affiliation, Peabody also, reasoning from "the genius of the primitive languages," sees in Western monotheism a radical fall from the identificatory spiritual idealism of the ancient East. Fortunately, however, there intervened what both she and Alcott view as its crucial pedagogical reembodiment in Classical Greece: "The theoretical philosophy of Anaxagoras was the reassertion in Greece, of the religious philosophy of the east. Mind is God, said the great teacher of Pericles and Socrates. And hence sprang up in Athens, the practical philosophy of *know thyself.* If the human being is a generation of that Spirit which preceded the existence of matter, (so reasoned Socrates,) then a consciousness of its own laws, i.e. of itself, must be the point from which all things else are to be viewed; and without affirming any thing, he began to inquire himself, and to lead others to inquire, into the distinction between the accidental and the real" (189). The view of Christian *Bildung* that Alcott and Peabody, and later Fuller, practice at the Temple School owes to the Eastward-looking Plato more than its Socratically dialogic form, conceiving, in Peabody's words, "that all other souls are potentially what Jesus was actually; that every soul is an incarnation of the infinite; that it never will think clearly till it has mentally transcended time and space; that it never will feel in harmony with itself until its sensibility is commensurate with all beings" (191).

🖙 Thus, although it was the first sutra translation in English, by the time *The Dial* published Peabody's pages from the Lotus Sutra—almost a decade after her *Record of a School*—the Transcendentalists were well aware that their exposure to Buddhism was scarcely virginal. They knew that the Ancient Greeks as well as the German Romantics, their two main points of identification in "Western" culture, wrote prolifically of Asia as a likely place of intellectual, linguistic, and spiritual origin (Halbfass 2–23, 69–138). Little as they were in a position to know about Buddhist and Hindu thought, their own thought, as they knew well, was not innocent of but to a great extent already constituted by it. They would even have posited with the midcentury Indologist Max Müller, "We all come from the East—all that we value most has come to us from the East, and in going to the East . . . everybody ought to feel that he is going to his 'old home,' full of memories, if only he can read them" (29).

Without dramatizing the Germanic uncanniness of Müller's image, I would like to pause and acknowledge in this New England moment a very indicative hermeneutic situation. It is, I believe, still that of many Western-raised inquirers who seek encounters with Asian thought, aware at once both of a blanketing ignorance and at the same time of the always already internal positioning of Asian within "Western" intellectual and spiritual culture.

There is an American brand of popularizing Buddhist audiotapes (Sogyal Rinpoche, Lama Surya Das, meditation music) called Sounds True. I used to think this an unfortunate choice of name for spiritual teachings, imagining it spoken with a skeptical shrug: "*Sounds* true, but . . ." More recently, though, I've noticed that for all its modesty, "sounds true" is a good description of how it feels to assent to or learn from these teachings. It describes mainly an exchange of recognition—at best, of surprising recognition. As if the template of truth is already there inside the listener, its own lineaments clarified by the encounter with a teaching that it can then apprehend as "true."

As with the Transcendentalists, it's hard to know how to think about this hermeneutic situation. It would be plausible to discredit such "learning" as completely tautological, the projection of Western commonplaces, our already-known, onto the glamorizing screen of a fantasied Orient. Or this encounter could be described as a scene of adaptation, where the Western consumer selects from a complex Buddhist tradition only those elements that symmetrically answer to specific situational needs, and arrogantly labels the result "Buddhism" tout court.

Another possibility is that the sense of recognition arises from bringing together with its Buddhist original some historically Buddhist idea now naturalized by its continued usage in Western thought. For example, any emphasis on nondualism is liable to "sound true" to me, and I'm not the first to have tried to trace a tropism toward the nondual historically through, say, deconstruction and its modern predecessors to a series of progressively more speculative Asian contacts extending backward through various Christian heresies, neo-Platonism, Gnosticism, Plato, the pre-Socratics, and so on.

This genealogical perspective, however, opens onto two kinds of infinite regress. One is historical: at the time of the Transcendentalists as now, there was already a strong tradition (it goes back at least to the Renaissance) of speculative reconstructions that share the same shape and goal. Thus, what begins as an empiricist survey of intellectual history quickly turns to a vertiginous mirror-play of what may be quite fantasmatic historiographies involving hermetic, esoteric, Masonic, theosophical, occult, Rosicrucian, and other such Western-based traditions. At the same time, the perspective of personal history is equally frustrating. If Sounds True tapes sound true to me, it can't be simply because they sound like deconstruction; after all, what made deconstruction sound true? As far as I can remember (for what that's worth), nondualistic teachings have always sounded truest to me.

A further possibility in this hermeneutic situation is that the teachings one gravitates to sound true because they *are* true, and that certain people, Eastern and Western, simply recognize them as such through some kind of individual access to an ahistorical, world-overarching stratum of the *philosophia perennis.*

Each of these divergent ways of viewing the situation has its own history and scholarship, and each makes very different appeals to the subjective groundings of experience, thought, and politics. They have in common, however, that they leave untouched the apparently tautological nature of the pedagogical scene itself. By the criterion of "sounds true," one can apparently learn only what one already knows—whether one knows it through one's "own" native culture, through long-term cultural introjection of historically foreign ideas, or through direct intuition.

Buddhist pedagogy is hardly the only kind that enters on this familiar hermeneutic circle. The Heideggerian paradox/impasse/scandal of being able to learn only versions of what you already know or find only what you have already learned to look for is both theoretically and strategically familiar across the disciplines of Western scholarship. Here the hermeneutic tautology is always available as a fulcrum of delegitimization, yet never fully integrated in the practice of any disciplinary protocol. For how could it be? At most, it is itself an object of study.

In Buddhist pedagogical thought, however, the apparent tautology of learning what you already know does not seem to constitute a paradox, nor an impasse, nor a scandal. It is not even a problem. If anything, it is a deliberate and defining practice.

When Elizabeth Palmer Peabody one day walked right smack into a tree, she was naturally asked whether she had not seen it in her path. "I saw it," she became famous for replying, "but I did not *realize* it" (Ronda 261). If the story points to a certain Transcendental fuzziness, it also indicates her interest in a distinctively Buddhist opening out of the psychology and phenomenology of knowing. In modern Western common sense, after all, to learn something is to cross a simple threshold; once you've *learned* it you *know* it, and then you will always know it until you *forget* it (or maybe *repress* it). In this model, learning the same thing again makes as much sense as getting the same pizza delivered twice.

Colloquially, though only colloquially, even English differentiates among, say, being exposed to a given idea or proposition, catching on to it, taking it seriously, having it sink in, and wrapping your mind around it. To the degree that these can be differentiated, of course, the problem of tautology disappears. In Buddhist thought the space of such differences is central rather than epiphenomenal. To go from *knowing* something to *realizing* it, in Peabody's formulation, is seen as a densely processual undertaking that can require years or lifetimes. Even to "tolerate" the incomprehensible idea that all things are unborn, for example — even for a bodhisattva — involves three separate evolutionary stages of knowing the same thing (Thurman, *Holy* 5). And one's developing understanding of form passes such distinct milestones as the seeing of form; the seeing of external form by one with the concept of internal formlessness; the physical realization of liberation from form and its successful consolidation; the full entrance into the infinity of space through transcending all conceptions of matter; the full entrance into the infinity of consciousness, having transcended the sphere of the infinity of space; the full entrance into the infinity of nothingness, having transcended the sphere of the infinity of consciousness; and the full entrance into the sphere of neither consciousness nor unconsciousness, having transcended the sphere of nothingness (153).

A likely reason Buddhism places its rich psychology of learning at front and center in this way, rather than deprecating any apparent circularity, as most Western thought does, is that the fact of recognition itself is an end as well as a means of Buddhist knowing. In many Mahayana manifestations especially, *realization* substantively means *recognition* — of the Buddha, the nature of mind, phenomena, the guru, emptiness, apparitions in the bardo — *as not other than oneself.* Clearly, such recognition can be no perfunctory cognitive event.

A new fold, then, in the Transcendentalists' hermeneutic situation and in some of our own. The Western reader drawn to Buddhist pedagogical thinking may be most at risk of decontextualizing and misrecognizing it, riding roughshod over its cultural difference, even recasting it in her own image — the worst Orientalizing vices identified by recent critical scholarship — just to the degree that she can apprehend it through a Buddhist sense of knowing rather than a Western one. Conversely, from within the framework of the Buddhist respect for realization as both dense process and active practice, a theorized scholarly skepticism as to whether Buddhism can be known by Westerners may reveal its own dependence on an eerily thin Western phenomenology of "knowing."

☞ Whenever I want my cat to look at something instructive — a full moon, say, or a photograph of herself — a predictable choreography ensues. I point at the thing I want her to look at, and she, roused to curiosity, fixes her attention on the tip of my extended index finger and begins to explore it with delicate sniffs.

Every time this scene of failed pedagogy gets enacted (and it's frequent, because I am no better at learning not to point than my cat is at learning not to sniff) the two of us are caught in a pedagogical problematic that has fascinated teachers of Buddhism since Sakyamuni. In fact, its technical name in Buddhist writing is "pointing at the moon," and it opens on a range of issues about both language and the nonlinguistic that became engaging to Western teachers and learners only in the twentieth century.

It seems likely that to Elizabeth Peabody, Bronson Alcott, and many other nineteenth-century Western teachers, the recognition/realization aspect of Buddhist pedagogy, discussed above, allowed for significant misrecognition above all in the image of their own hope for a seamless pedagogy of affirmative identification. As Thomas Tweed points out in *The American Encounter with Buddhism: 1844–1912*, even the most interested Americans historically resisted most of the crucially negative aspects of Buddhism. From the beginnings of European Indology, for instance, and despite expressions of the same preference in Classical Greece, Western scholarship presented a stony wall of incredulity to both the Hindu and Buddhist assumption that the happiest fate is not to be born (or reborn). Schopenhauer and the later Freud aside, to find a motive in nonbeing was thought, for some reason, to fall outside the definitional bounds of the human. The monism of the Transcendentalists, likewise, quite refused the whole negational turn in Buddhism; the intuition that nature and spirit are one, and solidity an illusion of the senses, never emerged onto a teaching of emptiness.

Similarly, the eager Transcendentalist apprehension of learning as a form of recognition never grappled, as have many Buddhist traditions, with the corresponding question of how—indeed whether—learning might proceed in the absence of spontaneous recognition. The multilayeredness and long duration of bodhisattva pedagogy, after all, point to its difficulty as clearly as narratives of sudden enlightenment point to its great simplicity. Bronson Alcott's sense of mental limits attached exclusively to the difficulty of conceiving anything negative. As Peabody notes, in one lesson "the word *none* was referred to its origin in the words *no-one*. Mr. Alcott asked them if they could think of *nothing at all,* or if they did not think of *some* or *one* in order to be able to get the abstract idea of nothing. . . . Mr. Alcott thinks it wise to let the children learn the limits of the understanding by occasionally feeling them" (Peabody, *Record* 29).

For Peabody herself, as for Alcott, the nature of language itself raised few pedagogical problems; if anything, it offered a providentially apt medium for spiritual instruction. "Language," she wrote, "being of both natures, spiritual and material, makes an elemental sphere for the intellectual life, beyond the material; in short, makes a metaphysical world, in which the finite and the infinite spirits commune with other finite spirits and the Infinite One" (*Lectures* 93). Even less problematized, however, was the theoretical priority of a resort to the nonverbal, ostentive method: essentially, pointing at things. Alcott's General Maxims include the instruction "To teach principally a Knowledge of things, not of words" and "To teach, illustrating by sensible and tangible objects" (318). Over the years, and under the increasing influence of the German Romantic educator Froebel, Peabody grew even more emphatic about indicating "things": "It is a first principle that the object, motion, or action, should precede the word that names them. . . . It is the laws of *things* that are the laws of *thought*" (*Lectures* 48).

Buddhist pedagogy is far less sanguine about both saying things and pointing to them. As Walter Hsieh summarizes, "Employing speech as a skillful means, the Buddha spoke many sutras, which should only be taken as 'the finger that points to the moon,' not the moon itself. The Buddha said, 'I have not taught a single word during the forty-nine years of my Dharma preaching.' The sutras often admonish us to rely on meaning rather than on mere words. . . . Readers should bear in mind that it is not the words themselves but the attachment to words that is dangerous. The crucial function of the sutras as a finger pointing to the moon should be upheld" (in Chang 23 n. 20). The implication of the finger/moon image is that pointing may invite less misunderstanding than speech, but that even its nonlinguistic concreteness cannot shield it from the slippery problems that surround reference.

To put the issue another way, the overattached learner—my cat, say—is mistaking the kind of speech act, or we can just say the kind of act, that pointing is: for me, the relevant illocution is "to indicate," while for her, it is "to proffer." It is the same kind of mistake that Stephen Batchelor finds in the creedal treatment of the Buddha's four noble truths as parallel, propositional *beliefs* ("'Life is Suffering,' 'The Cause of Suffering Is Craving'—and so on"), rather than as active and performatively differentiated *injunctions* (to "*understanding* anguish, *letting go* of its origins, *realizing* its cessation, and *cultivating* the path"; 4–5).

Perhaps the most distinctive way Mahayana Buddhism has tried to negotiate the "finger pointing at the moon" issue is through the ostentive language of thusness or suchness (Sk. *Tathatā*). As Kukai wrote, "The Dharma is beyond speech, but without speech it cannot be revealed. Suchness transcends forms, but without depending on forms it cannot be realized. Though one may at times err by taking the finger pointing at the moon to be the moon itself, the buddha's teachings which guide people are limitless" (in Hakeda 145–46). When a Buddha is referred to as the Tathāgata or "thus-come" one, or when a twelfth-century Japanese text advises that even momentary contemplation of the "suchness" of ordinary things is a guarantee of speedy enlightenment (Stone 199), the gesture of indication is being used in at least a double way. It alludes to the supposed self-evidence and immediacy of the phenomenon pointed at, but at the same time to its ineffability, ungraspability, and indeed emptiness of self-nature. "In its dynamic aspect," in W. T. de Bary's formulation, thusness is "manifestation, the phenomenon, the realm of Facts" (167). In this sense it could be compared to "hecceity," Duns Scotus's Latin word for thusness, which Deleuze borrows to designate the sheer presence or "perfect individuality" of, for example, "an hour, a day, a season . . . a degree of heat, an intensity" (Deleuze and Parnet 92). In its "static aspect" in Buddhism, on the other hand, de Bary says, "Suchness is the Void, the noumenon, the realm of Principle." And in this sense of emptiness, suchness may again correspond to Deleuze's hecceity: as anything that, while evoking perception, involves neither intrinsic identity nor a split between perceiver and perceived.

Thusness seems, then, to compact into a single gesture—the baseline pedagogical recourse of pointing—the double movement of an apperceptive attraction to phenomena in all their immeasurable, inarticulable specificity, and at the same time an evacuation of the apparent ontological grounds of their specificity and, indeed, their being. The endless vibrancy of this resonant double movement suggests what the Dalai Lama may mean when he offers, as an image of emptiness, the inside of a bell. Tathatā, moreover, besides involving form with emptiness, involves all forms with all others, nondually: "each identical with the totality of all that is and encompassing all others within itself" (Stone, 201).

Hence, finally, in the view of thusness, even the distinction between finger and moon dissolves, and with it perhaps the immemorial injunction against confusing them. As a contemporary Zen abbot notes, "The finger pointing to the moon is the moon, and the moon is the finger . . . they realize each other" (Loori, 8). A koan commentary elaborates: "When the monk asked about the meaning of 'the moon,' the master [Fa Yen] answered 'to point at'; when someone else asked about the meaning of 'to point at' the master replied 'the moon.' Why was it so? The deepest reasoning, probably, was in the Enlightened mind of the Ch'an master, where there was no distinction between what the ordinary mind called 'to point at' and 'the moon.' To him, the relation between the two was similar to the relation of an ocean to its waves" (Holstein 49).

However liberating conceptually, though, the compaction of such complexly realized meaning into "thus" and "such" also indicates a kind of pedagogical irreducibility. It seems to mean that Buddhist pedagogy offers no more elementary minim of understanding. When the pointing gesture that is the default for inarticulate teaching already itself comprises the difficult lesson, it may be a case of If you have to ask, you'll never know. (Not in this life, anyway.) In contrast to the democratic optimism of American education in assuming that every lesson can be divided into ever more bite-sized, ever more assimilable bits, the wisdom traditions of Buddhism, because of their holographic structure, have to assume that students have already surmounted a fairly high threshold of recognition.

☞ In the United States it seems to have fallen to the twentieth-century popularizers of Zen, after World War II, to begin to articulate the centrality in many forms of Buddhism of this radical doubt that a basic realization can be communicated at all. After all, if Zen practice cannot promise to bring one methodically over the high learning threshold of satori, it at least offers distinct practices, such as wrestling with koans, for dramatizing and perhaps exhausting the impossibility of methodical learning. Furthermore, the antischolasticism of Zen and the often anti-intellectualism of the counterculture merged in a durable consciousness of the limits of verbal articulation. The 1960s heyday of these explorations, even more than the Transcendentalists' heyday, was one when a critique of school institutions became the vehicle of almost every form of utopian investment; if Buddhist explorations were peripheral to the student movement, they nonetheless both enabled and were enabled by it.

As this form of negation gained prominence among Zen popularizers, it also made ideas such as emptiness more intelligible to Americans than they had been and showed that their importance was pedagogical as much as metaphysical. The influential and pragmatically detailed *Three Pillars of Zen*, for example, published in 1965 and introducing a wide audience to both the practice and theory of Zen teaching, revolves around advice like that of Rinzai: "There is nothing in particular to realize" (in Kapleau, 194).[1] Postwar readers responded with excited recognition to the sense of teaching and learning as (nearly) impossible tasks, lonely where they are not in fact conflictual. As Alan Watts wrote in 1957: "The basic position of Zen is that it has nothing to say, nothing to teach. . . . Therefore the master does not 'help' the student in any way. . . . On the contrary, he goes out of his way to put obstacles and barriers in the student's path" (163). In their pursuit, Zen practitioners of the 1950s and 1960s drew on an ethos of solitary existential heroics of the soul. Kapleau, for instance, quotes Mumon's advice for working on a first koan: "Do not construe Mu as nothingness and do not conceive it in terms of existence or non-existence. [You must reach the point where you feel] as though you had swallowed a red-hot iron ball that you cannot disgorge despite your every effort" (76). Through much of their tropism toward the negative ran a celebration of "sheer will power" (95); to that extent, Zen popularizers offered a version of selfhood whose relation to emptiness and nonbeing was hardly clearer than the Transcendentalists' had been.

Both the efflorescence of the 1960s counterculture and the sense of political discouragement at its collapse were among the conditions for development of the conscious dying movement in England and America after 1980. Closer influences have been the widening Tibetan diaspora, the high-visibility AIDS emergency, and the already ongoing movement for hospice and palliative care. One effect of the sudden appearance of AIDS among young, educated, articulate men (among the many whom it affects) — especially because the disease is both gradual and so far incurable — has been the carving out of a cultural space in the West in which to articulate the subjectivity of the dying. This space, until the 1980s rather imperiously foreclosed by the melodramas of modern medical delivery, has now also become increasingly available to some others facing the likelihood of early death, and indeed to some of the aged. Interestingly, though it has none of the communitarian ambition of some 1960s politics, the conscious dying movement has a far greater involvement with the Buddhist pedagogy of nonself.

Perhaps it is not surprising that those of us now moving through this subjectivity have an unusual sense of permission to explore aspects of Buddhism that were most troubling to Americans of the nineteenth century. To be sure there are still raucous voices adjuring us, *especially* in the name of "East-West mind-body medicine," that we are the last people who should be allowed to lapse from an unremitting regimen of positive thinking. But when the most damning of the West's historical epithets about Asian negativity — pessimism, quietism, extinction, exhaustion — already form an inescapable part of any given day's stream of consciousness, what sanction remains against exploring more of the vibrant realms of "no" in Buddhist thought?

The bardo that extends from diagnosis until death makes some people seek out Buddhist teachings; in many Buddhist teachings, however, it is also itself viewed as an extraordinary pedagogical tool. Perhaps nothing dramatizes the distance between knowledge and realization as efficiently as diagnosis with a fatal disease. As advertised, it does concentrate the mind wonderfully (even if by shattering it) and makes inescapably vivid the distance between *knowing* that one will die and *realizing* it. The effect is only heightened by all the very exigent lifelong uses that each of us has had for the idea of dying, whether shaped by depression, hysteria, hypochondria, stoic or existential dramas; these contrast starkly with the seemingly absolute opacity of one's own death to cognitive knowing. A reality index: when I was healthy, I assumed that Pascal's wager could only be seen as something quite ignoble.

The writings and practices around conscious dying seem to bring an aesthetic of rather Zenlike minimalism to the otherwise lush proliferation of Tibetan Buddhist teachings. From Baba Ram Dass's *Be Here Now* in 1971, to Stephen Levine's *Who Dies?* eleven years later, to Sogyal Rinpoche's *Tibetan Book of Living and Dying* eleven years after that, the account of the bardo teachings grows exponentially more detailed and expansive. Yet even Sogyal, as we have seen, keeps his reader grounded in an almost childish rhetorical simplicity; that seems a mode in which the reader can move freely through the severe cultural and ontological dislocations of the journey. To go from Sogyal's book to almost any other Tibetan text in English, moreover—to the many books that are not shaped by this particular Anglo-American-Tibetan conversation about dying—is still to be brought up short by the denseness of an alterity at which even he had barely hinted.

In calling the aesthetic of these writings Zenlike I do not refer to their affective tonality. All of them, including Sogyal's, are brimming with emotional expressiveness. The Zen aspect—maybe better called Tao-like—appears instead in the extremely high value placed on economy of means. The Buddha's own "skill in means," which always refers to pedagogical means, can take extravagantly elaborate forms throughout the sutras. In this modern project for teaching and learning to die, by contrast, quiet action or even negative action seem to represent skill. The attempt is to work as much as possible, in a formulation from Vimalakīrti, "by silence, inexpressibility, and unteachability" (Thurman, *Holy* 86). No one fails to die; at best, one can get out of one's way.

Thus, the instructions for dying are actually the same as the instructions for working with the dying. Both teaching and learning in this situation involve the most passive and minimal of performances. "Opening to" (a person or predicament), "opening around" or "softening around" (a site of pain), *listening,* relaxation, spaciousness, patience in the sense of *pateor* or lying open, shared breathing: these practices of nondoing, some of them sounding hardly more than New Age commonplaces, seem able to support a magnetic sense of the real far into the threshold of extinguished identity. As Sandra Butler writes, "It has been the liminal experience of caring for those who are dying, their flesh decaying, their minds trapped in failing bodies, their hearts pounding, life beating against narrow ribs, that has taught me the necessary silences between words, the pauses where breath emerges, the soundlessness of connection" (4). And it's a surprise, though it shouldn't be, that a nondoing verging on extinction would be the condition of possibility for *companionship* in these realms of unmaking.

As a pedagogical aesthetic, this self-effacing minimalism draws together "Eastern" and "Western" influences in a now familiar historical feedback loop. In 1836, for example, describing her ambition to offer spiritual and political Conversations for adult women in Boston, the Transcendentalist Margaret Fuller was unsure of even being intelligible to her correspondent as she struck a note apparently new: "I know it is very hard [for participants] to lay aside the shelter of vague generalities, the cant of coterie criticism and the delicate disdains of *good society* and fearless meet the light although it flow from the sun of truth. Yet, as without such generous courage nothing can be done, or learned I cannot but hope to see many capable of it. . . . General silence or side talks would paralyze me. I should feel coarse and misplaced if I were to be haranguing too much. In former instances I have been able to make it easy and even pleasant to twenty five out of thirty to bear their part, to question, to define, to state and examine their opinions. If I could not do as much now I should consider myself unsuccessful and should withdraw" (in Kornfeld, 98–99).

By the end of the next century, on the other hand, Robert Thurman's rather similar description of a Buddha's own pedagogy of self-effacement, in *Essential Tibetan Buddhism,* gives the impression of being as rooted in familiarly American cultural forms as are therapy groups or committee facilitators: "Thus a Buddha embodiment was supposed to be a manifestation of compassion with no other purpose than to open people up to their own higher potential. . . . A Buddha has no solid sense of center as we do. . . . A Buddha's energy is entirely with and for us when we encounter it; there is in it no energy scoop or surge opposed to our own. . . . Such a being, whatever his or her form, is the focal node of a field in which other beings find maximal opportunities for their own evolutionary advancement, gaining dramatically increased understanding, improved emotions, perceptions, and insights, feeling much better, often rising to the occasion and doing and understanding much better" (21–22).

I don't want to suggest that the American sound of Thurman's writing brands it as either distorting or appropriative. Instead, its very ways of being "Western" locate it in an ongoing, palimpsestic, but very dynamic conversation with, among, even within a variety of Asian teachings.[2]

☞ What can it mean to see the pointing finger and the indicated moon as finally inseparable? I understand this image as part of a continuing Buddhist meditation on how means relate to ends. A nonpedagogic image, such as seeing the journey itself as the destination, makes it easy enough to see means and ends as inseparable. But with an image that necessarily evokes a scene of teaching, and in the context of the long, highly self-conscious tradition of Buddhist hermeneutical thought, it is apparently considered necessary to emphasize the nonidentity of pedagogical means and ends on a routine basis, and only rarely to invoke their inseparability.

The pedagogy of illness and dying, however, as I have already suggested, brings means and ends into unaccustomed relations with each other, and dramatizes how hard it can be to assign the labels of pupil, teacher, and teaching on any stable basis. The invalid Vimalakīrti, for example, is said to "manifest himself as if sick" "out of [his] very skill in liberative technique" (Thurman, Holy 21). The bardo teachings treat death itself as "the key or tool that enables us to discover and recognize [opportunities for liberation], and make the fullest possible use of them" (Sogyal 104). It is a commonplace in the conscious dying movement—but also more than a commonplace— that, in Cicely Saunders's words, "Sooner or later all who work with dying people know they are receiving [from the dying] more than they are giving" (in Sogyal 177). In fact, there is a subgenre of popular spiritual books with titles like Lessons from the Dying and Final Gifts about how healthy people can learn from other people's dying. There is even a year-long self-help program that involves pretending to oneself that one has a fatal disease (Levine, Year).

Thus, while the sickbed or deathbed is continually produced as a privileged scene of teaching, the assignment of pedagogical roles is unstable and so is the assignment of means and ends. Do illness and death constitute skillful means to some further end, or are they problems to be solved by using (other) skillful means? To practice living as mindfully as if in the constant presence of death; to be able to die as one has lived, with consciousness and dignity; to be able, like Vimalakīrti, to learn or teach about emptiness through proximity to death; to experience the bardos of death and becoming in such a way as to achieve freedom from involuntary rebirth — these goals are not mutually exclusive, but they are certainly distinct. Among them all it is hard to tell which finger is pointing at which moon.

The writing of the entire conscious dying movement, even that of Sogyal Rinpoche, shares a nondenominational commitment designed to make it engaging to readers of various religious affiliations or none. The sense, that is, of the undecidable closeness of ends and means, indeed of their near inseparability, is a consistent hallmark of this movement — in fact, the most powerful manifestation of its economy of means. What remain irreducible in the Tibetan teachings, however, even in their most Western-friendly versions, are their pragmatic emphasis on rebirth and their confident narrative of the subjective experience of actually dying.

When I talk with healthy people about experiencing illness in the context of this movement, our discussion often breaks crudely on the shoals of reincarnation: Do I believe in that? The person with whom I'm speaking says she could never do so. These interlocutions tend to be isolating and defensive on both sides.[3]

From a pedagogical point of view, at any rate, the Tibetan teachings on the bardos and rebirth are irrepressibly rich. The framework of rebirth casts the single human life in the context of a much longer, very complex learning project. Instead of constituting a single, momentous master-class graded on a pass/fail basis, like Christianity — or even ungraded, like the secular version — the individual lifetime is more like a year of one's schooling, a year preceded and followed by other school years at the appropriate levels. Reincarnation differs from K–12 or college, however, in some crucial ways. Every summer, almost every student loses almost all memory of who he or she is. Come September, most have forgotten they are even enrolled in school. Although in principle there is an orderly sequence of grade levels, very few students move through it in orderly fashion; instead, they drop back five grades, graduate directly from kindergarten, or repeat fourth grade several thousand times. (There are no social promotions. But the annual amnesia keeps people from feeling shamed or discouraged by failure.) Students differ, as well, on the purpose of their education. Some just want it to go on forever. Others, disliking it, see it as preparing them to leave school behind for good. Others don't think about a world outside the school and look forward to going back to their classes in the role of student teacher. In fact, because of the memory problem, many in each grade are left to speculate that they or their classmates already *are* student teachers.

At least at present, I can't see what sense it would make either to believe or disbelieve such an account. The most and least I can say is that exposure to it, including less slapstick versions, has rearranged the landscape of consciousness that surrounds, for me, issues of dying. Specifically, the landscape has become a lot more spacious. I remember the very painful epistemological/psychological knots that I used to be able to wriggle into but not out of: Am I really afraid of death or not? How can I tell the difference between fatigue with living and attraction to dying? How do I know if my confident atheism will wither like a leaf under a hot wind? Do I really, *really* realize, even now, that I'm mortal?

The constricting, obsessional nature of these questions is probably evident enough from their grasp at the first-person singular, as though that were a specimen to be immobilized rather than a vagrant place-holder. A worse mark of their unskillfulness is that, while obsessed with them, even I found them numbingly boring.

The question Do I *really believe* in rebirth? might not work so differently from those or, indeed, be much more interesting. Responding to the insistence on rebirth of scholars such as Robert Thurman, Stephen Batchelor's 1997 book, *Buddhism without Beliefs,* tries to articulate a stance of neither believing nor disbelieving. Batchelor argues for a principled agnosticism as the best way of negotiating between "responsibility to the future" on the one hand (113) and "the cliches and dogmas of other epochs" on the other (104). Yet he depends on an often unquestioned twentieth-century empiricism. Even to speculate about rebirth, he complains, "lead[s] us far from the Buddha's agnostic and pragmatic perspective and into a consideration of metaphysical views that cannot be demonstrated or refuted, proven or disproven" (36). "An agnostic Buddhist would not regard the Dharma as a source of 'answers' to questions of where we came from, where we are going, what happens after death. He would seek such knowledge in the appropriate domains: astrophysics, evolutionary biology, neuroscience, etc." (18). (I was surprised to learn that any of these disciplines studies what happens after death.) And even at its least programmatic, Batchelor's agnosticism is marked by its unresting disdain for *consolation*. He deprecates belief in rebirth, for example, as "the luxury of consolation" (43).

For all its claim to openness and not-knowing, then, Batchelor's book often shares the feel of those tight, painful psychic knots such as Do I *really realize* . . . ? It isolates and immobilizes the self in a similar way, for example. Despite all his contemptuous usage of the word, I do not suppose that Batchelor, who speaks of "long[ing] to appease the anguish of others," really considers *their* consolation a contemptible thing (104). Instead, it is evidently he who must never desire or need consolation. His existential demands on, well, *someone* are unpitying; he expresses contempt for any "failure to summon forth the courage to risk a nondogmatic and nonevasive stance" on "crucial existential matters" (38). "Agnosticism is no excuse for indecision," *someone* is sternly reminded. "If anything, it is a catalyst for action" (38). To construct and maintain this morally muscular figure is an expensive undertaking. Among the things sacrificed is that consciousness of impermanence, or even emptiness, by which the figure might recognize itself as not permanently other than the "others" who have a need of more compassionate treatment. In this respect, the continually circulating pedagogy of the conscious dying movement seems more flexible, multidirectional, and effective.

I don't know that multiple samsaric rebirths sound all that consoling anyway. What is more palpable to me is the skillfulness of the Tibetan teachings as a presence in the world of people dealing with mortality. Being and learning to unbe a self are both less smothering in a space that already holds amnesia, metamorphosis, and ever-shifting relationality—indeed, that holds them as the crucible of all phenomena.

Simply to be with this teaching makes far more difference than would either believing or disbelieving it. Take, for example, the game or meditation—so likely to arise with the teaching of rebirth—of picturing your life, even your character, otherwise than as it is. So many questions emerge. Yet their emergence is not into a context of blame or self-blame, nor of will or resolve. The space is more like—what? Wish? Somewhere, at least, liberated by both possibility and impossibility, and especially by the relative untetheredness to self.

Suppose I am thinking about some good things I have never done because of shyness, for instance, or because of being so averse to physical discomfort. I find now that the question What would have made those qualities different?, askable to the depth of a life history and even beyond, is a surprisingly easy one to generate and follow. Many reflections are able to "open around" it as they have never been before, never when the question was really the shamingly constricted, deontological one about *me*. There is so much companionable space in the imaginable, tutelary difference of a being whom the present I will never know, and who in turn need never wonder about the thread of hope spun somehow into its own, characteristic courage. Does it make sense to ask whether such teachings concern the present or the future? For at least some people, through a number of histories, conceiving the Buddhist teachings pedagogically has long offered a way to keep recognizing their elusive ends in their skillfully intimate means.

NOTES

This essay is full of the memory of my friend and student Brian Selsky, who took his life on Yom Kippur of 1997.

1. The view of the Dharma as fundamentally resisting transmission hardly goes unchallenged in the sutras. Peabody found a very different, almost seamless view of spiritual education in translating from the Lotus Sutra. Even in Vimalakīrti, famous for an intractable silence, we read of a head-turning range of pedagogical techniques: "There are Buddha fields that accomplish the Buddha work by means of bodhisattvas; those that do so by means of light; those that do so by means of the tree of enlightenment; those that do so by means of the physical beauty and the marks of the Tathāgata; those that do so by means of religious robes; those that do so by means of food; those that do so by means of water; those that do so by means of gardens; those that do so by means of houses; those that do so by means of mansions; those that do so by means of magical incarnation; those that do so by means of empty space; those that do so by means of lights in the sky" (in Thurman, *Holy*, 86). And in the sutra on Skillful Means it seems as though a bodhisattva teaches through something like the physical extension of a mimetic force field: "Venerable Lord, it is like this. All sentient beings who stand before Sumera, the king of mountains, have the same color—the color of gold—regardless of whether they have thoughts of hatred, serenity, or attachment, or thoughts hindered in access to the doctrine. In the same way, venerable Lord, all sentient beings who stand before bodhisattvas, whether they have thoughts of hatred, serenity, or attachment, or thoughts hindered in access to the doctrine, all have thoughts of the same complexion—the complexion of omniscience" (Tatz 45).

2. It also speaks to an alternative, minimalist tradition within European Romantic pedagogy (see Rancière). And note that all three of these examples are taken from educational work aimed at adults; it makes sense that minimalist means in teaching would

emerge most readily in work with adults—a fortiori, with the dying—rather than children. It also bears emphasizing that the Transcendentalists' interest in adult education may be the most substantial of their legacies. Although Peabody, after studying with Froebel in Germany, became the pioneer of the immensely successful kindergarten movement in the United States, the Transcendentalists' commitment to continuing, nonremedial, spiritually oriented pedagogy involving adults of their own class was more original and arguably has been even more influential.

3. The fate of Bronson Alcott's Temple School may offer an indication of how divisive the question of rebirth can be in the West. The firestorm of public criticism that engulfed the school in 1836–1837 is usually attributed to "rumors of talk about conception and childbirth" (Ronda 128). But Peabody's own sense, at any rate, as she tried unsuccessfully to head off the controversy, was that the most sensitive issue raised by the school's discussions of "birth" did not involve sex education, but rather rebirth. She denied that Alcott taught the "Oriental doctrine of pre-existence and emanation," but wrote, "Mr. Alcott indeed believes that birth is a spiritual act and fact prior to embodiment. . . . For my own part, I believe that this is the only way of conceiving the unity of a spirit; and that it is the pre-existence meant in Wordsworth's ode on Immortality, and that which Plato himself meant to teach; and that it certainly is the doctrine of Christianity taught by Jesus Christ" (in Ronda 128). The conflation of sex scandal with reincarnation scandal is certainly striking, whether done by Bostonians of the 1830s or by later historians.

WORKS CITED

Adams, James Eli. *Dandies and Desert Saints: Styles of Victorian Manhood.* Ithaca, N.Y.: Cornell University Press, 1995.

Alcott, A. Bronson. *How Like an Angel Came I Down: Conversations with Children on the Gospels.* Ed. Alice O. Howell. Hudson, NY: Lindisfarne Press, 1991. Reprint of *Conversations with Children on the Gospels,* Boston: James Munroe and Co., 1836. 2 vols.

Anderson, Benedict R. O'G. *Mythology and the Tolerance of the Javanese.* Ithaca, NY: Modern Indonesia Project Monograph Series, 1965; rpt. 1969.

Austin, J. L. *How to Do Things with Words.* Ed. J. O. Urmson. New York: Oxford University Press, 1970.

Basch, Michael Franz. "The Concept of Affect: A Re-Examination." *Journal of the American Psychoanalytic Association* 24 (1976):759–77.

Batchelor, Stephen. *Buddhism without Beliefs: A Contemporary Guide to Awakening.* New York: Riverhead Books, 1997.

Benjamin, Walter. *Charles Baudelaire: A Lyric Poet in the Era of High Capitalism.* Trans. Harry Zohn. London: Verso, 1983.

Benveniste, Emile. *Problems in General Linguistics.* Trans. Mary Elizabeth Meek. Miami: University of Miami Press, 1971.

Berger, Peter. *Sacred Canopy: Elements of a Sociological Theory of Religion.* Garden City, NJ: Doubleday, 1966.

Bersani, Leo. *The Culture of Redemption.* Cambridge, MA: Harvard University Press, 1990.

Bishop, Elizabeth. *The Complete Poems 1927–1979.* New York: Farrar, Straus and Giroux, 1979.

Bora, Renu. "Outing Texture." In *Novel Gazing: Queer Readings in Fiction,* ed. Eve Kosofsky Sedgwick. Durham, NC: Duke University Press, 1997.

Broucek, Francis J. "Shame and Its Relationship to Early Narcissistic Developments." *International Journal of Psychoanalysis* 63 (1982): 369–78.

Butler, Judith. *Gender Trouble: Feminism and the Subversion of Identity.* New York: Routledge, 1990.

———. "Performative Acts and Gender Constitution: An Essay in Phenomenology and Feminist Theory." In *Performing Feminisms: Feminist Critical Theory and Theatre,* ed. Sue-Ellen Case. Baltimore: Johns Hopkins University Press, 1990.

Butler, Sandra. "A Writer Returns to Silence." *Women's Cancer Resource Center Newsletter* 9.5 (fall 2001):4.

Cavafy, C. P. *Collected Poems.* Ed. George Savidis. Edmund Keeley and Philip Sherrard. Revised ed. Princeton, NJ: Princeton University Press, 1992.

Chang, Garma C. C., general ed. *A Treasury of Mahāyāna Sūtras: Selections from the Mahāratnakūṭa Sūtra.* Translated from the Chinese by the Buddhist Association of the United States. University Park: Pennsylvania State University Press, 1983.

Cleary, Thomas, trans. *Entry into the Realm of Reality: The Text. A Translation of the Gandavyuha, the Final Book of* The Avatamsaka Sutra. Boston: Shambhala, 1989.

Cvetkovich, Ann. *Mixed Feelings: Feminism, Mass Culture, and Victorian Sensationalism.* New Brunswick, NJ: Rutgers University Press, 1992.

Dalai Lama, H.H. Oral teaching on dependent origination. Chuang-Yen Monastery, New York, 25–27 May 1997.

de Bary, William Theodore, ed. *The Buddhist Tradition in India, China, and Japan.* Rpt. New York: Vintage, 1969. New York: Random House, 1972.

Deleuze, Gilles, and Claire Parnet. *Dialogues.* Trans. Hugh Tomlinson and Barbara Habberjam. New York: Columbia University Press, 1977.

de Man, Paul. *Allegories of Reading: Figural Language in Rousseau, Nietzsche, Rilke, and Proust.* New Haven: Yale University Press, 1979.

Derrida, Jacques. "Signature Event Context." In *Margins of Philosophy.* Trans. Alan Bass. Chicago: University of Chicago Press, 1982.

Descombes, Vincent. *Modern French Philosophy.* Trans. L. Scott-Fox and J. M. Harding. Cambridge, England: Cambridge University Press, 1980.

Dickens, Charles. *American Notes.* 1842. London: Penguin, 2001.

———. *Dombey and Son.* Oxford: 1848. Oxford University Press, 2001.

Dickinson, Emily. *Complete Poems of Emily Dickinson.* Boston: Little, Brown, 1960.

Eliot, George. *Daniel Deronda.* 1876. London: Penguin, 1967.

———. *Middlemarch.* 1871–72. London: Penguin, 1966.

Felman, Shoshana. *The Literary Speech Act: Don Juan with J. L. Austin, or Seduction in Two Languages.* Trans. Catherine Porter. Ithaca, NY: Cornell University Press, 1983.

Foucault, Michel. *The History of Sexuality.* Vol. 1, *An Introduction.* Trans. Robert Hurley. New York: Pantheon, 1978.

Freud, Sigmund. *The Standard Edition of the Complete Psychological Works of Sigmund Freud.* Ed. James Strachey. Trans. James Strachey et al. London: Hogarth Press, 1953–1975. 24 vols.

Fried, Michael. *Absorption and Theatricality: Painting and Beholder in the Age of Diderot.* Rpt., Chicago: University of Chicago Press, 1988.

Gibson, J. J. *The Senses Considered as Perceptual Systems.* Boston: Houghton Mifflin, 1966.

Gramsci, Antonio. *Prison Notebooks.* Ed. Joseph A. Buttigieg. New York: Columbia University Press, 1996.

Gregory, Richard L., ed., with O. L. Zangwill. *The Oxford Companion to the Mind.* Oxford: Oxford University Press, 1987.

Hakeda, Yoshito S. *Kukai: Major Works Translated with an Account of His Life and a Study of His Thought.* New York: Columbia University Press, 1972.

Halbfass, Wilhelm. *India and Europe: An Essay in Understanding.* Albany: State University of New York Press, 1988.

Halley, Janet. "Sexual Orientation and the Politics of Biology: A Critique of the Argument from Immutability." *Stanford Law Review* 46.3 (February 1994): 503–68.

Hebb, D. O. *Organization of Behavior.* New York: John Wiley and Sons, 1949.

Heims, Steve J. *Cybernetics Group.* Cambridge, MA: MIT Press, 1991.

Hertz, Neil. *The End of the Line.* New York: Columbia University Press, 1985.

Hinshelwood, R. D. *A Dictionary of Kleinian Thought.* 2d ed. Northvale, NJ: Aronson, 1991.

Hocquenghem, Guy. *Homosexual Desire.* Trans. Daniella Dangoor. Durham, NC: Duke University Press, 1993.

Hofstadter, Richard. *The Paranoid Style in American Politics and Other Essays.* New York: Knopf, 1965.

Holstein, Alexander, trans. *Pointing at the Moon: One Hundred Zen Koans from Chinese Masters.* Rutland, VT: Charles E. Tuttle, 1993.

Jacobs, Harriet A. *Incidents in the Life of a Slave Girl. Written by Herself.* Ed. Jean Fagan Yellin. Cambridge, MA: Harvard University Press, 1987.

James, Henry. *The Art of the Novel.* Rpt. Boston: Northeastern University Press, 1984.

———. *The Golden Bowl.* Harmondsworth, England: Penguin, 1980.

———. *Notebooks of Henry James.* Ed. F. O. Matthiessen and Kenneth B. Murdock. New York: Oxford University Press, 1947.

James, William. *The Correspondence of William James.* Vol. 1, *William and Henry: 1861–1884.* Ed. Ignas K. Skrupskelis and Elizabeth M. Berkeley. Charlottesville: University Press of Virginia, 1992.

Jarrell, Randall. *The Complete Poems.* New York: Farrar, Straus and Giroux, 1969.

Kapleau, Roshi Philip. *The Three Pillars of Zen.* 25th anniversary ed. New York: Doubleday Anchor, 1989.

Kornfeld, Eve. *Margaret Fuller: A Brief Biography with Documents.* Boston: Bedford Books, 1997.

Laplanche, J., and J.-B. Pontalis. *The Language of Psycho-Analysis.* Trans. Donald Nicholson-Smith. New York: Norton, 1973.

Levine, Stephen. *Who Dies? An Investigation of Conscious Living and Conscious Dying.* New York: Doubleday Anchor, 1982.

———. *A Year to Live: How to Live This Year As If It Were Your Last.* New York: Bell Tower, 1997.

Litvak, Joseph. *Caught in the Act: Theatricality in the Nineteenth Century English Novel.* Berkeley: University of California Press, 1991.

Loori, Abbot John Daido, M.R.O. "Transmission of the Light." Talk given during the Soto School's Tokubetsu Sesshin. Zen Mountain Monastery. www.zen-mtn.org/zmm/talks/teisho2.htm, 1995.

Lopez, Donald S. *Curators of the Buddha: The Study of Buddhism under Colonialism.* Chicago: University of Chicago Press, 1995.

Luger, George F., and William A. Stubblefield. *Artificial Intelligence: Structures and Strategies for Complex Problem Solving.* Redwood City, CA: Benjamin/Cummings Publishing, 1993.

Lyotard, Jean-François. *The Postmodern Condition: A Report on Knowledge.* Trans. Geoff Bennington and Brian Massumi. Minneapolis: University of Minnesota Press, 1984.

MacGregor, John M. *Metamorphosis: The Fiber Art of Judith Scott. The Outsider Artist and the Experience of Down's Syndrome.* Oakland, CA: Creative Growth Art Center, 1999.

Miller, D. A. *The Novel and the Police.* Berkeley: University of California Press, 1988.

Miller, J. Hillis. *Tropes, Parables, Performatives: Essays on Twentieth-Century Literature.* Durham, NC: Duke University Press, 1991.

Moon, Michael. *A Small Boy and Others: Imitation and Initiation in American Culture from Henry James to Andy Warhol.* Durham, NC: Duke University Press, 1998.

Morris, William. *News from Nowhere and Other Writings.* 1890. London: Penguin, 1994.

Müller, F. M. *India: What Can It Teach Us?* London: Longman, Green, 1883.

Nathanson, Donald L. *Shame and Pride: Affect, Sex, and the Birth of the Self.* New York: Norton, 1992.

Newton, Esther. *Mother Camp: Female Impersonators in America.* With a new preface. Chicago: University of Chicago Press, 1979.

Peabody, Elizabeth Palmer. *Lectures in the Training School for Kindergartners.* Boston: D. C. Heath, 1888.

———. *Record of a School: Exemplifying the General Principles of Spiritual Culture.* Boston: J. Munroe, 1835.

———, trans. "The Preaching of Buddha." *The Dial: A Magazine for Literature, Philosophy, and Religion* 4.3 (January 1844): 391–401. (Published anonymously; long attributed to Thoreau)

Pope, Alexander. *The Poems of Alexander Pope.* Ed. John Butt. New Haven: Yale University Press, 1963.

Proust, Marcel. *In Search of Lost Time.* 6 vols. Ed. D. J. Enright. Trans. Andreas Mayor and Terence Kilmartin. New York: Modern Library, 1992.

Ram Dass, Baba. *Be Here Now.* San Cristobal, NM: Lama Foundation, 1971.

Rancière, Jacques. *The Ignorant Schoolmaster: Five Lessons in Intellectual Emancipation.* Trans. Kristin Ross. Stanford: Stanford University Press, 1991.

Ricoeur, Paul. *Freud and Philosophy: An Essay on Interpretation.* Trans. Denis Savage. New Haven: Yale University Press, 1970.

Roach, Joseph R. "Slave Spectacles and Tragic Octoroons: A Cultural Genealogy of Antebellum Performance." *Theatre Survey* 33 (November 1992): 167–87.

Ronda, Bruce A. *Elizabeth Palmer Peabody: A Reformer on Her Own Terms.* Cambridge, MA: Harvard University Press, 1999.

Śāntideva. 1995. *The Bodhicaryāvatāra.* Trans. Kate Crosby and Andrew Skilton. Introduction by Paul Williams. Oxford: Oxford University Press, 1995.

Searle, John R. *Speech Acts.* Cambridge, England: Cambridge University Press, 1969.

Sedgwick, Eve Kosofsky. *Between Men: English Literature and Male Homosocial Desire.* New York: Columbia University Press, 1985.

——. *The Coherence of Gothic Conventions.* New York: Methuen, 1986.

——. *A Dialogue on Love.* Boston: Beacon, 1999.

——. *Epistemology of the Closet.* Berkeley: University of California Press, 1991.

——. *Tendencies.* Durham, NC: Duke University Press, 1993.

Silverman, Kaja. "Too Early/Too Late: Subjectivity and the Primal Scene in Henry James." *Novel* 21.2–3 (1988): 57–74.

Sloterdijk, Peter. *Critique of Cynical Reason.* Trans. Michael Eldred. Minneapolis: University of Minnesota Press, 1987.

Smith, Barbara Lee. "Judith Scott: Finding a Voice." *Fiberarts* (summer 2001): 36–39.

Sogyal Rinpoche. *The Tibetan Book of Living and Dying.* Ed. Patrick Gaffney and Andrew Harvey. San Francisco: Harper, 1993.

Stone, Jacqueline I. "The Contemplation of Suchness." In *Religions of Japan in Practice,* ed. George J. Tanabe. Princeton, NJ: Princeton University Press, 1999.

Tatz, Mark, trans. *The Skill in Means Sutra (Upayakausalya).* Delhi: Motilal Banarsidass Publishers, 1994.

Thomas, Deborah A. *Thackeray and Slavery.* Athens: Ohio University Press, 1993.

Thomas, Elizabeth Marshall. *The Tribe of Tiger: Cats and Their Culture.* New York: Simon and Schuster, 1994.

Thurman, Robert A. F. *Essential Tibetan Buddhism.* New York: HarperCollins, 1995.

——, trans. *The Holy Teaching of Vimalakirti: A Mahayana Scripture.* University Park: Pennsylvania State University Press, 1976.

Tomkins, Silvan S. *Affect Imagery Consciousness.* 4 vols. New York: Springer, 1962–1992.

——. "The Quest for Primary Motives: Biography and Autobiography of an Idea." *Journal of Personality and Social Psychology* 41.2 (1981): 306–29.

————. *Shame and Its Sisters: A Silvan Tomkins Reader.* Ed. Eve Kosofsky Sedgwick and Adam Frank. Durham, NC: Duke University Press, 1995.

Walker, Alice. *Meridian.* New York: Harcourt Brace, 1976.

Watts, Alan. *The Way of Zen.* New York: Pantheon, 1957. Rpt. New York: Vintage, 1989.

Wilden, Anthony. *System and Structure: Essays in Communication and Exchange.* London: Tavistock, 1972.

Wittgenstein, Ludwig. *Philosophical Investigations.* Trans. G. E. M. Anscombe. 3d ed. New York: Prentice Hall, 1999.

INDEX

Anger, Kenneth, 150
Antiessentialism. *See* Epistemology:
    antiessentialist; Essentialism and
    antiessentialism
Austen, Jane, 90 n.2
Austin, J. L.:
    How to Do Things with Words, 2, 6, 44,
    67–72, 76, 90, 90 n.3;
    and marriage, 45–46, 67–72;
    and texture, 16–17.
    See also Performativity; Speech acts
Autotelic, the, 19–21, 24, 99–100

Baba Ram Dass, 174
Barnes, Djuna, 150
Barthes, Roland, 147
Basch, Michael Franz, 36–38
Batchelor, Stephen, 170, 178–179
Bateson, Gregory, 99
Benjamin, Walter, 14, 16
Benveniste, Emil, 6
Bersani, Leo, 126, 151 n.2
Binarisms. *See* Dualisms; Structuralism
Biology and biologism, 93, 101–108, 111–
    114, 120 n.9;
    and finitely many (n>2) values, 108–114
Bishop, Elizabeth, 3
Bloom, Harold, 134
Bodhisattvas. *See* Buddhism: bodhisattvas
Bora, Renu, 13–15
Borensztein, Leon, 22
Broucek, Francis J., 37
Buddha, Sakyamuni, 158–159, 161, 168, 170,
    178
Buddhism, 2, 21, 153–181;
    American, 154–157;
    bodhisattvas in, 160–161, 169, 180 n.1;
    emptiness in, 169, 177, 179;
    Mahayana, 160–162, 167, 170;
    Theravada, 157;

thusness (suchness) in, 170–172;
    Tibetan (Vajrayana), 157–160, 173–180;
    Zen, 157, 171–174.
    See also Identity; Indology; Pointing;
    Reincarnation
Burke, Kenneth, 145
Burnouf, Eugène, 138
Butler, Judith, 3–6, 7, 68;
    Gender Trouble, 2, 9, 129–133, 139, 149.
    See also Epistemology: antiessentialist;
    Essentialism and antiessentialism
Butler, Sandra, 175

Camp, 63–64, 149–150, 151 n.6
Cancer, 13, 28–34, 148–149, 156
Carlyle, Thomas, 81
Cats, 153–154, 168, 170
Cavafy, C. P., 90 n.1
Cavell, Stanley, 75
Chaos theory, 106.
    See also Complexity; Systems theory
Christianity, 166, 177, 181 n.3
Complexity, 18, 25.
    See also Chaos theory; Systems theory
Cornell, Joseph, 150
Curtain, Tyler, 151 n.3
Cvetkovich, Ann, 108–112, 120 n.8
Cybernetics. *See* Systems theory

Dalai Lama, the XIVth, 157, 171
Dante, 70, 90 n.1
de Bary, W. T., 170–171
Deconstruction, 7, 62, 77, 125, 146, 165–166.
    See also Epistemology: antiessentialist;
    Essentialism and antiessentialism
Deleuze, Gilles, 8, 146, 171
DeMan, Paul, 7
Depression, 38–40
Derrida, Jacques: 3–6, 68, 75, 93.
    See also Deconstruction

Descombes, Vincent, 119
Desire. *See* Drives
Dickens, Charles:
American Notes, 83, 87;
David Copperfield, 131;
Dombey and Son, 79–87;
Nicholas Nickleby, 42;
Our Mutual Friend, 42
Dickinson, Emily, 151 n.4
Digital. *See* Analogic and digital
Displacement, 15, 140, 144.
See also Proscenium: mobile; Psychoanalysis; Spatiality
Drives, 8;
vis-à-vis affects, 17–21, 101
Dualisms:
of agency, 8, 13, 14, 21, 24 n.2, 76–77,
93–94;
hegemonic vs. subversive, 12–13;
law of excluded middle, 8;
means vs. ends, 21, 99, 161, 167, 176–180
(*see also* Autotelic, the);
mind vs. body, 113;
nature vs. culture, 94;
on vs. off, 100 (*see also* Analogic and
digital);
presence vs. absence, 94;
self vs. other, 93;
stimulus vs. response, 103–104, 113;
subject vs. object, 8, 22, 93;
subversive vs. hegemonic, 9–14, 110;
true vs. false, 91 n.3;
yes vs. no, 91 n.3.
See also Lack; Nondualism; Repressive
hypothesis; Sexual difference
Duns Scotus, 171

Eliot, George:
Daniel Deronda, 75–78, 83;
Middlemarch, 15

Emerson, Ralph Waldo, 157
Empson, William, 145
Epistemology: antiessentialist, 6, 8, 17, 110,
138–139;
Buddhist, 156;
of death, 178–180;
of marriage, 72–77;
paranoid, 126–151;
Proustian, 137–138.
See also Phenomenology: of learning
Essentialism and antiessentialism, 5–6, 8,
109–118, 120 n.9, 138–139.
See also Epistemology: antiessentialist;
Epistemology: paranoid
Euripides, 77
Exposure. *See* Epistemology: anti-
essentialist

Fay, Michael, 140
Feedback. *See* Systems theory
Felman, Shoshana, 4, 71
Feminism. *See* Activism, political: femi-
nism and
Fetishism, 15
Firbank, Ronald, 150
Foucault, Michel, 93, 109, 110, 137, 140–143;
History of Sexuality, vol. 1, 2, 9–13, 111;
performativity and, 5, 77, 90 n.3.
See also Repressive hypothesis
Frank, Adam, 18, 93–101, 151 n.1
Freud, Sigmund, 17–21, 54, 93, 99–100, 118,
118 n.2, 124–126, 128–129, 131, 137, 147,
151 n.1.
See also Psychoanalysis
Fried, Michael, 7
Froebel, Friedrich, 169, 180 n.2
Fuller, Margaret, 162–163, 175

Gibson, James J., 13
Goodman, Paul, 99

Gothic, the, 74
Gould, Timothy, 120 n.9, 151 n.4
Gramsci, Antonio, 12
Greenblatt, Stephen, 93–94

Halley, Janet, 120 n.9
Hebb, Donald, 101–102
Heidegger, Martin, 166
Hermeneutic circle, 166.
    See also Phenomenology
Hermeneutics of suspicion, 124–125,
    138–146
Hertz, Neil, 76
Hinduism, 157, 163–164
Hinshelwood, R. D., 128
Hocquenghem, Guy, 126
Hofstadter, Richard, 142–143
Homophobia, 108, 119 n.3, 126, 146
Hsieh, Walter, 170
Hughes, Holly, 150

Identity, 98, 117;
    and Buddhism, 160, 171, 179;
    and shame, 36–38, 64–65
Illocution. See Performativity: illocution
Indology, 155–157, 160, 163–166
Inner child, 40, 44
Interpellation, 69, 158–160

Jacobs, Harriet, 87–89
Jacobs, John S., 89
James, Henry, 7, 13, 63;
    "The Altar of the Dead," 44;
    The Ambassadors, 43–44, 46–47;
    The American, 43, 57;
    anality and digestion in, 47–61;
    The Art of the Novel, 38–61;
    The Awkward Age, 41, 45;
    "The Beast in the Jungle," 44, 47;
    The Golden Bowl, 73–75, 83;

"Guy Domville," 38;
    New York edition, 38–39, 43 (see also The
    Art of the Novel);
    notebooks, 47–48;
    "Owen Wingrave," 60;
    relationships with younger men, 43;
    The Spoils of Poynton, 41;
    The Tragic Muse, 53;
    The Turn of the Screw, 43;
    Wings of the Dove, 51, 53, 56
James, William, 49–50
Jameson, Fredric, 110, 125
Jamyang Khyentse, 157–160
Jarrell, Randall, 27
Jung, C. G., 155

Kissinger, Henry, 127
Klein, Melanie, 128–138, 146, 150
Kukai, 170

Lacan, Jacques, 93, 99, 132–133.
    See also Lack; Sexual difference
Lack, 21, 23, 94
Laplanche, Jean, 129, 151 n.1
Lévi-Strauss, Claude, 93
Lewis, Matthew Gregory, 74
Liberalism, 8, 11, 139–143
Lincoln, Abraham, 67, 74
Litvak, Joseph, 39, 147
Loori, John Daido, 171
Lopez, Donald, 155
Ludlam, Charles, 150
Lynch, Michael, 33
Lyotard, Jean-François, 7

MacGregor, John M., 23
Mahayana Buddhism. See Buddhism:
    Mahayana
Marriage, 7–8, 45–46, 67–90.
    See also Proscenium

Marxism, 11, 77, 109, 124–125, 139
Masons, 166
Meditation, 157.
  See also Buddhism
Miller, D. A.:
  The Novel and the Police, 129–136, 139–144,
    150
Miller, J. Hillis, 7
Milne, A. A., 42
Milton, John, 134
Moon, Michael, 151 n.6
Morris, William, 16
Müller, Max, 165
Mumon, 172

Nathanson, Donald L., 119
Neo-Platonism, 166
Newton, Esther, 8
Nietzsche, Friedrich, 124–125, 139
Nondualism, 1, 165–166, 171;
  and finitely many (n>1) values, 108–114.
  See also Dualisms

Orientalism, 154–157, 165, 168.
  See also Indology

Paranoia, 123–151
Pascal, Blaise, 174
Patton, Cindy, 123–124, 129
Peabody, Elizabeth Palmer, 161–168, 180
  n.1, 180 n.2, 181 n.3
Pedagogy, 27–34, 44, 153–181
Performance, theatrical, 6–7, 29, 36, 115;
  in Henry James, 38–39, 44–47, 53.
  See also Proscenium; Slavery, U.S.
Performativity:
  explicit performative utterance, 4,
    67–68, 78;
  in Henry James, 44–47;
  illocution, 4, 68, 79, 91 n.3, 154;

performative utterance, 3–6;
  perlocution, 68, 78;
  queerness of, 3.
  See also Marriage; Queerness; Spatiality:
    performativity and; Speech acts
Periperformativity: 5, 67–91.
  See also Spatiality: periperformativity
    and
Phenomenology, 20–21, 145;
  of learning, 156, 166–172, 173–180
Philosophia perennis, 166
Plato, 120 n.9, 161, 166, 181 n.3
Pointing, 168–172
Political activism. *See* Activism, political
Pontalis, J.-B., 129, 151 n.1
Pope, Alexander, 48, 51
Powers, Hiram, 80–81
Pre-Socratic philosophy, 166
Proscenium:
  mobile, 8, 72–79, 83–90.
  See also Performance, theatrical
Proust, Marcel, 98, 106, 137–138, 147–148,
    150
Psychoanalysis, 11, 15, 23, 77, 109, 125, 132,
    154;
  Oedipal complex, 146–148;
  phallus, 54, 132–133;
  repression, 36, 54, 64, 98, 106, 167.
  See also Lack; Repressive hypothesis;
    Sexual difference
Psychology: behaviorist, 25 n.3, 103–104,
    113;
  clinical, 98, 154;
  cognitive, 106, 112–113;
  developmental, 98;
  experimental, 98;
  Gestalt, 91 n.3, 116;
  neuropsychology, 99, 101–103;
  perceptual, 13, 99, 107;
  self, 98;

social, 99.

See also Psychoanalysis

Queerness, 29, 61–65, 71–72, 125, 132.
See also Activism, political; Performance, theatrical; Performativity; Theory: queer

Ram Dass, Baba, 174
Rancière, Jacques, 180 n.2
Rebirth. *See* Reincarnation
Reincarnation: 158–159, 169, 177–180, 181 n.3
Reparative position. *See* Klein, Melanie
Repressive hypothesis, 9–14, 17–18, 64, 94, 98, 110
Ricoeur, Paul, 124–125, 138–139
Riggs, Marlon, 28, 34
Rinzai, 172
Roach, Joseph, 80
Romanticism, 162–164, 169, 180 n.2
Rosenblatt, Frank, 107
Rosicrucianism, 166

Saunders, Cicely, 176
Schachter, Stanley, 112
Schizoid/paranoid position. *See* Klein, Melanie
Scientism and antiscientism, 94.
See also Biology and biologism
Scott, Judith, 22–24
Searle, John, 6, 17
Sedgwick, Eve Kosofsky:
"The Beast in the Closet," 46;
Between Men, 18;
The Coherence of Gothic Conventions, 131–132;
A Dialogue on Love, 3, 21–22;
Epistemology of the Closet, 120 n.7
Self-help movement, 155–157
Selsky, Brian, 29–30, 180

Senile sublime, the, 24
Seventy, Sylvia, 23
Sexual difference, 132–133, 135, 146
Shakespeare, William, 48, 83
Shame. *See* Affect: shame-humiliation; Speech acts: shaming
Shelley, Mary: *Frankenstein,* 41, 74
Shyness, 63, 179–180
Silverman, Kaja, 54
Slavery, U.S., 8, 65 n.2, 79–90
Sloterdijk, Peter, 141, 143
Smith, Barbara Herrnstein, 24
Smith, Jack, 150
Sogyal Rinpoche, 157–170, 165, 171, 177
Sounds True, 165
Spatiality: beyond, beneath, and beside, 8–9;
centers and circumferences, 51–53, 68–69;
emptiness, 180 n.1;
performance and, 9, 68;
performativity and, 5, 68–70;
periperformativity and, 5, 68–70, 78–79;
reincarnation and, 179–180.
See also Activism, political; Buddhism: emptiness in; Proscenium; Slavery, U.S.; Speech acts
Speech acts:
civil disobedience, 28–29;
curse, 74, 76–78;
dare, 69–70;
demand, 31;
demonstration, 33;
disinterpellation, 70;
gift-giving, 76–78, 154;
manumission, 79;
pointing, 168–172;
promise, 76;
purchase, 79;
refusal, 29, 70;
sale, 81–82;

Eve Kosofsky Sedgwick is Distinguished Professor of

English at the CUNY Graduate Center. She is the author of books

including *Fat Art, Thin Art* (Duke University Press, 1994), *Tendencies*

(Duke University Press, 1993), and *Epistemology of the Closet*

(University of California Press, 1991).

Library of Congress Cataloging-in-Publication Data

Sedgwick, Eve Kosofsky.

Touching feeling : affect, pedagogy,

performativity / Eve Kosofsky Sedgwick.

p. cm. — (Series Q)

Includes bibliographical references and index.

ISBN 0-8223-3028-8 (cloth : alk. paper)

ISBN 0-8223-3015-6 (pbk. : alk. paper)

I. Frank, Adam.   II. Title.   III. Series.

PS3569.E316 T68   2002

814'.54—dc21   2002007919